The Art and Science of

COMPUTER ANIMATION

Stuart Mealing

intellect™

EXETER, ENGLAND

First published in Paperback in United Kingdom in 1998 by
Intellect Books
School of Art and Design, Earl Richards Road North, Exeter EX2 6AS, UK

Consulting editor: Masoud Yazdani
Copy editor: Cate Foster
Cover design: Sam Robinson
Text layout: Stuart Mealing

A catalogue record for this book is available from the British Library

ISBN   1-871516-71-4

Printed and bound in Great Britain by Cromwell Press, Wiltshire

For my mother

ACKNOWLEDGEMENTS

I am pleased to offer my thanks for help in connection with the production of this book to:

Roger Fickling, Dr. Wendy Milne and Coral Mealing for the many helpful comments and suggestions passed on after reading the draft copy of the book, many of which have been acted upon. Apple Computers Inc. for kind permission to reproduce the paper by Galyn Susman on 'The Making of Pencil Test' as an appendix. Program Now magazine for permission to reproduce passages from an issue. Paul Hooker of 3C Systems, Worcester, Bill Allen at Gromark Ltd (London), and Daphne Powers at Symbolics Ltd (High Wycombe) for generously taking time to produce material used in diagrams and plates. Mick Winning and Brian Carroll of Splash (Cardiff) for advice and for allowing me to browse through and photograph their artwork. Mark Watt of Digital Pictures, William Latham of IBM UK Laboratories Ltd, Craig W. Reynolds of Symbolics Graphics Division, Karl Simms of Optomystic, Professor Eihachiro Nakamae of Hiroshima University, Deirdre Warin at Pixar, Jarrett Cohen at University of Illinois and Alan Stone at Rediffusion Simulation for very kindly supplying slides for reproduction as plates. The Apple Centre (Exeter) for help and advice. Malcolm Kesson, Paul Reilly and Bill Tingle for specific advice and discussion. Professor John Lansdown and the staff at CASCAAD (Middlesex Polytechnic) for much information, acquired both formally and in casual discussion, which has percolated through to the book.

LIST OF CONTENTS

COLOUR PLATES

<u>Front cover</u> **A numerically severe storm** (a)
This animation is used to study the water and ice structure of a severe storm, the movement and rotation of air in andaround the storm, and the different physical processes which influence storm rotation near the ground. The cloud formation and movement, as well as the movement of other elements in the animation, was created numerically from mathematical equations which are based on contemporary laws of physics.The measurements for this model were taken from a severe storm that occured in Oklahoma on April 3, 1964. Produced by the Visualisation Group, National Center for Supercomputing Applications, University of Illinois at Urbana-Champaign.

<u>Back cover</u> **Particle Dreams** (waterfall)
This waterfall is part of a group of animations entitled *Particle Dreams*, which are all created using particle systems, created by Karl Sims at Optomystic.

<u>Back cover</u> **Wet, misty road**
This plate is taken from research at at the Electric Machinery Laboratory, Hiroshima University, into the creation of a light model aiming at drive simulators

<u>Back cover</u> **Flight simulator**
A two and a half ton flight simulator from Rediffusion Simulation. Its 6 hydraulic legs move the 'cockpit', in synchronisation with the cockpit display, to realistically reproduce the flight movements generated by the 'pilot'.

<u>Plate 1</u> **Storyboard**
Created by Mick Winning (now at Splash Computer Graphics Ltd., Cardiff) for S4C to demonstrate an animation idea (not transmitted). The scene opens with mountains reflected in rippling water, reflections turn into the number '4' and lift from the water, bands of light and water orbit the '4' and then form the letters 'S' and 'C'.

Plate 2   **Stills from the storyboard**
Three stills from the storyboard (Plate 1), generated on a Paintbox.

Plate 3   **Rendering sampler**
Examples of quick Lambert shading, smoother Gouraud shading and raytracing, which includes shadows and reflections.

Plate 4   **Luxo Jnr.**
From an award-winning animated short film created at Pixar in 1986 by John Lasseter with William Reeves, Esten Ostby and Sam Leffler. At the time, the fim broke new ground in its ability to imbue inanimate objects with personality and emotion using computer animation. It is the first 3-D computer animated film to be nominated for an Academy Award.

Plate 5   **Tin Toy**
This 1988 Pixar production is the first computer animated film to ever win an Oscar. A 3-D model of the baby's body was digitized from clay figures and merged with a skeletal description of the character. Special software fits the body model to animation of the skeleton, so that the body moved and flexed according to the animator's directions.

Plate 6   **Sunlight on water**
From *Light-water interaction using Backward Beam Tracing*, SIGGRAPH Proceedings 1990 by Mark Watt of Digital Pictures. A fuller treatment is given in *Advanced Rendering & Animation Techniques: Theory and Practice*, (pub) Addison Wesley 1991.

Plate 7   **Mutations**
Produced by William Latham with Stephen Todd at the IBM UK Scientific Centre, Winchester. The programs used were Esme, Mutator and Winsom.

Plate 8   **Numerically severe storm** (b)
See the description of the front cover plate.

Plate 9   **Quarry**
From an animated simulation of a quarry created for an environmental impact analysis (EIA) by 3C Systems, Worcester.

INTRODUCTION

One definition of animation is that it is 'the condition of being alive'. This book tells how computers are being used to breathe life into static images and dry data.

Computer animation is a heady mixture of visual poetry and mathematics, a search for the realisation of impossible dreams and a genuine tool for visual enlightenment. It is a discipline which can be, and is, approached from the directions of science, art and just plain curiosity. This book aims to make understandable to the reader from any of these backgrounds, the means by which computer animations can be created and the rich potential of the medium as a whole. It is a book about what can be done, what will be done and how it might be done. It presents an overview of the whole of the new, challenging, and above all exciting area of computer animation.

There is a large, and fast growing, resource of books dealing with the mathematics, geometry and programming of computer graphics, but few of them deal at any length with animation. This book aims to be both comprehensive enough to describe the many ways in which computers can be used in the production of animation, and general enough to be of equal use to the mathematician, programmer, designer, artist or to any reader with a particular interest in this emerging discipline. It will discuss the general principles of creating moving images on a computer, investigate the growing number of applications of the medium, review the current state-of-the-art and consider its future. These subjects will be approached without the presumption of prior expertise on the part of the reader, and will thus provide a foundation from which to approach the more specialist sources which are cited in the text and listed in the bibliography. For this reason readers coming to the book with a particular expertise may feel able to pass by chapters outlining the basics of their subject. (For the reader who wilts at the thought of mathematics it is worth pointing out that good computer systems make their methods transparent to those who prefer not to know.) In particular, the proceedings, course notes and videotapes of the annual conference of SIGGRAPH (Special Interest Group on Computer Graphics of the Association of Computing Machinery) are strongly recommended and are often mentioned in the book.

It is obviously not possible to deal fully with every development within the discipline, and the necessary abbreviation sacrifices detail in favour of a broad general understanding. To anyone who finds the work of years summarised in a paragraph I apologise. In some cases I have described relatively few examples from a popular research area, with the intention of giving a flavour and local understanding of the work, which the reader can choose to follow up in greater depth using the bibliography. For instance, whilst I select only a couple of examples of work being done in the area of facial animation from the many approaches that have been developed over a number of years, I hope it is sufficient to suggest to anyone new to the area both the breadth and rigour of the research field as a whole. It will also be noticed that in some cases two spellings of a word occur (e.g. colour & color, modelling & modeling). This is because the book is written in England, but retains the native spelling in references from American sources.

The book falls into two main parts. Part one explains the background and basic science for computer animation, whilst Part two moves up a level and deals in greater detail with some of the latest developments in the area. It is arranged as follows: Chapter 1 considers the nature of animation, traditional techniques and the role of the computer. Chapter 2 describes the varied applications of computer animation from TV graphics to flight simulation and from scientific visualisation to special effects. Chapters 3 to 8 deal with the basic principles of computer graphics, movement control and with hardware, language and software considerations relevant to computer animation. Chapters 9 to 12 look at the current state-of-the-art in the discipline, and include issues such as soft modelling methods, dynamic animation, artificial intelligence and the construction of synthetic humans. Chapter 13 looks at future developments, and extrapolates from the material that has gone before, to make suggestions about applications of imminent hardware and of virtual reality. Appendices, a glossary of terms and a comprehensive bibliography conclude. In order to emphasise that the book is applicable to work on any size of computer the illustrations show images produced on a range of machines.

As well as hoping to explain and demystify, I would like to share with the reader my own excitement in this rapidly developing medium and my belief in the significant role it can play in a wide range of areas. There is no conflict between computer animation being serious and being fun. It is a good moment in time to be able to review the discipline, as it has survived most of its teething problems and has come to be recognised as offering a new dimension in the presentation and dissemination of information in science, commerce, education, entertainment and art. It represents one of the biggest growth areas in computing, and, to bring to full maturity, will need the dedicated attention of enthusiasts with the vision and understanding to work across the many discipline areas it encompasses. I hope this book can contribute a little to their efforts.

PART ONE

CHAPTER 1

THE NATURE OF ANIMATION

It is often desirable to produce animated images. The motive may be entertainment, scientific clarity, commercial persuasion or other, but the means is to present a sequence of images, called frames, at a rate such that the observer will accept the succession of discrete images as being one of continuous movement. The rate at which this illusion of movement is considered adequate is normally between twenty and thirty frames per second, and will often be determined by a secondary medium onto which the animation is saved, i.e. film or video.

The ability of the viewer to construct the illusion of movement from discrete images is strong, and if the movement being watched is understood at an intellectual level then relatively few visual clues may be needed to support the illusion. For example a walking figure is so familiar that a few frames from the gait cycle may be 'padded out' by the viewer's experience to match the known experience. The frequency of these frames may be low enough for them to be recognised as being separate without the illusion being lost. The illusion is particularly easy to sustain if the frames are synchronised to the tempo of the 'real life' experience.

1.1 FRAME RATES

It is therefore possible to simulate continuous time with a sequence of discrete frames (analogue to digital?), but at what speed does the description of this as animation become justified? The question is probably more interesting than the answer, which varies according to context and is ultimately subjective. Persistence of vision has been claimed to be sufficient at 12 frames per second (fps) but is more often considered acceptable at between 18 and 24 fps. There are, however, fixed frame display speeds associated with different media, which should be listed. Old 16-mm home movies run at 18 fps, standard movie films run at 24 fps, TV in the United Kingdom runs at 25 fps and in the USA at 30 fps. (In order to show films at the correct speed on American TV every fourth frame is shown twice, on British TV films just end earlier.) On a computer, frames can usually be run at varying rates, and it is interesting to find for yourself the lowest speed at which you are satisfied with the credibility of an animated sequence.

Whilst talking about timing, it is a good moment to introduce the concept of 'real-time'. Often used in connection with visual applications of computing, it is used to imply that there is a one-to-one relationship between the speed at which things are displayed on the screen and the speed at which they happen in real life. In the context of computer animation, a real-time display is one in which the computer displays the images at the same number of frames per second at which they should be finally viewed. It might be that they are generated AND displayed in real-time, or merely that they are generated over a longer period and saved up for subsequent real-time display. The reason for the latter method, as we will see, is that the computer may require minutes, or even hours, to generate complex frames.

In more general terms, real-time can be used to refer to the computer's ability to display an image as it is input. This is a desirable feature in a paint system, for instance, where any delay between drawing on an input pad and seeing the corresponding mark appear on screen creates problems. Since the computer's electronics has to do some work on the input before it can be displayed, it can never be truly real-time, but is described as such if the delay is not perceptible. In the case of interactive animation, it is essential that generation and display are both done in real-time, which either requires a powerful computer or simple images.

1.2 ANIMATION DEVICES

Mechanical devices with wonderful names like the Thauma-trope, the Phenakistoscope, the Zoetrope and the Zoopraxiscope date back to early last century, and brought the wonder of simple animation into Victorian parlours. Flicker books, and their grown-up cousins the peep shows (or 'What-the-butler-saw' machines) can still be seen today, and are not to be derided. Only recently, I was obliged to make a flicker book from computer plots, in order to see the movement I was attempting to construct, because the main-frame computer was taking half a minute to produce each frame and video problems prevented the sequence being recorded. It can also prove a quick and effective way of bringing a storyboard to life, and of carrying it around in your pocket. A flicker book is simply made by building a stack of sequential images on paper, fixing them at one edge, and flipping through them with your thumb. (It is necessary to align the sheets cleanly at the edge you flip, or preferably cut that edge after the book is assembled.) It is also quick and practical to draw the images roughly on sequential pages of a sketch book, though aligning each image with the previous one can be a problem.

1.3 STORYBOARDS

Animations need to be planned to be effective. It is possible to improvise at the computer keyboard, without any prior plan, but nothing of any ambition is likely to arise this way. A central most usual device for planning an animation is the storyboard, a sequence of pictures illustrating key moments in the script, which not only forces the transition from ideas to images, but does so in a form which is easily communicated to all those involved (Plates 1 & 2). The storyboard may be preceded by discussions between artist, production team and client, and by sheets of source material and drawing where environ-ments and characters are developed, depending on the context in which the animation is being created. The variety of applications of computer animation will be discussed in the next chapter, when it will be seen that the general case implied here is subject to various degrees of modification. A scientific simulation, for instance, would require different planning to a TV commercial.

At the storyboard level, aesthetic changes can be made, the technical consequences considered and the cost calculated in both financial and computing terms. In a production environment accurate assessment of time and cost determines whether your firm still exists to make any more animations, so expensive ideas may not be given the free reign that an academic or research environment might be able to offer. The requirements for producing a three-year doctoral thesis are different from those for producing a thirty-second commercial on a two week deadline. Many of the techniques described later in the book are too close to the sharp end of the discipline to be viable production tools at the moment, but the history of the field is one of very rapid development. Also, commercial pressures and the animator's own satisfaction will both demand that new things be tried.

Whilst a good storyboard presents a clear visualisation of the animation to come, it takes experience to picture how the images will look in movement and how long different passages of movement should be. It is likely, for instance, that each picture in the storyboard will not represent the same amount of display time, a number of pictures perhaps being needed to adequately describe a second of complex activity. A simple improvement is to produce a cross between a storyboard and a flicker book, by putting the storyboard images into the computer and displaying each image for the same time that the sequence it represents will last. At this point the time steps can be interactively tuned. Alternatively, a rough animatic can be produced quickly, probably on a small micro, sacrificing detail in order to preview movement and general layout, before making the commitment to full scale production. Such an animatic is particularly helpful to the client, who may well be inexperienced in picturing the final result of his large investment. A comprehensive storyboard does not, of course, preclude changes during production or post-production.

1.4 TRADITIONAL METHODS

Before considering the role of the computer in animation, let us look briefly at the most common traditional techniques. Hand-drawn animation, with each frame individually crafted by an artist, requires a lot of skill, a lot of patience and very little equipment. The drawing is usually done on a cel (a clear sheet) which allows previous frames to show through, or on backlight paper, and the cels have alignment holes punched out so that they can be registered by pegs. Each frame can be recorded on film or video, and the amount of work going in to an animation of any size is staggering. A feature film containing the production of 250,000 individual drawings would take fifty years of labour if all were to be drawn by one person [Halas 1974]. Needless to say it is not often done by one person. It will be coordinated by one person, but worked on by a number of artists who will delegate jobs, such as filling in areas, to juniors. The senior artists will draw the key-frames (frames where something significant changes) and junior artists will draw up the frames coming between the key-frames. It is remarkable to see vast rooms, filled with rows of tables, at each of which sits a figure with a paintbrush, all to produce a few minutes of a children's cartoon perhaps.

Whilst all the detail can be painted on to every frame, it is more likely that the frame will be compiled from several cels at the point of filming. The background may be on one cel, static characters on another and the moving character on top. In this way the bottom two cels can be used in a number of frames. It might also be that the cels are moved relative to one another in successive frames, without being redrawn, so that, for instance, a background could be scrolled past to suggest the movement of the character in front. Because of the potential enhancement of the sense of space in the picture by creating movement on several superimposed layers, it is sometimes referred to as 21/2-dimensional (21/2-D).

The source images may come straight from the artist's imagination (established by years of critical observation), or can be taken from live-action film or video. The process of tracing images, one at a time, off a screen is known as rotascoping. The source material may be already available, perhaps archival footage, or might be specially created in order that the animator can work from it. Whilst it is very convenient to be able to copy directly from live-action material, it is only appropriate to do so if the material exactly matches the script. Film of a horse galloping past the camera is no help if you are required to draw a horse galloping towards the camera.

1.4.1 MODEL ANIMATION

In the same way that two dimensional drawings can be individually recorded in a sequence, it is equally possible to manipulate objects in front of the camera. This is known as model animation, and is a sort of staccato puppetry, where, instead of drawing something at each stage of its movement, you move and film the thing itself. The subject can be a rigid object, an articulated object or even a flexible, transforming object (can everyone remember the ball of clay that turns itself into a man then into an animal then back into a ball?), and the process can be recognised in many children's TV shows. Sometimes it is the camera that moves, rather than the object, and very large sets may be built for model animation, perhaps a miniature town covering a thousand square feet. In this case, a 'fly through' of the town is likely to require a 'motion-control rig', in which a specialised camera, fixed to overhead tracks, is controlled along a very precise path through the scene. The camera may record the scene through a 'snorkel lens' (an inverted periscope) which allows it to work in the heart of the model, where the main camera body will probably not fit.

A technique sharing some properties of cel animation and others of model animation is the manipulation of two dimensional cutouts under the camera (if the camera points down, gravity holds your scene in place). It is most easily achieved using a rostrum camera. The rostrum camera is a versatile tool, in which a vertically mounted, movable camera points down at a movable, horizontal bed on which the artwork is held. This setup allows for a flexible range of camera and subject movements relative to one another, and can be enhanced by replacing the single bed with several transparent levels for multi-level cel work and 3-dimensional (3-D) effects. All the moving parts are controlled with a high degree of accuracy according to a detailed shooting script. The various animation techniques described are not exclusive, but can be, and often are, combined.

1.5 KEYFRAMING

An important concept in animation, which has already been mentioned in passing, is that of the key-frame. If an object was to move smoothly (and unchanged) in a straight line from A to B, it would be possible to draw the two end positions, and then rationalise all the positions that the object had passed through from those two end positions. A more complicated motion can usually be decomposed into shorter sections, between the extremes of which, further positions can be interpolated. This incremental change from one key-frame to

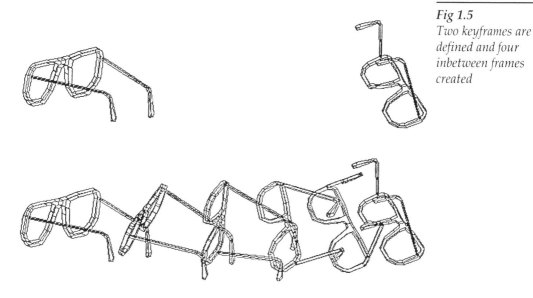

Fig 1.5
Two keyframes are defined and four inbetween frames created

another is known as 'in-betweening' (Fig 1.5).

It might be that different parts of an object, or scene, can be seen as having different key points, for instance, the first and last frames of a cartoon figure dropping from the top of the screen to the bottom might suffice as key-frames, but if the mouth is moving as the figure drops it will require more detailed attention. Therefore, although the term 'key-frame' will often be applied to the entire frame at a key moment, it will soon be seen that the concept can usefully be applied to different elements within a scene. It will also be seen that the movement path between key-frames is often defined by a curve instead of by a straight line, and that both the rate of change of the curve and the timesteps along the path need not be equal.

1.6 THE ROLE OF COMPUTERS

If a feature film containing the production of 250,000 individual drawings would take fifty years of labour if all were to be drawn by one person, it is clear that automation of parts of the animation process could be very productive. It is often said that the role of computers should be to relieve humans of the need to undertake tedious chores, and there are certainly some repetitive chores involved in traditional animation. Whether the fresh chores brought by the use of computers are preferable to the existing ones is a matter of personal opinion (and financial assessment), but their use pushes forward the creative and production horizons of the medium.

Computers can be used in animation in two main ways: as tools to improve the application of traditional methods; and as a means of generating material not possible traditionally. Between these two poles lies the possibility that computers may sometimes be able to improve on the speed, cost or accuracy of traditional animation techniques to the extent that projects which were previously technically possible, but impractical in scale, could be attempted. An example of this is the computer control of a motion-control rig, where camera movements of much greater precision and flexibility are possible, and with the major advantage of total repeatability. By storing a complete record of all parameters digitally, any sequence can be repeated, in whole or part, with the total accuracy vital for multiple exposures.

It is often necessary to synchronise motion-control shots with material generated within the computer. A recent advertisement for 'Smarties' (a button-sized chocolate sweet) had the camera sweeping through school classrooms following the progress of flying Smarties. The Smarties, and incidents during their flight, were computer generated, and had to be synchronised exactly to the film shot by the camera in a set of classroom models. Because the computer controlling the camera held a complete digital record of all camera positions and angles against time, it was relatively straightforward to use the same information in the computer generation of matching images. Similar numerical control can also be applied to the rostrum camera.

The production of program titles and credits is particularly suited to computer assistance. Two-dimensional typography can be produced by a paint system and three-dimensional letter forms by a modelling system, with all the consequent advantages of scaling, positioning and colour changes being made simple by the computer. Text can be 'wrapped' around objects with an ease that encourages experiment, rather than with the labour that discourages subsequent change. Most applications have their own built-in range of fonts, and specialised machines exists just to produce captions electronically, having up to a thousand different fonts included and the ability to accept fresh ones created by the graphic designer. The 'Aston' caption generator ('cap-gen') is to be found in the corner of most studios that I have visited, and in one studio, heaving with the latest computer wizardry, was cited as their single, most reliable source of income. It can also be used during live transmission for presentation, for instance, of sports results.

1.7 MANIPULATION BY COMPUTER

By their very nature, computers are good at doing certain things. Repeating a set of instructions any number of times is one thing they are good at, and animation often gives them scope to prove it. Interpolation between key-frames involves repeated incremental steps of sufficient quantity to match the action to the required time span. If an object has to move 20 units along the X (horizontal) axis and at the same time rotate once around its Y (vertical) axis, taking two seconds to complete the move, then we can derive a set of instructions to achieve the necessary change between successive frames. Given a frame rate of 25fps then we have 50 frames to complete the 2-second move. In the course of 50 frames there are 49 frame changes, so the amount the object must move in each frame is 20/49 units, and the amount it must rotate is 360/49 degrees. We can therefore say:

> For each frame from 1 to 50:
>   move the object 20/49 units along X
>   rotate the object 360/49 degrees around Y

This is virtually the way that we would write it in a computer program using the common structure called a 'loop', though the need to do so could well be hidden from us by a friendly interface. We would merely define for the machine the start frame, the end frame and the total movements required, and then leave it to get on with it. In the example above, the changes between frames are even, but it would take little extra definition to introduce acceleration or other change of pace. If you consider an army of similarly mindless objects moving across a surface, it can be seen that the same rules determining the movement of one object can be applied to all the others. The addition of a single line to our loop could lead to the movement of a hundred objects through the fifty frames:

> For each frame from 1 to 50:
>   For each object from 1 to 100:
>   move the object 20/49 units along X
>   rotate the object 360/49 degrees around Y

The saving in time and effort over doing the same job manually is obvious and the ease with which repetitive things can be done has sometimes lead to them being done for their own sake. It is equally easy to produce an incremental change in a 2-D shape or in the form of a 3-D object by defining the two extremes of shape, the number of frames over which the change must occur, and then having the computer calculate a percentage change at each frame. This transformation must not confuse the 2-D representation of a 3-D object with the 3-D object, which serves to distinguish between image based and

Fig 1.7
Transformations

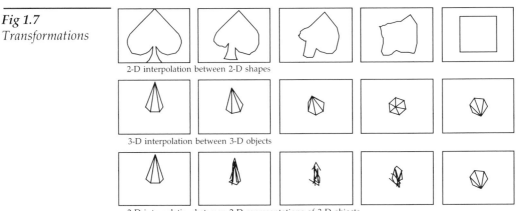

2-D interpolation between 2-D shapes

3-D interpolation between 3-D objects

2-D interpolation between 2-D representations of 3-D objects

parameter based keyframe interpolation (Fig 1.7).

Another repetitive function is the production of patterns. These can be generated mathematically or created by repeating any image or part of an image. Even the most basic systems allow you to 'cut out' and then manipulate areas of the image which can be repetitively combined to form patterns. The cut areas can often also be moved around under machine or hand control to invite fresh variations on animation procedures. The block of screen defined could represent a character, or part of a character, and this is the basis of 'sprite' animation. The animation in a games program might include a little figure who walks around the screen (albeit in a rather wooden fashion), and it takes little observation to see that each position in which he is shown is composed from a library of body parts, each drawn in a range of different attitudes. Various techniques allow the computer to compose and move the various figure combinations at great speed, enabling the animation to be interactive if desired.

1.8 PAINT SYSTEMS

Paint systems have been mentioned several times, and, although they are not tools specific to computer animation, they usually become involved in the production process at some point. A paint system is a combination of computer, software, monitor and input device, which allows the electronic simulation of drawing and painting on a screen (technical drawing being best handled by other specialist systems). Input is often via a stylus, held and manipulated like a pen, the movements of which on a sensitive surface are translated, in real-time, into marks on the screen. These marks can be predefined to appear similar to those created by different size brushes, with paint of different transparency, or to other mark-making devices offering different textures, such as charcoal, pencil or airbrush. The ability to draw straight lines, curves, boxes and to use text is included, and the more sophisticated machines duplicate almost all the tools a graphic designer could want, including powerful masking functions. Images can be input from other sources via a video camera, digitiser or scanner, and utilised in conjunction with all the other tools. Colours can be defined and mixed up to a total palette size of several million.

This is the briefest summary of a piece of equipment which is revolutionising the practice of graphic design, but it hopefully gives an inkling of its potential. At any stage the current image can be saved digitally for recall later, permitting numerous permutations on a visual idea to be developed quickly. Different colour ways and combinations can be tried in seconds, (red swapped for green, the green darkened a little, no, let's try the red again but make it warmer, and so on) and limited animation facilities may be included. It is more likely, in the context of animation, however, that the paint system will be used to create art work which is manipulated elsewhere or else be used for post production work on imported frames of animation.

One part of the traditional animation process which it would be very advantageous to automate, is that of painting-in the cels by hand. Currently labour intensive, and, therefore, often farmed out to distant places where labour is cheap, the chore of filling in thousands of consecutive images of the same subject with the same colours seems a job ideally suited to a computer. It can now be undertaken with specialised resources, but is not as straightforward as it might at first sight seem. A level of intelligence on the computer's part is necessary in order to enable it to follow each area as it is transformed from frame to frame (i.e. recognising changing views of the figure's head). There is also the problem created when an area leaves and rejoins the screen, where the clean edge of an area breaks up and where a clean edge is not intended between adjacent areas. Difficulties such as these mean that currently available techniques are of limited application, and that the hand still reigns supreme.

Surprisingly, perhaps, it has been possible to persuade computers to colour old black and white movies. The computer is given a colour model for each new set and character and can then be 'trained' to recognise that character when it reappears. If John Wayne changes his shirt, the machine is given details of the new one, and continues following its progress. Whilst I do not think that a colour version of 'Stagecoach' or 'Battleship Potemkin' would be at all desirable, as it flies in the face of the aesthetic judgments brought by the original directors, in a society used to TV and films being in colour there is a market for these new renderings, some people apparently feeling cheated with mere monochrome. The technique seems more appropriate for recolouring old and faded film stock, and apparently the new, improved 'Gone With the Wind' has been given a fresh lease of life at the box office. I do not currently have much information on that system, but projecting forward from possible methods suggests the future use of intelligent edge detection to automate rotascoping.

1.9 OTHER ROLES FOR THE COMPUTER

One further area where computers are set to revolutionise animation, and film production in general, is in the storage and subsequent manipulation of digital media. Instead of recording images on film or video tape, it is increasingly possible to save them digitally on a range of media. This offers a massive improvement in the flexibility of post-production work (work, such as editing, which is done after the initial images have been produced). Any frames can be accessed, almost instantly, in any sequence and rearranged, combined or altered (possibly many times) without loss of quality. The ease of handling and improved image quality allow techniques which were previously impractical, such as the building of sequences with, perhaps, forty or more layers of images. This would result in an unacceptable loss of quality if built up on video tape.

These, then, are ways in which computers can aid, complement or update traditional animation. Much more interesting, however, and the main subject of this book, are the ways in which computers offer a completely fresh set of tools for the animator to use. They push the limits of the discipline far forward, allowing work of unimagined sophistication and complexity to become an everyday reality, and, at the leading edge, cement a new marriage between art and science. They can also be used to do the accounts.

It has become a truism to point out that computers can only push numbers around, and, in the final analysis, can only distinguish between zero and one. They can, however, do so extremely fast, and as we have come to understand that much of our knowledge about the world can be meaningfully reduced to numbers, we are in a position to use computers to manipulate that knowledge. Objects and scenes from the real world, or from an imaginary world, can be conjured out of these numbers, can interact, can be subjected to the application of physical laws, and, most importantly, can be made visible and hence accessible. Modern communication and media ensure that the results of this newly acquired skill is made available, for better or worse, to hundreds of millions of people throughout the globe, in their very homes.

1.10 THREE DIMENSIONS

One of the most impressive advances that new technology offers animators, is the ability to build three dimensional objects and scenes in the memory of the computer. Instead, then, of having to invent and draw separate cels for each change of viewpoint or object movement, it is now possible to define all the ingredients of the scene in three dimensions (form, scale, colour, surface qualities, lighting conditions, camera position) and to animate any or all parts of the model at will. Much of the book will look at how this can be done, but it is the conceptual leap as much as the technical one that is astounding. Actually to have enough information about Midtown Manhattan stored in a few micro-electronic components, to allow you to 'fly' down Broadway from Central Park, turn left at West Thirty-third Street and sweep up the elevation of the Empire State Building still seems remarkable, even when it can be done (at a simple level) on a cheap home computer. Today's 'simple level' is, of course, yesterday's 'state-of-the-art', and it can be safely assumed that everything described here as pushing the discipline to its extremes will be commonplace in a few years using the cheapest equipment.

The automatic calculation of perspective, which enables our imaginary 3-D scene to be rendered on our 2-D monitor screen, still seems a breathtaking piece of magic, whose wonder is not diminished by understanding the mathematics and programming involved. New developments which allow us to enter and explore that same scene, with all the apparent sensory clues of true 3-D, herald the dawning of a new way of looking at, responding to and understanding our world. They promise to vastly extend the role of animation (perhaps now 'hyper-animation'?), and find it new and exciting uses within a range of fresh disciplines.

Less dramatic conceptually, but visually remarkable (some might say insidious), is the manipulation of flat, 2-D surfaces in 3-D space. The ability to 'turn' a page of electronic type, to 'wrap' a picture of a politician around a dustbin (which has been created as a 3-D computer model), to fragment and 'blow away' the image of a woman's face in a cosmetics advertisement, or to 'roll' a flat electronic image into a cone and 'spin' it around the screen, is taken for granted many times during every night's television viewing.

1.11 KINEMATICS / DYNAMICS

The work of the animator to date has been mainly kinematic, which means that the operator has to specify the position of everything in the scene at any moment in time. This may be relieved by setting key-frames, between which we now know we can interpolate, and by defining relationships between objects which the program will be forced to observe (such as determining that the forearm must remain connected to the upper arm by a hinge joint with a defined range of movement). It still leaves the animator to mimic the effects of forces on all his 'actors', to decide how high a ball should bounce or how flat a cat should be squashed. (A useful convention has arisen whereby objects interacting with one another, or with their 'set', are referred to as 'actors', a term coined by Hewitt in 1971. He defined an actor as an object that can send or receive messages, a definition which is helpfully intuitive, and derives from an object orientated approach. Using similar references Reynolds [1987] calls an actor the computational, abstraction that combines process, procedure and state.)

In a dynamic animation, physical laws, such as the effect of gravity and collisions, are 'known' to the program, which can then derive an object's movement from their application. Being able to describe these rules to the computer and then leave it to deal with all the movements and interactions, relieves the animator of much work and increases the complexity of the material which can reasonably be dealt with. It also presents the opportunity for direct simulation, where the animator may establish the starting conditions and then sit back as a spectator. The amount of information that needs to be specified for a scene of any complexity is enormous, and rapidly outstrips the ability of the user to supply it directly, so that any attempt at realistic motion suggest the computer's intervention.

1.12 RULE-BASED SYSTEMS

Rules that can be specified include those of the animator or storyboard (e.g. the logo will continuously rotate about all three axes during its move from A to B), those imposed by physical laws (e.g. once the ball has been thrown, it will decelerate, fall to the ground and bounce) and behavioural rules (e.g. the bees will fly from A to B in a compact swarm, without flying into one another or the ground). The animator's rules may, of course, have been derived intuitively, or by observation, from physical laws. The level at which the animator chooses, or is forced, to work varies from the highest level ('implicit') where it is necessary to specify the actors, their starting points plus constraints, if appropriate, and leave them to work out how to move themselves; to the lowest level ('explicit') where every motion, through every degree of movement, of every actor, for every frame, has to be specified individually. In some circumstances, of course, the user may want to 'interfere' with a 'high-level' animation in order to refine movement details at a 'lower' level.

Consider the case of a cartoon cat leaping off a cliff. Typically, it is suspended in mid-air at cliff-top height for some seconds, before being overcome by a sudden and dramatic plunge to the ground, probably hitting the ground some seconds before its ears catch up with it. Now consider an attempt to model accurately the movement of snooker balls across the green baize. In both cases the movement is proscribed by rules. In the first instance the rules are the intuitive 'falling cat' rules of the animator, at once based on, and yet suspending our understanding of, gravity. In the second instance the rules are exclusively those of dynamic analysis, dealing with the mass of the balls, the compression of the cushions, the friction of the baize, the force of the cue's strike and the angles of collision.

Perhaps one rule-based system could control both instances. If all the Newtonian laws of motion were somehow built into the system, together with rules for the actor(s) to obey, it would be easy for the animator to set one rule for the snooker model: "Obey the laws of motion", and three extra for the cat. 1: "gravity is ten times the normal for falling cats", 2: "there is a 2-second delay for the effect of gravity on cats" and 3: "there is a 3-second delay for the effect of gravity on cats' ears". He could then set the boundary conditions and take a lunch break while the animations create themselves. A crucial difference between kinematic and dynamic animation, however, is that the first can be storyboarded but the second is open-ended. Therefore in the kinematically specified world things can happen in a specified sequence and take a specified time, but once the dynamic snooker balls have been set in motion there is no external control over when they stop (if ever).

1.13 ARTIFICIAL INTELLIGENCE

A further removal of the need for operator intervention can be achieved by applying 'artificial intelligence' (AI). This scientific field is involved with building features associated with natural intelligence into machines. Dealt with at greater length in Chapter 11, AI offers the potential for creating actors that can be given scripts and then left to get on with producing their own animation! If an actor (remember that we are using the word in the broad sense to refer to anything that interacts in our scene) 'understands' how to respond in any given situation, then we need give it much less direction. This understanding could encompass not only physical responses (such as how to modify a gait pattern as speed changes and how to respond to collisions), but environmental ones (such as how to plan an optimal route from A to B and how to avoid obstacles) and also behavioural ones (such as what positional relationship to hold with other actors and how to react to conflicting demands). Actors could be given motivation and emotions which would condition their responses to situations they find themselves in, but could hopefully be stopped short of temperamental refusal to work. Work on applying AI techniques to animation is in its early stages but interest is strong, as the concept is very much in tune with the time, and the development complements other current research.

Simulation is an area which can make good use of dynamics and AI. Part of the real world can be isolated and reproduced by obeying rules that are deduced from scientific observation, a simple example being the snooker balls mentioned earlier. Parameters can be changed in order to observe their effect in a theoretical world (e.g. gravity could be doubled, the mass of the balls decreased, the roughness of the baize changed, etc.) and the simulation run with the same, or with fresh, starting conditions. This discipline has many applications, as will later be shown, but in any context there is a very special appeal about watching a story unfold on the screen, apparently of its own volition, without having written the ending. It is worth pointing out that whilst visual 'cheating' plays a big part in commercial animation it can obviously have no part in a simulation.

CHAPTER 2

APPLICATIONS OF COMPUTER ANIMATION

The increasing ability to produce computer animation at an acceptable cost and speed, and to employ it on a wide range of machines, is opening up many new opportunities for the medium. Almost everyone in the western world is being regularly exposed to the medium through commercial and entertainment uses on television, with dreaded "flying logos" swooping past the eyes at frequent intervals (very neatly parodied in a showreel from Conn, Homer and Associates). This increased exposure leads, of course, to increased familiarity and then, as the medium is accepted along side more traditional ones, to increased demand. Things in the real world are constantly moving, and the ability to mimic or simulate that quality breathes life into the inanimacy of the frozen image. A single image can capture "the decisive moment", which might have become lost during a sequence, but many situations demand greater truth to turbulent reality.

In science, business, entertainment and education, frontiers are being pushed back through the insights which computer animation alone can offer. Finding visual form for impenetrably large collections of numbers has offered revelations to mathematicians, doctors have been led to new diagnoses and treatments, space missions have been rehearsed in safety and TV graphics has been revolutionised. Some phenomena in the world are only visible when they are moving, a fact demonstrated by a square of dots seen against a field of dots (where the square is invisible until it moves). Although this might seem an obscure example, it shows how much information could be hiding in a stack of data, and how animation could provide the vehicle for extracting it.

2.1 TV GRAPHICS

Because it is the most public use of the medium, TV graphics is a good place to start considering current applications of the medium. It has been taken on board so readily by producers and designers, wanting their programme introduction or promotion to have more punch than its rivals, that it has almost become the de facto standard. As a spin-off, it has unfortunately brought to millions of people, in the privacy of their homes, some of the most vulgar and needlessly expensive images of the century. The best examples of the genre have, however, become minor classics which enlighten and contribute to the discipline of graphic design. It will be interesting to see what effect the imminent proliferation of satellite TV stations has on the cost and quality of computer animation. The medium is properly used when it either extends the range of things the designer can do visually, or makes easier, quicker or cheaper an existing part of the design process. Whether the presentation and manipulation of a logo is poetic or crass depends on the skill of the designer and the sensitivity of whoever commissions it, it is not a property of the medium itself. It is, however, often the case that a medium stimulates ideas and visions to grow in a particular direction. If the designer is constrained by the hardware and software available, with a machine designed for typographical aerobatics and with a "chrome" rendering option, then the results may be predictable, and the existence of those features on his machine will be the partly the result of market forces. The good designer will always be breaking new ground, and consequently pushing hardware and software to its limits, but he will rarely be in a position to write software to push beyond the current limits of his application. There is, therefore, at graphics' leading edge, a growing liaison between designers, programmers and engineers.

Quantel has been the name associated with computer paint systems for a number of years and is still the yardstick against which others are measured. It may or may not be the best, but it is clearly identified with the revolution in TV graphics, and helped moved designers to a more central role in production. Designers at the BBC found that it so speeded up their jobs that they were prepared to forsake their families and work during the night if that was when the machine was free. Its relevance to animation was less marked until the Harry system was coupled to it. Harry is a digital editing suite which gives enormous flexibility in the manipulation of images from a range of sources, including live action video, without the generation loss which inhibits normal video work. It allows an animated sequence to be worked on (either frame by frame or in its entirety), added to and processed indefinitely without loss of quality, and with intuitive ease.

The combined system, perhaps with the addition of an effects generator, gives the animator great creative freedom. Although its uses are often so unassuming as to pass notice (for instance replacing a car numberplate throughout a sequence, or 'painting' out the lighting rigs in a studio shot and adding a fresh surround), it permits the accretion of hand drawn images, images input from photographic sources, and computer generated images together with existing stock in an animatic potpourri which is currently popular in pop videos. It is not a system for the creation of 3-D scenes (though scenes generated on suitable machines can be imported and worked on) but successive layers of images can be added to build 2 1/2-D scenes. The mixing of computer-generated images with computer-amended images and with straightforward live film in a single sequence should be noted, as it is very commonly used in a range of contexts, though it is not to be dealt with in this book.

One of the most well known and enduring examples of computer animation on British television is of the Channel 4 'ident' (station identity): a brightly coloured figure "4" breaking into sections which fly and tumble past the camera before reforming. Certainly the work of Martin Lambie-Nairn, and with many other people claiming part of the credit, the piece has a simple elegance which has endured since 1983. The apparent simplicity of the image does not mean that it was easy to create, and, just seven years ago, it was not possible for all the work to be done in this country. The rate of development of systems, however, means that many home micros today could match the choreography, if not the resolution, of that sequence. (An interesting detail is that the Channel 4 logo is shown in orthographic projection, which means it has no perspective. Since it needed to be shown in a perspectival projection in order for its flight to make visual sense, it was necessary to "cheat" a little in the opening and closing frames to move from one system to the other.)

It is hard to generalise about the use of computer animation on television as its function and form will vary according to the context, but there are several areas where it is currently popular. Station idents, programme title sequences, information graphics and advertisements all make heavy use of the medium and it is almost universal, at the moment, for news programmes to employ computers in the production of their introductions. News programmes are something of a flagship for the stations, and are an important part of establishing their housestyle. The graphics may need to evoke quali- ties of honesty, seriousness, topicality and grittiness, define the relevant locality, reinforce the station's image, and be accompanied by a matching soundtrack. The images used are usually iconic (the globe, the parliament building), the typography prominent, the movement smooth and pacey, and the overall feel often symbolic (reaching out across the airways, flying to the nation's pulse).

Strings of letterforms, in 2-D, or more often 3-D, lend themselves to geometric manipulation in 3-space and are able to retain a high degree of legibility throughout major transformations. In simple cases it is also very straightforward to accomplish with rela- tively basic machines (Fig 2.1), and so is frequently seen, though it is interesting to notice that these animations can last as little as half a second, possibly just re-establishing the station ident between two separate pieces of programme material.

The use of basic machines can even include the use of home micros to provide broadcast material. Relatively crude pieces of animation, often used in games shows, are found acceptable at a low resolution, with a limited range of perhaps sixteen colours, and can be produced quickly and cheaply on sixteen-bit machines such as the Atari ST and Amiga. The short, hectic animated graphics on pop music programmes is often made using similar machines, and in some cases combined with more sophisticated hardware in the production of 'quality' images. (Some of these machines also have excellent music and sound control capacities using a 'midi' interface.) The next generation of home computers will be able to produce broadcast quality material as a matter of course.

Television weather forecasts usually employ a range of

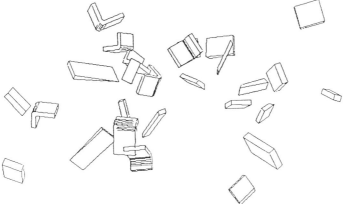

Fig 2.1
Exploding letterforms
from a student project

computer animated material, in addition to their 'intro', and are interesting in that the weather charts themselves, need to be remade, perhaps several times each day. A system is therefore required which will allow the rapid production of fresh images from meteorological information. This might be the animation of digitised satellite photographs, moving isobars or 'raining' clouds and 'shining' sun icons. This means that information must be received at regular intervals from a meteorological source, and that there must be a quick method of getting from production of the charts to the point of broadcast. One method, allows the charts to be compiled on cheap micro computers using a customised library of icons, which then automatically controls a Quantel paintbox in down-time to produce top quality graphics. In the Cardiff studio of Stylus Video Graphics, who developed such a system, there is an infrared video link to the TV station using their weather material.

2.2 SCIENTIFIC VISUALISATION

Weather is also a subject for scientific visualisation. In order to study the growth and development of weather patterns, a vast amount of numerical information on winds, temperatures, barometric pressures and other relevant data must be accumulated. This information arrives in the form of millions of numbers, which need to be presented in a way which will make sense of them. The data relating to any one moment in time can be plotted manually, or with the aid of a computer, but the development of any meteorological phenomenon requires that it be observed over a period of time. The computer can readily build a sequence of diagrams which can be played back as an animation. This is the essence of visualisation (sometimes called Visual Data Analysis or ViSC - Visualisation in Scientific Computing): to convert impenetrably large amounts of data into a visual form which will prove revealing. It is possible to select from the data in different ways in order to reveal different things, and to find different forms of presentation to show the relationship of several variables. There are several neat quotations to be taken from McCormick [1987]: 1: "Richard Hamming observed many years ago that 'The purpose of (scientific) computing is insight, not numbers'. The goal of visualisation is to leverage existing scientific methods by providing new scientific insight through visual methods." 2: "Today's data sources are such fire hoses of information that all we can do is gather and warehouse the numbers they generate." 3: "Scientists not only want to analyse data that results from super-computations; they also want to interpret what is happening to the data during super-computations." 4: "The ability of scientists to visualize complex computations and simulations is absolutely essential to insure the integrity of analyses, to provoke insights and to communicate with others."

Several hundred years ago, overlaying the location of deaths from cholera, on a map of available water pumps, traced the cause of a London epidemic. Held separately the two pieces of information yield nothing, but the importance of the knowledge gained from combining the two, explains the search for increasingly sophisticated methods with which to draw conclusions from separate pieces of data. The need for this development has been accelerated by the quantity of data which computer technology can generate, and the impossibility of making useful judgments about it. Papathomas [1988] points out that storage capacity increases are not keeping up with those of computational speed and quotes Upson as concluding that a researcher can compute more than he can store and can store more than he can comprehend. Visualisation can lead to revelation.

A graph showing acceleration, for example, plots speed against time, and has a clarity and immediacy which is lacking in the raw data from which it is constructed. A two-dimensional graph shows the relationship between factors whose proportions are indicated on two axes (i.e. plotting X against Y, plotting house prices against year). A three-dimensional graph extends the factors that can be compared by adding a third axis (i.e. plotting X against Y and then extending into Z, plotting house prices against year in different regions). The information from several 2-D graphs can thus be condensed into one 3-D graph with a potential increase in clarity (Fig 2.2). It is necessary to be careful about the scale of axes to preserve accuracy, and to find an appropriate presentational form to prevent 3-D information being obscured. The 3-D contour map which can be created in a 3-D graph, can have its surface overlaid with a further layer of data, effectively creating a 4-D image. It is also possible to plot diagrammatic information over a 'realistic' 3-D form, such as overlapping an operating temperature map for a disc brake over a 3-D model of the disc [Jern 1990].

In business graphics today, histograms (bar charts), pie charts

Fig 2.2
3-D graph

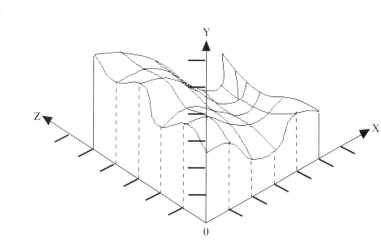

and other devices have become a common place, but the trend is now towards animated presentation which adds another axis, that of time. Whatever the form of presentation, it is not likely to be practical commercially if a visualisation specialist with esoteric programs is required to produce the material. Demand has therefore given rise to a range of accessible applications which can be used 'in house', or quickly and relatively inexpensively by a bureau. At the other end of the scale, the magnificent animated study of a numerically-modelled severe storm (Plate 8 & front cover), from the Scientific Visualisation Program at the National Center for Supercomputing (USA), required a range of workstations and computers including a Cray-2, and lists thirteen people in its credits for animation, research, support, script and audio. It shows very graphically in a 3-D animation, the growth of a storm using a cloud-like simulation containing within it diagrammatic information about air flow and other relevant features. The ground plane is divided into a grid mapped out with temperature distributions and colour coding continues throughout the model to make the storm's development understandable at several visual and intellectual levels. It is also richly impressive as an image in its own right, and conveys both the power and complexity of the phenomenon to the viewer, regardless of its meteorological content.

2.3 SIMULATION

An American firm specialises in creating animated computer simulations for use in lawsuits. It recreates car crashes which have involved the litigants, incorporating parameters based on those present in the actual accident, in order that the incident can be studied in court. This is in accord with one definition of simulation as: the reproduction of the conditions of a situation, etc. as in carrying out an experiment. It is more problematic as a piece of legal evidence if an alternative definition of simulate is tried: to make a pretence of, to feign. A simulation must embody truth about the situation it seeks to reproduce, but at the same time need not pretend to be that actual situation. Whilst recognising that we are looking at organisations of pixels denoting two automobiles on a flat screen, we can derive useful information about what two real vehicles would do in a given situation, if the representations have been programmed to make accurate responses in terms of the masses, forces and frictions involved in real life. Simulations seek to model reality with different levels of fidelity.

As well as being able to recreate an incident from the past, it is practical, and more usual, to want to create a simulation of a theoretical event. What would happen if one of the cars had been travelling twice as fast? At what point would a bearing fracture if it were put under an increasing load? By providing the right forces to a model which "knows" how to respond, we can watch the event unfold before us, then vary the parameters and observe the changes. This also allows us, in the right circumstances, to build and animate a scene by describing the physical rules which will apply, rather than having to kinematicaly control every element. The suspension of a car, for instance, can be tested in a dynamic model, and in some circumstances the operator can be interactively involved with the simulation, providing feedback which determines the model's future behaviour.

'Man-in-the-loop' simulation has developed over the last few years to the point where it can play a real part in the development of engineering projects, and in the case of the automobile, in subsequent driver training. In aeronautics, engineers can study the effects of stresses and strains on the airframe by simulating meteorological extremes, G-forces, etc., and subsequently check modifications against the same conditions. This leads to an understanding of the operational limits and to the definition of the aircraft's flight envelope.

2.4 FLIGHT SIMULATORS

A 'top-of-the-range' flight simulator will model the experience of flying an aircraft with such accuracy that flight sickness can be a genuine problem. At the cost of several millions of pounds, the pilot can sit in the aircraft of his choice, confronted with an authentic cockpit display, with a full set of 'working' controls, a realistic view of his chosen airport visible through the windscreen, appropriate engine noises, and can 'fly' the plane in any chosen conditions, with the correct flight characteristics. Hydraulic rams under his 'cockpit' tilt and rock him just as a real aircraft would do (see back cover), and the combination of physical and visual stimuli is so convincing that it is necessary to concentrate very hard in order to have any doubt in the reality of the flight experience. In some military simulators, the addition of snug hydraulic suits through which pressure can be increased on the body, and seat belts which can exert sudden tension on the pilot, allow the stresses of acceleration and increased G-forces to be reproduced. Even the relatively crude visual display of a flight simulator on a home micro is considered, by qualified pilots, to have a useful level of realism.

Our interest is centred on the visual display, and a number of clever shortcuts may be implemented in order to be able to move realistically through a scene in real-time. Dusk and night simulations require less detail to feel realistic, and point light sources alone (which are easier to manipulate than polygons) may provide much of the visual information about an airfield at night. Instead of 'building' a city from polygons it might be possible to 'stick' pictures of the city onto highly simplified shapes, similarly it is sometimes appropriate to produce authentic looking clouds by 'sticking' cloud pictures onto simple blocks, and shadows will often be acceptable if they are exist as silhouettes in an idealised ground plane and fail to adapt to contours and obstructions.

Flight simulators, of course, are more than just sophisticated fairground rides. They save aircraft, lives and money by allowing for efficient ground training, where landings and take-offs from obscure airports can be practice repeatedly, responses to in-flight emergencies rehearsed and pilots 'converted' to new types of aircraft. Military pilots can practice bombing runs, in-flight refuelling and landings on aircraft carriers without risk of dangerous and expensive mistakes. These principles can also be applied to other types of vehicle and equipment, train cabs, oil tanker bridges and anti-aircraft guns can all be simulated using similar techniques. A rather sombre spin-off from using flight simulators, is that crash investigators can sometimes use the data from the 'black box' flight recorder, salvaged from a crashed aircraft, to relive, and to analyse, the problems that caused the accident.

2.5 MILITARY

The military has always been an important client for many applications of computing, and graphics and animation provide no exceptions. Noakes [1988] points out that the initial impetus for the development of computer animation came from experiments with simple analogue computer systems originally used in anti-aircraft viewfinders, and says that it was John Whitney Snr. who reversed this military application of computers, enabling him to develop computer controls and imaging in the early 1950s. Interest by the military in a discipline can result in significant research funding, the findings of which can spill over into other applications, and is said that cruise missile technology was important to computer paintbox development.

Simulation is an area of obvious military interest, both for developing and testing possible confrontation scenarios, and for crew training with transport and weapon systems, etc. The difficulty of testing out many military projects in peace time, and, indeed, the possibility that some systems can never be tested until the time comes for them to be used in anger, renders the option of evaluation through simulation vital. It also imposes great pressure on the simulation to prove accurate. Recent developments in aircraft cockpit displays, which include projection on to the helmet visor, enhanced stereoscopic vision, night vision ability, simulated vision through animation in headsets, and interfaces operated by speech and glance, are all being exploited in other computer graphic contexts.

2.6 SPACE

It is even more difficult to rehearse something which will happen half way across the solar system, and so space research makes heavy use of simulation and visualisation. The resulting material is also important in the fight for project finance, and it has been suggested that the fine computer animated previews of the Voyager spaceprobe played a big part in winning funding for the mission. The quality of movement of objects in space - that smooth, slow, cleanly defined pace - seems well matched to the sort of motion which computer animation produces most easily. Its silky accuracy often looks odd when applied to earthbound activity, but outside the earth's atmosphere everything appears to move like a flying logo. The particular clarity, and spatial depth of images from space, with its limited number of light sources, is well mimicked by the computer, and it is also convenient that most of the man-made objects, which are the subject of these animations, are constructed using the geometry which computers most readily generate.

The Voyager example does bring to light an interesting question about the ethics of changing things to make them more visible. If a 20-hour flypast of Jupiter is condensed into 3 minutes, how true to the real event can the simulation be said to be. Similarly, it is often desirable to change the contrast ratio of an image to facilitate its reproduction in a newspaper, or to change the colour range to suit television reproduction, but this could be seen as tampering with evidence on which scientific judgement is based. When images are returned from distant places in the universe, the colours used in their reproduction are likely to be altered in order to make certain features more visible, and any notion of a "true" record must be balanced accordingly.

It is particularly important for astronauts to have access to simulators of the vehicles and conditions which space will present since the moon is not a good place to make your first attempt at flying a lunar module. Specialised variations on flight simulators provide that opportunity. Space scientists can also rehearse proposed trajectories without the risk of losing a valuable payload, and data from unmanned space missions can be used to generate authentic looking flights over the surface of distant planets prior to manned landings. The construction of space stations can be rehearsed, amended, demonstrated and practice in an environment where gravity can be switched on and off at will.

2.7 ARCHITECTURE

Towns and buildings are straightforward to model on a computer, and this ability is increasingly utilised by architects, not only to experiment with different structures but also to demonstrate their choices to the client before large amounts of money are spent. Having modelled a proposal within its local environment (Plate 9), it is then possible to move around the model, viewing the building (or structure) from any position, viewing the surroundings from within the building and assessing the total physical relationship of the building to its surroundings. The shadows cast by the building, by its neighbours and by trees on site can all be anticipated with far greater ease than previously possible, and on a sophisticated model it might be possible to simulate airflow around and through the new site.

It is equally possible to travel through the building to preview the internal appearance and layout, to try different permutations of lighting, different decors, changes of ceiling height and position of windows, for instance. The same data base from which the model is constructed might be accessed by an expert system to calculate percentage area of windows, heat loss under different conditions and conformity to changing building regulations. The possibility of anticipating traffic flow problems by watching them develop on screen, or of seeing the shadow from the new office tower creep round to engulf the nearby housing estate, is sufficiently clear to believe that it will become a major planning tool. An architect designing a child-care centre has already been able to 'test out' his design by moving around it 'as a child', in this case exploiting technology (described later) which enabled him to actually move like a child as well as see from a child's viewpoint.

In a simpler case, the remodelling of a foyer or a domestic kitchen can be previewed much more clearly by a client who has no experience of reading plans, than traditionally, where those plans were likely to be supplemented only by an artist's impression or single perspective view. A floor plan can be entered into the computer and 'extruded' to make a basic 3-D model in a few moments, after which you can 'move around' anywhere inside or outside that space. This offers the improved efficiency of making and viewing changes in company with the client, and together with others in the design team. A reservation about computer modelling is that it has an immediate believability and appearance of finality which a rough sketch avoids. The sketch is somehow pregnant with possibilities which the computer model has tidied out of the way, and the two techniques can most usefully co-exist. There is also a superficial credibility about a clean computer model which might disguise flaws and design weaknesses from the layman.

2.8 ARCHAEOLOGY

It would be possible to pick on almost any discipline area and find applications for computer animation, this chapter, therefore, selects just a few. Since the examples given tend to be the more obvious ones, I include mention of a perhaps less expected example of the use of the medium in the field of archaeology. An archaeological excavation involves the investigation of a 3-D space over a period of time, and the acquisition of large amounts of data. Computers have already proved their use in the management of the data that accrues, but the vital recording of continuing changes to the site, and the locating of finds, suggests a 3-D model able to reflect those sequential changes.

Paul Reilly [1990] describes a simulated excavation site named Grafland, of which he built a three-dimensional computer model showing soil layers with various features (such as pits and post holes) cut into them, which constitutes a record of the data inevitably destroyed in the course of excavation. An animation shows a green 'field' falling away to leave a block of ground which represents the excavation volume. This volume is manipulated to show various features: the major layers, sections through pits and post holes, buried items, etc. Individual features can be isolated and observed, a hypothetical artifact assemblage can be shown in situ, and layers can be removed in sequence or added in reverse sequence. The whole piece provides a graphic record of the site, and changes to it, which traditional methods would find hard to match.

Computers are also being increasingly used to construct models of buildings, and such like, from the parts revealed by excavations. It is much easier to hold components in the spatial relationships in which they are found in the gravity-less computer model, than in a real world model, and to subsequently manipulate them and, perhaps, change the model's scale. Much more complete structures, such as the Roman baths at Bath, can be explained and explored with animated computer models, and are becoming a familiar educational resource at such sites. The reconstruction of artifacts from a complex jigsaw of pieces has also been facilitated by computers, although the spatial manipulations which are required to be enacted are not usefully discussed as animation.

2.9 MEDICAL

The ability to extract data from scans taken of patients, and construct from it 3-D computer models, is proving an important new diagnostic tool. Previous technology only presented 2-D pictures of internal structures, and it was necessary to resort to surgery in order to confront organs in 3-D. This new method makes it possible to build skulls, vertebrae, hearts and brains in the computer and then to manipulate them on screen. Volume visualisation (described later) permits a 3-D model of a body to be peeled back in layers to reveal the organ the doctor requires to see. Ambiguities about the exact form are then removed as the part is animated. The animation can even provide a reconstruction of the patient's pulsing heart, through which abnormalities can be seen that no other method would so clearly reveal. Similarly blood flow through a faulty artery or organ can be shown more dynamically than before, acting as a teaching tool as well as a diagnostic aid.

In all cases of medical imaging (and indeed any specialised area), it is important to recognise that the computer operator must be working with someone who knows what is being looked for and what needs to be seen. Whilst I can look at a computer animation of a group of articulating vertebrae and be impressed with the clarity with which their movements are shown, the animation is useless if it does not reveal what the doctors need to see. It is the person with medical skills who must decide what is needed and the job of either the system or the operator to manipulate the data to provide it. Increasingly friendly and intelligent systems are likely to mean that the doctor and the operator are often one and the same person, but at this stage of development that is unlikely to be the case.

The reconstruction of shattered bones or rebuilding of a deformed skull, involves a 3-D jigsaw that can be rehearsed on the computer model. Also of assistance to plastic surgeons is a skin simulation which will allow intended operations to be tried on the computer before being used on the patient, and more general operation simulators are being developed which will permit doctors to practice surgery in simulated 3-D reality. This idea extends to operations being carried out by doctors hundreds of miles from the patient, which is seriously suggested as a future space flight scenario.

2.10 FILM

At some point in this book, John Lasseter must have special mention, and this is the moment. Working at Pixar in California, he is a key figure in the team which has produced several of the most stunning pieces of computer animation. In each of the last four years the films 'Luxo Jr.', 'Red's Dream', 'Tin Toy' and 'knicknack' have provided the yardsticks against which all the other entries in computer film festivals have been judged. Their strength lies in the combination of skills which are brought together in the team. Lasseter worked for Walt Disney and brings to the films all the professional skills of a top animator, whilst others at Pixar are leading programmers, artists and computer researchers. The films are remarkable for the seamlessness with which the varied skills brought to their creation merge. They operate at the technical limits of the discipline yet are unassuming in the demonstration of that skill.

An earlier Lasseter computer animation is 'The adventures of Andre and Wally B.' which broke new ground in the way that it used a storyboard which made few concessions to the limitations of production on a computer, and incorporated technical advances such as motion blurring, but it does not use the new medium as unselfconsciously as his later work. 'Luxo Jr.' (Plate 4), however, is a miniature masterpiece in which the medium has become completely invisible and we enjoy the animation for itself. The stars are two anglepoise (Luxo) lamps, mother and child, who act out a scene (in which the youngster plays with a ball watched by his parent) with a level of characterisation that is close to human. It is a classic example of the technology being handmaiden to the art, though in this case the technology has been developed to a very high level of sensitivity. Telling details include the understated set and palette (in computer graphics all the colour knobs are too often set to maximum), the pinpoint accuracy of the few sound effects, and the proportioning of the child lamp. Instead of being a small version of the parent, it is proportioned in the same relationship of human child to adult - small light shade but same size bulb, shorter support rods and springs but with the same diameter [Lasseter 1987].

'Red's Dream' followed, with a wonderful level of detail in an early scene, where the interior of a bicycle shop, including shadows from two of the five light sources, was rendered using the equivalent of 4.5 million polygons. This was followed by 'Tin Toy' (Plate 5), which won the first Oscar awarded to a computer animation, and which was estimated to be the result of twelve trillion calculations per image (*Time Magazine*, May 1989). Despite the fascinating attempt in this film to model a human baby crawling across the floor, it does draw attention to the fact that computers much prefer to build from geometric shapes (as in the tin toy of the title) than to deal with flexible baby skin. After taking on the massive technical challenges of the previous films, the team chose to enjoy themselves with 'knicknack', which is again a superbly made, and very funny, animation attempting to break down fewer technical barriers, but which brought the house down at SIGGRAPH 89. It is also shown in 3D, which is now becoming commonly available.

Computer animation in this context is an art/entertainment medium. It does exactly the same job as 'Tom and Jerry', 'Fantasia' and 'When the wind blows' (the nuclear war parable) but is able to call on the computer as an additional tool in the process. The same production motives can be attributed and the same value judgments applied. Lasseter says that it is interesting to hear people call his work pioneering but that it is not, it is just a matter of applying fifty-year-old principles from Disney to a new way of working [Swain 1987].

In the context of much else in this book, it is interesting to be reminded that what Lasseter and his team do is largely subjective. The application of Newton's laws of motion is not for Wally B., his is the world of 'squish and stretch', terms from traditional animation which describe the way a character distorts in order to accentuate a movement. In this world the character also displays anticipation of what is to come, priming the audience and involving them as more than mere spectators. The formulae for making an anglepoise lamp look excited come from animators not physicists, and much of the excitement of working at Pixar must come from the intimate mixing of science and art.

2.11 SPECIAL EFFECTS

As the credits roll on many feature length films today, reference will be seen to computer special effects. The ability to generate impossible visions 'realistically' is all in a day's work for the computer, and has come to be widely exploited. The classic example is in space films, where computer modelled spacecraft, planets, meteorite showers and the like can be created and choreographed with some ease, often intercut or merged with live or model shot material. One advantage of computer generated sets, as oppose to hand built models, is that they can be destroyed as often as you like and then restored at the touch of a button. This has to be set against the additional time currently taken to construct and render a complex computer model, though improving hardware and techniques will soon give the computer method a clear edge. Computer control of equipment, in particular the camera, is also of great use in coordinating shots.

It is estimated at Industrial Light & Magic, a company renowned for special effects production, that only about two percent of their effects currently use computers, and that whilst that per centage will increase, it will not take over entirely from the model makers who have honed their skills over a number of years. One of their stocks-in-trade is dirt and the ageing of models, which often seems alien to computer graphics programmers, and is not always easily implemented when required. It is also difficult, at the moment, for computer models to match the subtlety of lighting that exists on a real set, and the primary requirement of special effects is that they MUST match the look of the rest of the film. A major advantage of computer graphics and animation, however, is that the 'virtual' camera and lights have zero dimensions. There is nowhere that the computer camera cannot go, no gap is too narrow for its passage and it can pass through walls to order. Similarly, scenes can be illuminated without the physical presence of real lights to contend with, so there are no cables to hide, nothing to keep out of shot, and no problems with heat or power.

Much of the use of computers in special effects is in details rather than in the construction of complete images, undertaking tasks such as removing supporting wires from shots of real models. Also, most special effects involve combining together a number of pieces of image in each frame, only some of which may be computer generated. One well known space sequence has nearly two dozen separate parts composited together in each frame, though the complexity is, of course, invisible to the viewer. Optical compositing is versatile but suffers from generation loss (a degradation in image quality with each successive process) whilst the digital computer medium avoids generation loss but currently has lower resolution than film. This is a problem on a 50-foot screen. Film can be scanned into digital form, manipulated digitally, and then scanned back to film, but with the above limitations. (Filmed images also tend to take up more memory than computer generated images, as adjacent pixels are less likely to be similar on grainy film. Data compression is dealt with in Chapter 6.3.)

'Tron', from Walt Disney, was one of the first attempts at using a lot of computer animation (about 15 minutes' worth) in a full-length feature film, though unfortunately its limited commercial success inhibited similar developments. 'Star Trek II' contained the 'Genesis Demo' sequence (which is discussed in Chapter 10.1) which shows the creation of life on a distant planet, but it was the 'Star Wars' series that really perfected and popularised many of the techniques with which we are now familiar. It is strange to feel convinced by the flight of an imaginary space-fighter through channels on the surface of an imaginary death-star or by the aerial acrobatics of imaginary combatants in deep space when we have no direct experience against which to judge it. The film makers, however, have looked carefully at archival footage of World War Two dog fights, at film coming back from NASA space flights and at planetary simulations, to create rules for motion that can be credibly extrapolated from our second hand experiences. The sci-fi scenario where a live actor steps into a machine/space/alien world is tailor made for a computing solution.

In 'The Abyss' a remarkable special effect from Industrial Light & Magic shows a pool of water growing an arm-like tentacle which retains all its clear, reflective and transparent properties while it extends, moves towards actors, transforms its end into a face, and is touched by an actress. Its smooth, gently rippling motion makes it totally like water and yet doing things wholly impossible for water. The brilliant sequence took six people, with the assistance of part-timers, six to eight months to produce 75 seconds of film (close to one second of animation per person per month). It also took four and a half hours to render each frame, with a number of steps to ensure that fog, shading, reflection, refraction and highlights were all correctly shown. By coincidence, the research team at London's Electric Image, was developing a similar effect at the same time, which serves to suggest that the leading edge of the discipline is internationally spread.

Transformations can sometimes use digital technology to advantage, and are quite common in fantasy films where a frog might metamorphose into a prince, for instance, or into an icecream. In the film 'Willow' an interrupted transformation from goat to ostrich to turtle to tiger to woman was required, and was achieved by computer animating between animatronic puppets of the creatures. In 'Indiana Jones and the Last Crusade' a major character had to disintegrate from flesh to dust, and director Spielberg insisted it be accomplished in one continuous take. The 'morfing' technique pioneered on 'Willow' was adapted to metamorphose seamlessly between three puppet heads successively mounted on the same motion-control rig. In 'Willow', however, the individual elements were composited optically, whilst for 'Indiana Jones.' the image was entirely composited digitally within the computer. Similar transformations can be carried out in 2-D with much less difficulty.

2.12 ADVERTISING

There is nothing unique about the computer animation techniques used in advertising, which distinguishes advertisments from material produced in any other context. Their existence is justified by their ability to sell their product, and very large budgets may be available for very short animations. It is an area where art directors have to be responsive to stylistic fashions, and where the sensitive balance of cost and creativity is in the client's hands. A production is likely to be handled by an agency using designers and facilities which may be found both in, and out, of house. Specialists firms may be brought in to deal with motion control, rendering, post-production, etc., or one company may deal with everything from design to final tape. The brief may be tightly defined by the client, or the design team may be given a great degree of freedom.

2.13 CORPORATE VIDEO

Increasingly firms are using video for point-of-sale promotions, for corporate presentations and for staff training. Since these applications do not necessarily require the highest sophistication or resolution they can be produced in-house or by small companies. A team of one or two people with a video camera and 32-bit computer can produce cost effective material, and can develop a house image through working for the one firm. Desktop video (DTV) is briefly discussed later.

Presentations which have, in the past, been given as slide shows, can now be animated at little, or no, extra cost, but with great extra effect. The 'pulling power' of a moving image can be used in traditional or innovative ways to enrich either the firm's product or their message, according to the context. In-house training material can more easily be updated with video and subsequently overlaid or inter-cut with animated material to produce visually rich instruction.

2.14 EDUCATION

The use of video material in education has grown with the technology, and it is a natural development that computer animation should become one of the production tools. The increase in specifically educational programs shown on television, such as the Open University in the UK, has created a market which can utilise both high-end and low-end animation. Sometimes the presentation can be simply like business graphics, with bar charts and such like, but in a learning situation these basic visualisation techniques can be most valuable. At other times more sophisticated techniques may be appropriate, and whilst the educational budget is rarely high, if production times are less rushed then economies can be made. The product can also be expected to stay on the market for a number of years and benefit a large number of users (though, no doubt, at a time of education cut-backs, the employment of such media will be seen by some as an excuse for staffing reductions).

A particularly inspired set of videotapes called 'Project Mathematics!' has been produced by Jim Blinn (long-time computer graphics guru and past simulator of the Pioneer and Voyager missions) to teach high-school mathematics, with funding from several sources, including SIGGRAPH. It is, perhaps, easy to imagine how the mathematics underlying all of computer graphics could be readily employed in the service of explaining that same mathematics. How immediate the relationship between a viewing transform (which converts data about 3-D space in order to display it on a 2-D screen) and an animated demonstration of aspects of trigonometry. Once again, however, it is the coming together of mathematical and visual skills which proves so productive.

In common with other fields, educationalists are very interested in multi-media presentation, where sound, live video, still images, animation and text can all come together. The laser disc is the medium which has precipitated development in this area, though it might be overtaken by other digital media. Also the increased memory of the latest, and future, computers, together with greatly improved data compression techniques, suggests multi-media in a single, intelligent box. A particular advantage of this technology is that it need not be linear, and is rarely designed to be so. It is not switched on and followed from beginning to end, but is used interactively, with the user determining the route, and speed, taken through the information. Each user, therefore, effectively constructs his own course according to his own interests and pace of learning, although hopefully under qualified supervision.

Improvements in machine speed also make viable interactive animation, which can be used in a learning environment. A research project running at Exeter University, which utilises artificial intelligence techniques in a text-based application for teaching English as a foreign language, has considered an animated 'front end'. What better way to show the user's microworld, or to explain concepts about spatial relationship, than to have them acted out on screen, ideally being 'driven' by the user? Computer-based microworlds have been built for children on the simplest micros, enabling them to explore the vocabulary and interactions within a limited, specified domain, and the added resource of interactive animation makes them that much richer.

2.15 GAMES

Animation is almost a prerequisite of computer games. Whether it is Pac-man gobbling up opponents as he traverses a maze, space creatures advancing to be destroyed in a 'shoot-em-up' game, or just chess pieces moving themselves in response to your move, games abhor a static screen display. Because the display is attempting to be interactive on a simple home computer, the complexity of the moving image has to be relatively simple, but games creators take great pride in optimising routines and hacking corners to improve their performance. The big brother of the home computer game is to be found in amusement arcades, where more advanced graphics on more sophisticated hardware lets you crash cars and kill aliens much more spectacularly. Arcades also have a brash, noisy atmosphere and add a social dimension which enhances the games for aficionados.

Arcade games can be exciting, involving and even addictive. Dramatic perspective, colour and speed are typical features, but some of the latest machines borrow heavily from state-of-the-art simulators to condense the sensation of landing a jumbo-jet, or flying a spitfire in battle, into a small cubicle at a cost of, perhaps, one pound. The realism is eerie as you battle with the controls of an aircraft coming into J F Kennedy airport in the corner of a pub in Soho, and is still credible sitting in your living room at the keyboard of your home micro. On a grander scale, the 'Body Wars' ride at Walt Disney World EPCOTT Center in Florida simulates a journey through the human body for the audience of a small theatre mounted on a hydraulic platform. The ride is not interactive, but consists of 2 minutes of computer animation, generated at film resolution, matched by the movement of the platform.

Other games require less effort in their participation but can prove just as addictive. It was suggested that the game of 'Life', devised in 1970 and introduced through the Scientific American magazine, was responsible for more than half the world's computer time being stolen, as fanatical users sat mesmerised at their screens. Probably an exaggeration, but I can remember the widespread enthusiasm for this simple game, and as someone without my own computer at that time I was resigned to covering my floor in sheets of graph paper as hand-played games developed. It is hardly a game at all, as no-one wins or loses, it is necessary merely to set the starting conditions, and watch as a few simple rules (the number of neighbouring cells at any point in time determines whether a cell is destroyed or created) create patterns which take on an apparent life of their own. The fascination is in the feeling that the game is underwritten with some universal truth.

Other non-games, which involve little user input, are more like house pet substitutes. One involves little computer figures inhabiting a cross-sectional house on the screen, living their lives, albeit rather restrictedly, for the entertainment of the user, whilst another has computer fish swimming on the screen. Although these games might not be very meaningful, a number of scientists are creating stimulus-response animations, in which cellular automata respond according to rules governing their behaviour. The rules can involve response to environment, to 'hunger', to population density, etc., and the social orders achieved can be controlled by varying the rule parameters and can be studied in relationship to those of real creatures.

2.16 ART

It is, unfortunately, neither practical nor closely relevant to discuss the nature of art here, nor to find wherein it lies the role of the computer. Suffice it to say that artists use computers, that some use animation, and that whilst all art is not visual, animation is necessarily so. The aesthetic criteria for the judgement of computer generated art should be no different from those applied to other media but unfortunately they have tended to become suspended for judgement of this new art form and most 'computer art' to date has been rather bad. One reason is the usual one for a new medium, that it starts by mimicking existing media before it learns to stand on its own two feet (as did photography in the early years). Another is that 'computer art' has often been merely the output which computer scientists thought attractive. Brian Reffin Smith [1989] expresses his views forcibly:
"Let us first agree that most 'computer art' is old-fashioned, boring,

meretricious nonsense; and then that most of it is done by people whose knowledge of contemporary art and its problems is more or less zero; and then that most of this 'art' is actually a demonstration of the power of a few companies' graphics systems; then that most of the 'art' is really graphic design, produced for graphic design-like (and thus not art-like) reasons; and finally that there is a sort of 'mafia' of people who produce, teach, write about, judge at competitions and generally celebrate and curate this 'art' (the present author not excluded)."

There are, however, signs that the medium is not all bad. William Latham has created sculptures on a computer which could not exist in real life (Plate 7), and the obvious way to view an imaginary sculpture is to move round it and through it in an animation. He uses constructional solid geometry and texture mapping (both described later), to create delicate, magical structures sometimes resembling hallucinogenic seashells. These are variously presented as photo-graphs, on computer screens or in animations where the viewer is 'flown' through the intricate coloured tunnels of the sculpture without the inhibitions of gravity or reality.

The mathematical basis for some forms of art (remember 'op art'?) leave it open to obvious development by computer. This readily applies to work in 2-D and 3-D, where there has been a consistent interest for a number of decades, but can also be extended into the fourth dimension. It has been exploited with film but can be explored with much more flexibly on a computer, where experiments with the time-base might be compared sympathetically to tempo in music, music also having a strong mathematical basis.

Artists are also creating expressive, abstract animations and exploring formal problems with the added dimension of time. Art colleges often have a media area where time-based studies are available, together with computers, and in that situation the two are obviously going to get used together. The distinction between 'art' and 'film' as discipline headings becomes too blurred to be relevant. Sometimes animations made in a completely different context, perhaps scientific visualisation, could be said to have the beauty and integrity to take on the additional mantle of art objects.

2.17 MULTIMEDIA

Multimedia is not a separate discipline area, but a much vaunted merging of a range of different media, including animation. The ability to combine text, graphics, animation, video and sound into a single, interactive, screen-based medium is hyped as a communications revolution which will make books obsolete. These claims are balanced by critics expressing strong reservations about the impact and potential of the new medium, and, in fact, questioning whether it can be described as a new medium at all. It seems clear, however, that people's expectation of communication media will grow to encompass all these forms.

Many of the discipline areas described in this chapter would be able to make obvious use of a medium which combined all these different ways of communicating information into one friendly package. Most obvious, perhaps, is education. A student could interactively learn from (and with?) the system at the best pace to suit the individual, drawing on the richness of all the media at the system's disposal. Educationalists might have reservations about the desirability of this means of gaining knowledge, and I would be cautious about the degree to which it might be substituted for real experience, but it seems destined for heavy use in some areas. Business presentations will be sure to incorporate multimedia, and how much more useful would a car manual be if it was possible to animate the diagrams at will, call up a video of a process being carried out, have a voice talking you through, and interrogate the manual when it was not clear.

Already multimedia is providing the environment for manufacturers to demonstrate their latest hardware, and computer trade shows abound with screens showing multiple, resizing windows containing all of the above media being displayed simultaneously. The animation one can envisage being used in such a context stretches across the whole range from animated bar charts to photographically realistic 3D. The success of the medium relies on the newly available high-capacity storage devices such as optical discs, on fast, high-resolution hardware, and on improved video interfacing. It remains to be seen whether the visual capability of those taking up the medium is always adequate for the task, and bad multimedia will surely be more intrusive than bad desktop publishing. The medium might also prove vulnerable to copyright problems, with material too easily copied without regard for necessary permissions.

2.18 CONCLUSION

None of the application areas described is exclusive, they overlap to varying extents, sometimes almost entirely. For instance, the only difference between flight simulators and arcade game simulators is in the level of sophistication and the motivation for using them. Visualisation, in particular, is a label which could be loosely applied to all the other areas, as computer animation is very much about making visible ideas about experiences which are visual, conceptual and/or narrative. Computers have revolutionised mathematics, directing attention towards iteration for example, and animated visualisation is providing a window onto previously inaccessible areas of the discipline. It offers very real potential as a tool in man's search for understanding of himself and his universe.

CHAPTER 3

BASICS OF COMPUTER GRAPHICS

This chapter will outline sufficient of the basic principles of computer graphics that anyone new to the area should be able to make sense of the rest of the book. It does not pretend to go into much depth as the main focus of this book is movement, but it should provide a familiarisation with the main concepts involved in producing and displaying an image. In the main, issues that are likely to be 'transparent' to us as animators, such as the algorithms for polygon filling or clipping are not discussed, we will merely leave it to the machine to take care of them. We will concentrate on working in 3D, the principles for 2D usually being similar and simpler, but less relevant to the rest of the book. It is hoped that the brevity does not introduce too much imprecision, and it is expected that many readers will have enough experience of the area to skip the chapter. A few books, from the vast range on the market covering these topics in greater detail, are listed in the bibliography for those requiring more information.

3.1 PIXELS

The basic unit with which an image is built up on a normal computer monitor, or a television screen, is the pixel (a word shortened from 'picture element') which can be round, square (Fig 3.1a) or rectangular. In the same way that a newspaper photograph is made up of many rows of dots, rows of pixels (each row a 'scan line'), shoulder to shoulder across the screen (Fig 3.1b), give the illusion of a continuous image if they are in sufficient quantity and viewed from an appropriate distance. The horizontal rows of pixels are scanned by an electron beam in the cathode tube of the monitor, and the pattern of scan lines is known as a 'raster'.

Fig 3.1a (left)
An enlarged letter-
form showing its
construction from
square pixels

Fig 3.1b (right)
Round pixels form-
ing two intersect-
ing lines

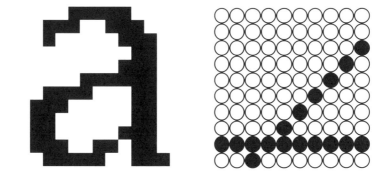

The density of pixels largely determines the resolution of the image. The more pixels, the higher the resolution, and the clearer the picture. The screen I am working at to write this has 400 rows with 640 pixels in each row, i.e. a little over a quarter of a million pixels on a screen about 220mm by 150mm, and is described by its manufacturer as being high resolution. In other situations this might be thought of as a rather low resolution, but unfortunately there is no standard for defining what is to be called high, medium or low resolution and the definition shifts according to manufacturer, machine type (i.e. micro or workstation), and the current state of the technology. On my monitor the pixels are either 'on' or 'off'. If they are switched 'on' they are illuminated and display as white, if they are 'off' they appear as black, thus giving a black and white display. A pattern of black and white pixels, in suitable proportions, gives the appearance of grey. Other machines may be able to display a 'grey scale' by varying the intensity of illumination of each pixel. On a colour monitor each pixel will be illuminated as a colour defined as a mixture of red, green and blue (the three primary colours of light) in an 'RGB' system. All red, with no green or blue, produces a red pixel. An equal mixture of all three colours produces a white pixel and by varying the intensity of the three primaries a range of colours (including greys) can be produced. Other systems exist for defining colours, such as 'HLS' where the colour is defined by parameters of hue, luminance and saturation. The size of the palette, and the maximum number of colours which can be displayed on screen at the same time, varies according to the machine. The number of 'bits' (a unit of computer memory) allocated to each pixel determines how large the maximum palette can be. A 16 bit home micro may be able to display 16 colours from a palette of 512 at a resolution of 320x200, whilst a 24 bit workstation may display any of a palette of 16.7 million at a resolution of 1280x1024. Three common standards established for PCs are:

'CGA' with 320x200 pixels, 4 colours
'EGA'   640x350   16
'VGA'   640x480   16

Boards with 4096x4096 pixels (16,777,216 colours) are available while resolutions exceeding 8000x8000 are being developed and the highest currently available resolutions produce images almost as fine as hand drawings. Although one would expect the realism of an image (taken from the real world) to increase with the size of the palette, there is a point at which the eye can no longer discriminate between close colours. Beyond this point, which is considered to be about 350,000 colours, little advantage is gained in increasing the palette but larger numbers are often available due to hardware/ memory considerations. The smooth gradations available with a large palette give an illusion of higher resolution than an image using a smaller palette.

3.2 COORDINATES

An individual pixel can be defined by its column and row number, for example: 'column 3 row 3' addresses a pixel near the top left of the screen, '320,200' addresses one at the centre of my screen. (Some systems internally define '0,0' at the bottom left, some at top left.) In the same way that a point on a map can be referred to by its grid coordinates, so any point on the screen can be referred to by its Cartesian coordinates, a system developed by René Descartes, the 16th century philosopher and mathematician. A horizontal axis (labelled 'X') and a vertical axis (labelled 'Y') are sufficient to locate any point in 2 dimensional space relative to an origin (0,0) (Fig 3.2a).

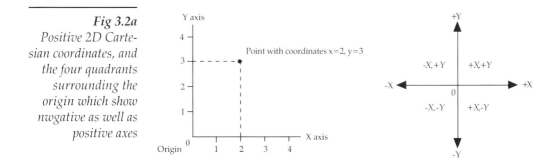

It is often convenient to set the origin at the centre of the screen, and to convert pixel co-ordinates accordingly, the coordinates being either positive or negative. In 3-space (meaning 3-D space) an additional 'Z' axis is required, orthogonal to the plane of the XY axes (Fig 3.2b).

Fig 3.2b
3D Cartesian coordi-
nate system

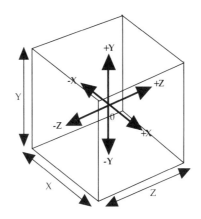

This is slightly complicated by the fact that some systems are 'left-handed', in which the Z coordinate numbers increase as they go away from the viewer, and some are 'right-handed, in which the Z coordinate number increases as they come towards the viewer (Fig 3.2c).

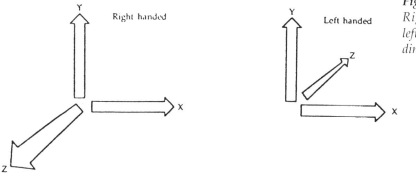

Fig 3.2c
Right-handed and left-handed 3-D coordinate systems

A commonly used 2-D alternative to the Cartesian system is the polar coordinate system (Fig 3.2d), in which distance (from the origin) and angle (between the positive X axis and a line from origin to the point) are used to determine position.

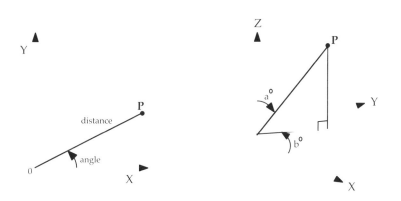

Fig 3.2d
Polar coordinates (left), spherical coordinates (right)

In 3-D this becomes the spherical co-ordinate system, requiring two angles plus the distance from origin to point. This can be useful in the real world where it more naturally matches our assessment of spatial position, and it also lends itself to trigonometric investigation, but is normally converted to the Cartesian system within the computer. (In order to simplify the mathematics used to manipulate coordinates a

55

3-D point can be represented by a four number vector to create an 'homogeneous coordinate system'. Whilst this will not concern us here it is mentioned in order to account for the extra number that might otherwise appear confusing in some calculations.)

The coordinates used for defining an object in the real world need not be the same as those used for defining its position on screen (or any other output device), and in fact rarely are. In fact the co-existence of several related coordinate systems can simplify object description. For example: a stamp could be defined as being near the top right hand corner of an envelope whilst the envelope is at the centre of a table and the table against one wall of a room. If the table is then moved within the room it is not necessary to redefine the position of the stamp as it has maintained a fixed relationship to the table. The local coordinate systems of the envelope, which defines the position of the stamp, and of the table, which defines the position of the envelope, are unchanged, only the position of the table within the local coordinate system of the room is new. It is also clear that since the monitor screen is in 2D, some manipulation of 3-D coordinates must take place in order that they can be displayed in a meaningful way. In fact a mathematical viewing transformation is used to create a 2-D perspective view of a 3-D scene from a given viewing point in 3-space (Fig 3.2e). The required position of the observer of the scene is defined using the world coordinate system. It is simple to display objects using projection systems other than the single viewpoint system (e.g. an orthographic engineering drawing) and to distort perspective at will.

Fig 3.2e
The viewing
transform

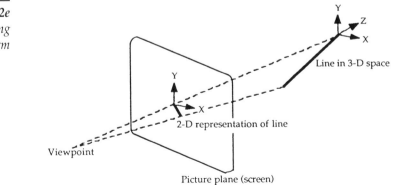

3.3 RASTER/VECTOR

It is, of course, possible to use a 2-D, single viewpoint description of an object, as in a photograph. This, however, does not contain the information necessary to manipulate objects in 3-D though the 2-D image can be manipulated in the plane of the screen. (For example an image can be can be broken up and the different elements moved about the screen. Those elements might correspond to individual objects and can be handled as 'sprites'.) Sprite animation is widely used in computer games.

If an object is represented by the pixel intensities which make up its two dimensional image, it is described as a raster image. If it is represented by the spatial relationships between the 2-D or 3-D vertices that define the object, then it is a 'vector' image. For example a square could be defined as being all the pixels from columns 100 to 200 in rows 350 to 450 (a raster description), or (if a 'unit' was set to be the same size as a pixel) as 10 units up, 10 across, 10 down and 10 back, starting at a particular point represented by screen coordinates 100,450 (a 2-D vector image), each unit being displayed as ten pixels in this case.

It is easy to overlook the need for an algorithm to draw lines on screen, but few line descriptions are likely to map exactly to pixel locations.

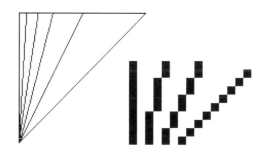

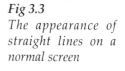

Fig 3.3
The appearance of straight lines on a normal screen

Newman [1984] points out that a straight line should appear straight, should terminate accurately, should have constant density, should have a density independent of line length and angle and should be drawn rapidly. One of the most widely used algorithms is that of J E Bresenham, which was originally developed for use on incremental plotters, and neatly avoids the repeated use of division or multi-plication (which are relatively slow calculations for a computer). It can be seen that whilst a vector description of a line is completely accurate, the accuracy with which it can be displayed is limited by the resolution of the output device (Fig 3.3).

3.4 TRANSFORMATIONS

Once an object has been defined using a coordinate system it should require only simple mathematics to modify or to move it (Fig 3.4).

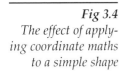

Fig 3.4
The effect of apply-ing coordinate maths to a simple shape

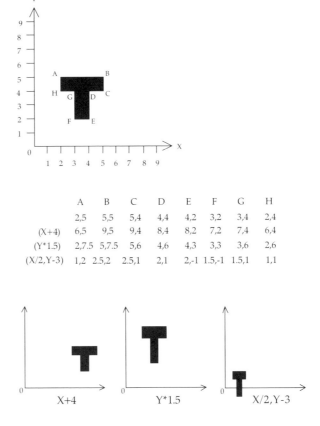

	A	B	C	D	E	F	G	H
	2,5	5,5	5,4	4,4	4,2	3,2	3,4	2,4
(X+4)	6,5	9,5	9,4	8,4	8,2	7,2	7,4	6,4
(Y*1.5)	2,7.5	5,7.5	5,6	4,6	4,3	3,3	3,6	2,6
(X/2,Y-3)	1,2	2.5,2	2.5,1	2,1	2,-1	1.5,-1	1.5,1	1,1

X+4   Y*1.5   X/2,Y-3

For instance, working in two dimensions, if we take a square we can see the effect of simple operations on the coordinate numbers. Add 2 to all the X coordinates, replot the square, and it has moved 2 units to the right, do the same to the Y co-ordinates and it moves up. This is known as 'translation' and already we have the means to animate the square by sequentially adding to the coordinates. Subtracting from the coordinates will move the square in a negative direction and the application of some basic trigonometry will allow us to rotate it about itself. We can scale it by multiplying the X and Y coordinates by a scaling factor, either proportionately or by different factors in each axis. Shearing results from proportional translation.

If it is required that the transformation is about the centre of the object then rotation, scaling and shearing require that the object is translated to the origin before being manipulated and then returned to position afterwards. If it is necessary to perform several transformations then the operations can be carried out in sequence. A particular form of mathematics is often used for these manipulations, with each transformation being represented by a matrix and the separate matrices representing a compound transformation can be concatenated into one. Compound transformations, however, are likely to produce different results according to the order in which they are carried out, and give rise to easily made errors.

These transformations can all be applied to 3-D objects with little extra complication. With the added refinement of their being carried out relative to an arbitrary point, hinging and jointing of compound objects becomes possible. If a hierarchy of local coordinate systems is established, each one positioned with a fixed relationship to the next one (a 'parent/child' relationship), then an object such as an arm can be articulated. The upper arm jointed about the shoulder, the lower arm hinged about the upper arm, the hand about the lower arm, etc., down to the sets of finger joints. We will see later, that in a case such as this, it is possible to define the limitations of movement at each joint so that undesirable movement is avoided, i.e. the arm bending backwards at the elbow.

3.5 MODELLING

A number of types of descriptions are available for 3-D objects, the commonest in the context of computer animation being the boundary representation method, known as 'b-rep'. This polygonises the surface of an object and stores the description as a list of vertices (the corners of the surface polygons), a list of lines joining the vertices (the edges of the polygons) and a list of faces (identifying the individual polygons). For the purposes of rendering the object these polygons are usually triangulated (since triangles are necessarily planar and so unambiguous surfaces) but this is not necessary to the description of the object.

Fig 3,5a
A bottle shaped template and the object created by spinning it

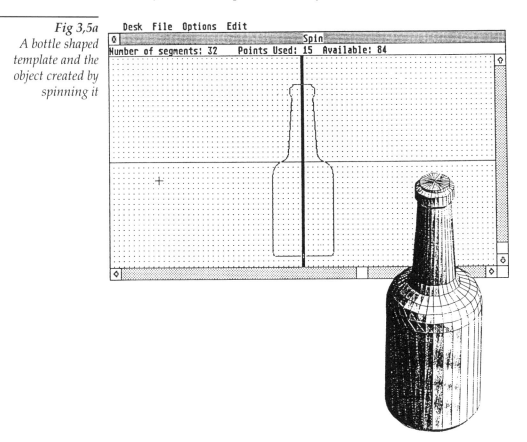

Fig 3.5b
*A triangular tem-
plate spun to form
objects with 3, 10
and 75 sides; a tem-
plate spun 250
degrees and a
template offset from
the centre of rota-
tion, spun 250
degrees*

A 2-D section can be swept through 3-space to define a 3-D object, creating a 'swept surface' model. If the section is described in X and Y, a rotation of the section about either of those axes (normally around Y) would produce a 'spun' object, such as a bottle (Fig 3.5a, 3.5b). If the sweep is in a direction orthogonal to the section the object is described as 'extruded', a simple case being a square section extruded along a straight path to produce a cube (Fig 3.5c, 3.5d). It is possible for the section to change at points along the extrusion path, in which case a more complex object, like a ship's hull, could be defined. The path need not be straight, however, and subtle objects can be created by extrusion along curved paths.

Fig 3.5c
A cube extruded from a square template

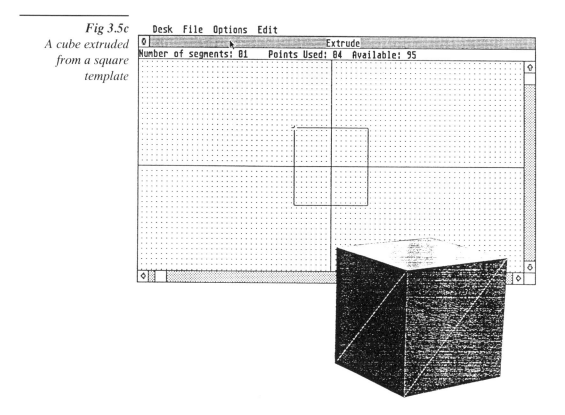

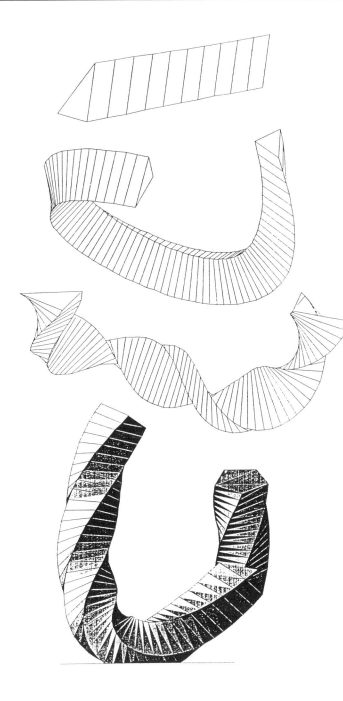

Fig 3.5d
*A triangular
template extruded
along a straight line;
along a curved path;
and along a curved
path with twisting.
The bottom object
was created by
extruding a
pentagonal template
along a path with a
smooth bend and an
angular bend.*

This is similar to 'lofting', a widely used technique in which cross-sections through an object are joined by 'triangulation', which is a standard technique for creating an optimal surface of triangular patches between the edges of consecutive sections. The cross-sections could be thought of as being similar to geographical contour lines defining a hill, and the triangular patches as describing the surface of the hill itself. The precision of the technique obviously depends on the detail of the cross-section and the closeness of the sections. It is likely that the sections would be input using a digitising pad, and the triangulation then computed with a simple program, which may have to deal with problems like the sections having different numbers of points.

A curve can merely be approximated by a continuous sequence of straight lines but can be accurately described mathematically. Bezier, working for Renault, evolved one of the most commonly known formulations in order to be able to describe the curved panels of car bodies. The Bezier curve is defined by a parametric equation which uses 'control points' to establish varying degrees of curvature along a line (Fig 3.5e, 3.5f).

Fig 3.5e
A spline curve changed by the movement of control point 'P'

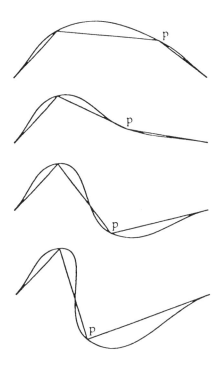

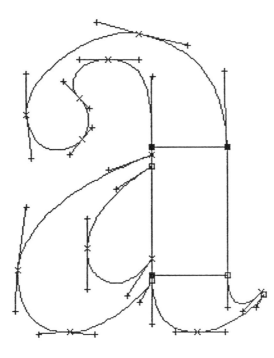

Fig 3.5f
A letterform created
using Bezier curves.
The image is taken
directly from the
screen in order to
retain the tangents
(which are made
visible as an aid to
editing the shape.

Moving the points changes the local curvature and the fact that the curve is tangential at the endpoint means that continuity of curve can be maintained with any other curve sharing that endpoint. If a curved surface was defined using the b-rep method, it too would only produce an approximation, since polygons drawn onto a curved surface would have curved edges and would not be planar. A complex surface (a teapot is the classic example) can be broken up into surface 'patches' which can be individually defined by extending the principle of the Bezier curve into three dimensions. The simplest Bezier curve or patch is quadratic (to the power of 2) but greater control can be achieved with cubic (to the power of 3) or higher order equations, at the cost of requiring more control points and more maths.

A further modelling method, popular in CAD systems, is constructive solid geometry, referred to as CSG. In this approach, an object is represented as a combination of simple 'primitives' such as cube, sphere and cylinder. These basic solids are used as building blocks for more complex objects by the use of Boolean set operations of 'union', 'intersection' and 'difference'. The primitives can be scaled, joined (union), subtracted from one another (intersection) and an object can be defined by the area of overlap of two other intersecting objects (difference) (Fig 3.5g).

Fig 3.5g
CSG modelling
illustrated by an
intersecting cube
and wedge

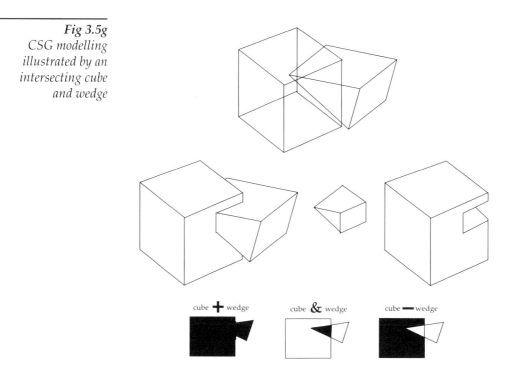

It is also possible within the system to define primitives by the use of 'half-spaces', which are infinite surfaces dividing 3-space into solid or void, to define objects. Any point exists either in the solid, the void or on the division, and several half spaces can combine to define the space enclosing an object. CSG is very economical in the information it needs to store but may need to be converted to b-rep in order for the object to be rendered.

A simple method which is of increasing interest, and which has found particular application in the field of medical imaging, is 'spatial occupancy enumeration'. 3-space is divided into cubic units called 'voxels', of whatever size is suitable, and the object is described by recording the units it occupies (Fig 3.5h). Because this method currently requires extensive storage in order to define an object at a useful resolution, the technique of 'octree decomposition' is often employed.

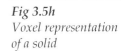

Fig 3.5h
Voxel representation
of a solid

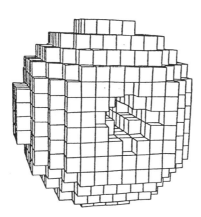

This starts with large units and allows the unit size to be reduced in steps only in those areas where greater resolution is required. Although the method awaits the wider availability of computers with big memories in order to come to fruition, it does have a number of advantages in some contexts, and is easy to render. Particle systems are a particularly interesting, though rather specialised, method of modelling. They consist of a large number of 'particles' (typically between 10^4 and 10^6) each of which represents a single point in 3-space. In quantity, a group of these particles can constitute an object, and it is a method associated with modelling fuzzy phenomena such as clouds, fire and grass. Reeves [1983] describes as advantages of the method, that a particle is very easy to define, create and move.

Another means of modelling irregular surfaces is to use fractals which build the surface in a semi-random or probabilistic way. They have the intriguing property that the mathematics which defines them can generate an infinite level of detail. This real world property is obvious when you consider approaching a mountain range, which the technique has typically been used to generate. The mountains reveal the same level of detail whether viewed from ten miles or ten inches, but it would be impossible to store, in a computer, all the detail of a mountain range down to the level of each grain of sand. In one dimension, fractals can be used to recursively subdivide sections of a line with a predetermined offset to create a 'crinkly' line with a degree of crinkle proportionate to the offset (Fig 3.5i). The same principle can be applied in 2D to polygons (Fig 3.5i), and in three dimensions to the facets of an object, as is used in the construction of fractal mountains. Applied in four dimensions, fractals can be used to control the motion of complex irregular moving objects, such as a leaf in the wind [Magnenat-Thalmann 1985].

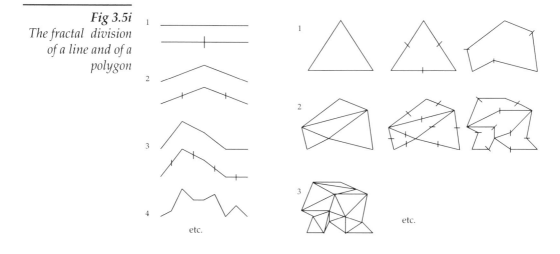

Fig 3.5i
The fractal division of a line and of a polygon

It can be seen that the techniques which are appropriate for describing a cube (or the spheres much loved by manufacturers when promoting their products) are unlikely to be the best for describing fog or water. Nature tends to avoid right angles but CAD systems, for designing man-made objects, revel in them. Angular planes can be efficiently defined by a collection of edge vertices, but curved surfaces lend themselves to more abstract mathematical descriptions. Whilst a usable representation of a sphere can be created with a b-rep system it is impossible to use that method to describe a perfect sphere for, however small the polygons used, they can never be more than an approximation of the surface. It might require the storage of 45,000 coordinates alone to describe a moderately smooth b-rep sphere (in addition to the necessary edge and face information) whilst a perfect sphere can be defined in a CSG system by four numbers: the three coordinates of the centre point plus the radius. It may be necessary to model flexible or articulated objects, and the methods described lend themselves readily to the construction of elements which can be hinged together. One way of building a flexible object is to define its surface by facets whose vertices are point-masses connected into a mesh by dampened springs (Fig 3.5j).

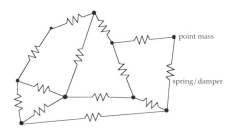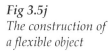

Fig 3.5j
The construction of
a flexible object

Rooney [1987] says "there exist two fundamentally different approaches to the problem of describing objects and systems, namely: 'declarative' representations and 'procedural' representations. The difference between them is essentially that between a description of the state of the object, and a description of the process needed to obtain the object. It is a bit like the difference between the physical shape of a cake and the recipe for making the cake." He goes on to suggest that both forms must represent both topological and geometric aspects. Attributes of the declarative form include: vertices, edges and faces; points, lines, surfaces and volumes; positions and orientation; equality and inequality. Attributes of the procedural form include: paths and cycles; translation and rotation; algorithms and procedures; (also pointers and records, which are structures used in programming).

3.6 HIDDEN SURFACES

Having created a numerical description of the desired model it is necessary to decide on a form in which to display it on the computer screen. The simplest representation (and quickest to display) is a 'wireframe model' in which all of the edges are shown as lines. Because it was the earliest form of representation of an object on a computer screen it is still sometimes called for when a scene is required to have a 'computer generated' feel to it. This can be confusing to view, however, as we are able to see the back as well as the front of the object and this lends itself to the manifestation of optical illusions. Some improvement can be achieved by using intensity modulation to strengthen close lines and make distant lines fainter, but unless it is transparent, the front surfaces of a real object obscure the back surfaces, an important factor in our visual understanding of the object. In fact, even a transparent object usually has the back surfaces modified in some way by being viewed through the front ones, either changed by a shift in colour or tone or by refraction. A wireframe view can only be constructed, of course, from a model which has been built from vertices, such as in the b-rep system, or else can be converted to such a system at this stage. An improvement on a wireframe model is a 'hidden line' version in which the front surfaces obscure those behind, resulting in a marked decline in ambiguity.

This ability to create a more realistic view is so important that many algorithms have been created to do the job (Fig 3.6a). The manner in which they work depends on the way in which the model data is held and on the level of accuracy required.

Fig 3.6a
The legibility of a model using four representations: wireframe, hidden line, shaded and shaded with edges of facets shown

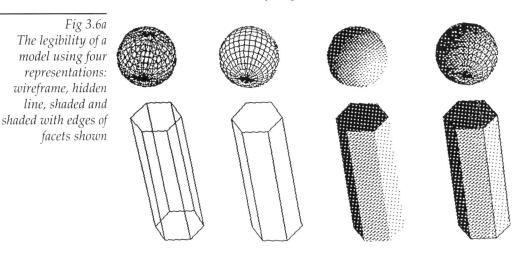

There is usually a trade-off between sophistication and speed, as a general purpose algorithm (which might not be able to deal with special cases) is likely to be much faster than one which is built to test for, and resolve, all conflicts it might meet. Applications often provide a quick method for draft work, at which stage errors might be more acceptable than time delays (Fig 3.6b), and a more efficient method for final work when the extra time taken is an acceptable overhead.

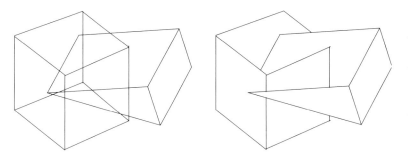

Fig 3.6b
An example of the errors which can arise with unsophisticated hidden line routines. (This can also be seen in Fig 2.1 although it is not visible when animated)

The simplest way of using hidden line removal to improve on a wireframe model is by 'back-face culling' in which surfaces pointing away from the viewer are removed. The direction in which a face is pointing is established by checking the angle between the viewer's line of sight and the 'surface normal', a perpendicular to the surface in question, using vector mathematics (both surface normals and vectors have many applications in computer graphics). The back-face cull is a rather crude method, however, as it does not deal with objects overlapping one another and usually proves inadequate for objects of any complexity.

A number of more efficient methods are available, employing different principles, to achieve the goal. Commonly used is the 'z-buffer' method in which the spatial depth of each surface is checked at each pixel location, and the the closest surface (i.e. the one with the smallest Z value) is displayed. Another is the 'painter's algorithm' which displays the furthest surface and then works forward through space "overpainting" with closer surfaces (although the distance of a surface can often prove ambiguous).It is in the nature of some rendering methods, such as 'ray tracing', to solve the hidden surface problem as we will briefly see.

3.7 RENDERING

The description so far, of the generation of computer images, suggests a rather diagrammatic representation of the real world.To create a realistic image of the world our objects need more treatment than just having their hidden surfaces removed. Objects in the world are illuminated by light of different colours and qualities coming from a range of sources and directions, they cast shadows, they have different degrees of reflectivity and transparency, they have different surface qualities. The interaction of these qualities gives us a rich understanding about them and the scene they inhabit.

There are several lighting types, available in even the simplest applications. A 'point source' is a light source such as a spotlight, in which the beam spreads out from a specific point and may be restricted in its arc by a shade of some sort. It can be subject to the 'inverse square law' in which the light intensity decreases in proportion to its distance from the source. To simulate a source such as the sun, however, the rays are given direction but are treated as parallel and of consistent strength (not strictly accurate, but the distance of that particular point source is so great that the approximation is adequate). A third light type is 'ambient', which is calculated to illuminate all surfaces with consistent strength and without direction, and is often found useful in relieving the totally shadowed areas created by directional light sources in simpler lighting models. It is possible, of course, to fill in surfaces, pixel by pixel, with a painting program but it is rather more practical to employ algorithms for dealing with the effects of light on surfaces. As you will have come to expect, they range from fast, crude renderings that are almost immediate, to slower, more subtle methods that can take hours, or even days, to complete.

The simplest one is 'Lambert shading' (Fig 3.7a), which uses the cosine of the angle between the ray of light hitting the surface and the surface normal, to establish what the intensity of the surface should be (hence its alternative name of 'cosine shading'). As the light source comes to be closer to a perpendicular from the surface, so the angle decreases and the surface becomes lighter. When the light is at right angles to the surface the angle is zero and the light intensity is at maximum. Despite its simplicity, it adds enormously to our perceptual understanding of the object and, since it can be applied extremely fast, is usually included as the basic shading method in applications. It does, however, produce flat shaded polygons which emphasise the artificiality of the model, and lacks any gradation across planes.

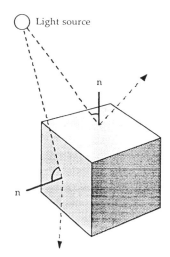
Light source

n

n

Fig 3.7a
Lambert shading.
The cosine of the
angle between the
surface normal 'n'
and the light ray is
used to calculate the
intensity of the
surface

Henri Gouraud gave his name to an improved shading model published in 1971 (Plate 3). It averages the light intensities at the edge of each polygon and then interpolates along each scan line across the plane lying between these averages to give a smooth, eggshell like gradation. An extension of his model also allows the individual facets to become hidden by interpolating across facet edges. Two years later, a paper by Bui Tuong Phong introduced a method which added specular highlights to smooth shading. Phong shading calculates the intensity at each point along a scan line from its approximated normal, that approximation being arrived at by interpolating from the normals at the edges on that scan line, which are in turn interpolated from the normals at the points bounding that edge. Surfaces with different levels of shininess can be simulated by employing a gloss parameter to determine the size of the highlight area. This 'specular' highlight depends on viewpoint, unlike a diffused surface which is independent of the eye position.

An odd effect of both these methods is that an object, such as a polygonised sphere, can be beautifully smooth across its surface, but will still have an horizon made up of the straight polygon edges. This requires additional treatment. It is also necessary to make sure that objects which are meant to look polygonal do not unintentionally have their edges smoothed over. The surface can also be made to approximate that of specific materials by the addition of some extra calculations (derived from real materials by James Blinn) to the Phong algorithm, and applications often have a small library of surface types, such as silver and brass, available.

A more recent method, called 'ray tracing' (Plate 3), employs a different technique to great effect. The principle is simple, tracing a ray back from the viewing position through each pixel to the first surface it meets. The ray is then reflected from this surface on into the scene, reflecting off subsequent surfaces until it reaches a light source or leaves the scene. The pixel is then set according to the intensity and colour of the light remaining after the contribution of intervening surfaces. A lot of computation is required, increasing with resolution, and a limit must be set to the number of times a ray can be allowed to reflect before a final result is accepted. The more reflections each ray is allowed, the more accurate the result. The method produces arresting images and automatically deals with shadows with refraction and with transparency but is currently too slow to be practical in many situations. It is good at dealing with specular light but poor with diffuse light. It is useful to have shadows dealt with automatically as they can otherwise be time consuming to calculate, and a number of shadowing algorithms have been developed over the years. Chin [1989] describes previous work and presents a method which achieves interactive performance for polygonal environments of modest size on appropriate hardware, and uses a shadow volume approach as one of its two methods.

Even slower, though good at dealing with diffuse light, is the 'radiosity interchange method' which developed with the field of architectural design in mind. It works from the assumption that the light energy striking a surface must equal the energy reflected, transmitted and absorbed. The first requirement is that the whole scene is divided up into surface patches (which may prove to be the way it has already been modelled) and each patch is effectively treated as a secondary light source. Extensive calculations consider the effects of every one of those patches on every other and would be almost impossible to compute if it were not the case that most of the patch pairs will prove to have a nil relationship. This method produces very credible subtlety within shadows and penumbra, and has the advantage that the computations are independent of viewer position which means they need only be done once per scene (provided that nothing within the scene changes). This would be convenient for animating movement through a fixed scene but impossibly painstaking for moving anything within the scene, since all the calculations would have to be repeated each frame.

New lighting models are being developed all the time, to deal with some of the subtle and complex situations that can arise in real life. By way of example, we can look briefly at two that have been presented this year. Mark Watt [1990] uses a variation of backward ray tracing (where the ray starts at the light source rather than at the eye) to render specular to diffuse phenomena such as the interaction of light with water. His method incorporates information about caustics, which deals with reflection and refraction by curved surfaces. With this technique he has produced some elegant and convincing animations of the delicate patterns that dance around on underwater surfaces (Plate 6). It is fascinating to see how evocative they are of other qualities we are all familiar with in swimming pools, recalling the memory of being actually in the water. Nakamae [90] looks at rendering road surfaces under various weather conditions, which has particular relevance to the development of driving simulators. His team has presented animations of road surfaces drying out, in which muddy puddles evaporate (requiring analysis of the minute undulations of the asphalt), but more exciting are those of cars driving at night. In order to simulate the effects of oncoming headlights he had to allow for diffraction due to the pupil of the human eye and even that due to eyelashes. The results are uncannily effective (see back cover), and the most significant clue to the computer origination of the sequence, lies not in the rendering, but in the smoothness of the car's motion.

3.8 TEXTURES

Most real objects do not have the smooth, uniform, unblemished surfaces which most of our shading models will produce. They are patterned, rough surfaced, reflective, transparent and probably dirty. One way of increasing the realism of our models is to wrap them in suitable surfaces, which has the advantage of adding surface detail without increasing the complexity of the model itself. The texture can be either two dimensional, like the graphics on a carton, or 3-D, like the surface of a shag-pile carpet. The technique is called 'texture wrapping' or, more accurately, 'texture mapping', and often offers the bonus of increasing depth perception since the scale of the texture can be seen to decrease as it recedes in space. Mapping functions for a flat surface are quite simple, but curved surfaces require more complex parametric descriptions, and models with complicated surfaces (consider the teapot again) will need to be broken into separate patches. This lends itself to awkward discontinuities of texture which require careful planning to avoid. 'Image mapping' transfers a 2-D image, which might be a photograph, a pattern or a graphic, from its location elsewhere in memory to the object's surface using an appropriate mapping function. A typical use would be to put the world map onto a sphere. The image which is mapped may be animated, as may the surface it is mapped to, and it is common to see a rotating cube with animated images on each face. 'Reflectance mapping' simulates a reflective surface by mapping a picture of the object's environment onto its surface. 'Procedural mapping' uses a suitable mathematical procedure to generate the texture values, and has been used to employ fractals in the simulation of rust on a surface. 'Bump mapping', or 'perturbation mapping', creates 3-D textures by perturbing the surface normals according to a function or a bump map. The illusion is created because the shading model (which uses the surface normals to decide which way a surface is facing in order to set the intensity) is now presented with a variety of normals across a single plane. The surface of an orange is the standard example.

An alternative to surface texture is 'solid texture' which involves mapping from a 3-D texture space to the 3-D object. This is a very simple exercise, involving little more than scaling, and has the advantage that it is independent of the surface complexity of the object being mapped to. The texture can be thought of as running right through the object (like the old "gob-stopper" sweet) which means that the object will reveal consistent texture if it is cut or modified. This makes it ideal for modelling the grain in wood but not for laying a graphic onto an object. Because of the enormous storage requirements of a 3-D texture map, and the complications of trying to input data digitised from a 3-D source, the information is usually generated procedurally when required.

3.9 ARTIFACTS

A number of errors commonly arise in the production of computer generated images (CGI), usually as a result of the fact that computers, and their display devices, work in discrete steps whilst the world we operate in is smoothly continuous. This results in our often having to match specific points in time and space to the nearest available points in computer time and space, with a small margin of error proving unavoidable. It might, for instance, be that our viewing transform converts a point in 3-space to an ideal screen location which is not exactly centred on a pixel. The best we can then do is to set the point at the nearest pixel, introducing an error (the potential magnitude of which will increase as the screen resolution decreases). This type of error is described by a branch of mathematics known as 'sampling theory' and is particularly evident in CGI as spatial aliasing. A straight line drawn on screen horizontally or vertically will appear perfectly straight since it will run along one row or column of pixels. A line drawn at 45° will run diagonally through pixel locations lying in a straight line, but consider a line lying at an angle close to, but not at, those described. The requirement to match the desired line to the nearest pixel locations results in an uneven, stepped effect. As jagged edges ('the jaggies') can be quite destructive of the illusion we wish to create, much effort goes into removing it, or, more accurately, disguising it.

'Anti-aliasing' is a technique (which might be considered counter intuitive) for disguising these effects by "softening" the edges of the line (Fig 3.9).

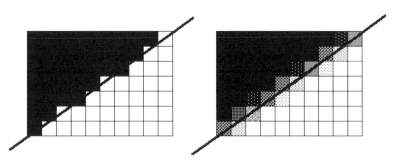

Fig 3.9
Anti-aliasing the border between a light and a dark area

Instead of representing the line with pixels entirely of the required intensity, the intensity of each pixel crossed by the line is set at a level between that of the line and that of the background, in proportion to the percentage of the pixel covered by the line. Where the line coincides with a pixel exactly it takes the line intensity, where the line crosses the boundary between two pixels they are both set at an intensity half way between the line intensity and background intensity. The percentage is arrived at by dividing the pixels into 'sub-pixels' for the purposes of the intensity calculations, and then averaging the values to arrive at an intensity for the screen pixel. (This is an example of 'super sampling', which is the academically correct means of dealing with aliasing problems.)

On a micro-computer, where its low-resolution display would most benefit from anti-aliasing, it is likely that the palette will be too small for it to be carried out effectively, and on the highest resolution machines the problem is far less important. In the middle area, however, the technique is so important that a long, expensive, legal battle has recently been fought in the London High Court over patent rights associated with it. Other methods of dealing with the problem are the 'dither matrix' which changes the intensity of a pixel on each scan sequence, and 'pixel phasing' where the screen location of individual pixels can be shifted fractionally by automatic adjustment of the electron beam.

'Temporal aliasing' is a manifestation of the same problem in time, rather than space, and therefore of interest to us in animation. One of its manifestations is clear in old TV westerns, where the stage-coach wheels sometimes appear to be static or rotating backwards. The spokes of the wheel are frozen in each frame of film, and the apparent direction of movement is determined by whether the spokes have been frozen before or after their relative position in the preceding frame. If the wheel takes 1/25th of a second to rotate and the camera shutter is recording it 25 times a second, then it will appear to be in the same position in each frame. According to whether it rotates faster or slower than the shutter speed (or a multiple of the shutter speed) it will appear to be rotating forwards or backwards. Super sampling again provides a solution. By rendering more frames per second than required, and merging them together, the artifact is replaced by 'motion-blur' which is visually acceptable.

'Mach banding' is a phenomenon, particularly associated

with Lambert shading, in which a surface that should be smoothly shaded appears to have dark streaks on it. This anomaly is a product of our edge detection abilities and is most easily improved on by decreasing the size of the polygons.

'Illegal colours' can be a problem at a production level, since it is possible to generate colours on screen which can not be accurately recorded onto video tape or broadcast. A waveform device monitor, which is like an oscilloscope, can be used to spot the offending colours.

'Precision errors' are inherent to digital computers. The computer can only allocate a limited amount of memory to each number it uses, and if this space is insufficient to store the complete number it becomes truncated. The imprecisions thus created can accumulate to create noticeable errors, but their avoidance is a programming issue which will not concern us. It is interesting to see, however, that in an engineering drawing application I have used, if 10 inches is converted to millimetres, and then straight back to inches again, the result is not exactly 10 inches. In another context, these rounding errors have been blamed, in the past, for false nuclear alerts!

3.10 HARDWARE

Although mentioned elsewhere in the book, it is worth briefly noting at this point, that the fast running of some of the algorithms described in this chapter has been found to be crucial to the practical production of computer animation. In some cases, therefore, these algorithms have been built into the machine itself, often then being referred to as 'firmware', since it embodies 'software' in 'hardware' form. Examples might be anti-aliasing, hidden line removal, fast polygon filling and shading algorithms. Data compression, described in Chapter 6.3, is an area of current interest in which algorithms built into chips are becoming standard in workstations, and in specialised situations, such as flight simulation, it might prove cost effective to custom build chips for a specific job. It is also now common, even in home micros, to include specialised chips such as graphics management chips to relieve the CPU (central processing unit) of the chore of looking after the graphics, and thus allowing it to work much faster on other jobs.

3.11 EXPENSE

It is interesting to compare the computational expense of different actions relating to graphics, by measuring them in terms of the number of assembly instructions necessary to carry out each action. This gives an insight into the relative time that various operations will take, though the scale of the action must also be considered. The following examples have been given:

Zoom : 24

Pan : 24

Pan + zoom : 40

Back surface cull : 40 (per facet)

3-D rotation : 72

Perspective : 150 (per point)

Clipping : 1000 (per line)

Depth cueing : 3200

Anti-aliasing : 4000 (per line)

Polygon shading : 8000

Hidden surface removal : 10000

Light-source shading : 20000+

CHAPTER 4

MOVEMENT CONTROL

Movement control is the very heart of animation. To point out that the difference between an animation and a static image is that the animation moves, is a truism which disguises the subtle complexity of the distinction. It is often the case that it is the quality of movement that establishes the credibility of a piece of animation, and the refined skills of a true animator are not readily matched by a simple program loop. It is, however, very easy to achieve certain types of movement with a computer, and this ease could tempt the less critical, or less experienced, animator to minimise the problem which needs to be tackled. If you are working at a machine which offers you one particular way of moving an object, it is inconvenient to admit that the method offered is inappropriate. I prefer the term 'motion control' to that of 'movement control', but since the former is normally used to refer to the control of a moving camera, I will use the latter.

It is by closely observing the real world at first hand and at second hand (through media such as film and photography) that you come to understand how real things move. It also sensible to be familiar with animation precedent, and to accept, in passing, the possibility that the conditioning it offers might be inhibiting. When a motion is one of pure invention, such as tumbling letterforms across the screen, the roots of its credibility may still lie in the viewer's knowledge of movement in the real world. It is this knowledge that enables a triangle to not only walk or run, but to do so cheerfully or miserably. I'm sure that many people have identified motion as having been generated by a computer because of its unworldly adhesion to a clearly mathematical path, perhaps a dead straight line or a perfectly formed curve, but paths such as these can still provide the basis for believable movement. We sometimes need to be presented with a facsimile of real life, and at other times can accept conventions which distort, enhance or idealise.

Early paintings by the artist Edgar Degas depict galloping horses with both front legs stretched forward and both rear legs stretched backward like a rocking horse. He was a critical observer of life, but the horses' gait was simply too fast to be caught by the human eye. It was only after the analytical photographs of Edweard Muybridge had shown the true pattern of equine locomotion that Degas, and subsequent painters, were able to represent moving horses in what we now understand to be correct postures. Despite the proven 'correctness' of the new paintings, they were castigated by some leading contemporary critics who accepted the truth of the images but recommended the old representation as being more attractive. Images of the horse throughout history, and through different cultures, have struggled to find ways of displaying the power, grace, speed and functionality of the animal, with means that were acceptable at that time and in that place. Our own (Western) views about representation are based on post-Renaissance and post-photographic single viewpoint perspective, and it is interesting to speculate about how animation would be achieved within other aesthetic frames. In a system which uses size to indicate importance rather than distance from the picture plane, or a system which incorporates several viewpoints into a single representation of an object, animation as we think of it might contradict the illusion the system strives to create. Our acceptance of the representation of movement is likely to be as constrained by the visual conventions with which we have grown up as our acceptance of any other image.

4.1 PATHS

It is often useful to think of the movement of an object in terms of the path along which it travels. Different parts of an object can have their own separate paths which might be defined within the object coordinate frame or within the world coordinate frame. The overall path of Betty Boop might be straight, but she will not move along it as a frozen mass. Her hips will be swaying, her arms swinging and her legs striding, but each of these parts of the actor could be considered to have its own repetitive path within the overall character. A complex path might also be considered as a number of subpaths, the termination points of which might define key-frames (a change of direction will often provide an appropriate moment at which to define a key-frame). Having picked on Betty as an example, it is only fair to point out that her particular gait and mannerisms are very much the product of hand-drawn animation, and the principles of paths and subpaths, whilst still valid, would be very intuitively applied.

The transition from one point in space or time (or one keyframe) to another, is likely to be achieved smoothly, though not necessarily in even steps. In the simplest case, an object might move from A to B in a straight line (i.e. along a straight path), and if we create equally spaced points along that line, corresponding to the number of frames the sequence must take, those points will identify the position of the object in subsequent frames. Since, in that instance, the object would be moving at a constant speed throughout its journey, it would be satisfactory for dealing with an object which had already reached its travelling speed, and which was to continue at that speed beyond the final point. The even spacing of the points, however, does not allow for acceleration at the beginning of the move (if the object had been stationary), or deceleration at the end of the move (if the object was to stop). In order to accelerate the object from standstill to its cruising speed, we need to start the path with points much closer together, and then stretch the gap between points until they are at their constant distance. This is known as 'cushioning' (or 'easing' or 'fairing') and is frequently applied to a motion to avoid sudden jerky transitions. It can also be applied between sub-paths to smooth changes of speed.

4.1.1 CURVED PATHS

It is likely that a path more complex than a straight line will be needed, and much of movement control (and motion control) is concerned with defining suitable curved paths along which to move actors. It is not easy to draw by hand a smooth line encompassing all the points on an object's proposed route, but aids have evolved in other disciplines which can help. The 'French curve' is a template of curve profiles which draughtsmen utilise, and from shipbuilding comes a more complete solution. In order to draw the smooth curves of sections through ships' hulls, thin, flexible strips of wood or metal (called 'splines') were held down at key points by weights (called 'ducks'), and their natural, internal tension led them to take up a smooth curve through the weighted points. Mathematical equivalents of the shipbuilders' spline have been developed, to provide us with a ready method of establishing a smooth path defined by a few controlling points. This is in contrast to a circle generated by a mathematical equation, for instance, whose smoothness depends on the number of points which have been used in its generation and display.

In order to generate a curve by specifying only a few key points, rather than have to specify every point along the curve, we must turn to these methods (Fig 3.5e). The Bezier curve (already mentioned) and the B-spline curve are two of the most commonly used, their main functional difference being that all control points in a single Bezier curve influence the final curve, whilst those in a B-spline curve (which is made up of a number of curve sections) have only local influence. This results in a consistently smooth curve with the Bezier formulation, but one in which isolated local changes can be difficult to make. The curves do not necessarily pass through the control points, and are, in fact, likely not to do so. A ß-spline (beta-spline) is a formulation of B-spline curve segments in which additional parameters (such as 'tension') are added to give global control over the curve. Amongst other curve types, less frequently referred to, which can be compared to those of Bezier (who developed them for Renault) are Ferguson or Hermite and de Casteljou (after a scientist working for Citroen). NURBS (non-uniform rational B-splines) do not require control points to be evenly placed and are associated more with surface modelling than with movement control. They add a 'weighting' to control points. Most accounts of splines and curves back up their explanations with some fairly serious mathematics, but since I intend to avoid doing so here, I select Watt [89] as being one of the clearest of the many references the reader might choose to follow up.

A spline is defined as a piecewise polynomial satisfying continuity conditions between the pieces, and it is necessary to

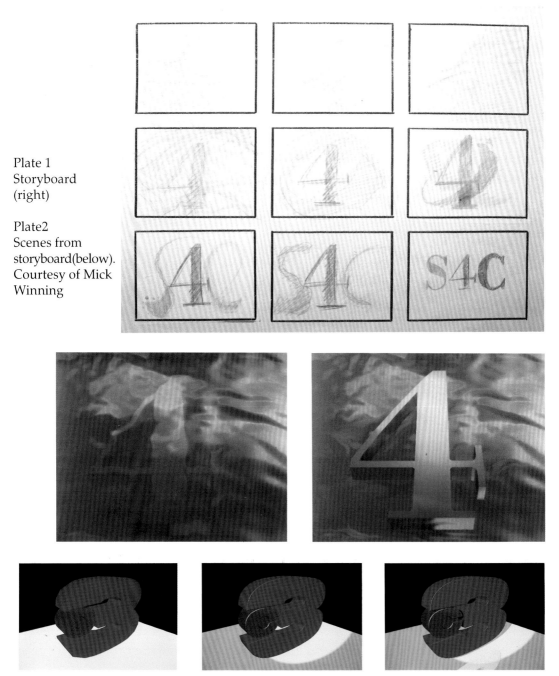

Plate 1
Storyboard
(right)

Plate2
Scenes from
storyboard(below).
Courtesy of Mick
Winning

Plate 3   Rendering samples courtesy of 3C Systems.
Lambert shading (left), Gouraud shading (centre), Raytracing (right)

Plate 4 Luxo Jnr.
© 1986 Pixar

Plate 5 Tin Toy.
© 1988 Pixar

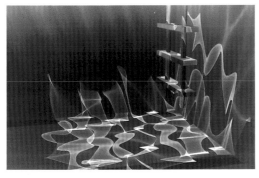

Plate 6 Sunlight on water.
Courtesy of Mark Watts

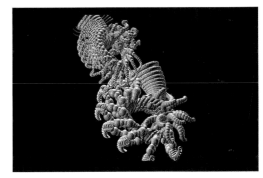

Plate 7 (from) Mutations.
© William Latham + IBM UKSC

Plate 8 A numerically severe storm.
Courtesy of the National Centre for
Supercomputing, University of Illinois

Plate 9 (from) Environmental impact
analysis simulation of quarry.
© 1991 3C Systems

mention this in order to explain several other terms that are often associated with splines. A polynomial is a mathematical expression consisting of a sum of terms which include variables raised to a power. If the highest power used is 2 (i.e. the variable is squared) the polynomial is 'quadratic', if it is 3 (i.e. the variable is cubed) the polynomial is 'cubic'. Whilst higher powers offer the ability to represent more complex curves, it is usually found in practice that quadratic polynomials are insufficiently sensitive, that high order polynomials are too complicated (involving a lot more mathematical calculation and therefore slower), but that cubic polynomials offer a satisfactory compromise. A complex curve is most easily divided into pieces which can each be described by cubic polynomials. 'Continuity' refers to the way in which the different pieces of the curve meet up with one another, it usually being necessary that one piece should blend into the next one smoothly, giving a continuous curve. There are several mathematical orders of continuity which define the various possible relationships between curve sections.

In order to create a 3-D spline path we input the XYZ coordinates of the control points for the spline. Since the curve will be controlled by the points without necessarily passing through them, we need to pay special attention to any point which we specifically require the curve to visit, ensuring that it is at the end of a curve section. A friendly interface is particularly helpful for designing a path through 3-space, ideally showing you the 3-D path within the scene through which it will be passing. The typical CAD display with separate top, side and front views, together with a movable 'camera' view, is good for this, allowing you to position the control points directly within the scene, and view the path they create relative to other scene elements. It may, of course, be necessary to employ the accuracy of numerical input, but whatever method is used, the path can be amended locally by repositioning control points until satisfactory, and it is for this reason that the B-spline is particularly suitable for animation. The speed of movement along the path is also required, and a particularly helpful interface is available in some applications (such as S-Dynamics from Symbolics), where an intuitive graph of speed against time can be drawn, and the acceleration thus expressed converted by the software into frame positions along the path.

To animate the object, it is then only necessary for it to be positioned at subsequent frame points along the path (it is important to distinguish between the control points which are used to create the curve, and the frame points which are later created along the curve when it is divided up according to the length of the sequence). Rather than drag the object impassively along the spline, it might be necessary to relate the object's local coordinate system to the spline, and to animate the object within that system (possibly even using localised splines). It would thus be possible to have one set of movements rotating the Moon in its orbit around the Earth (within the Earth's local coordinate system), while the Earth's coordinate system orbits the Sun (within the Sun's local coordinate system) and so on. Alternatively, Betty Boop's hips sway and her eyes roll within her local coordinate system, while her local coordinate system travels along the spline path.

4.1.2 OTHER USES

Splines have a wider use than moving actors around. They can equally well be used for moving the virtual camera in an application or the real camera on a motion control shoot. If computer-generated material has to be synchronised with motion control shot material, the spline data can be shared by the real and virtual cameras. Viewpoint can similarly be controlled, so that one spline can control the position of the camera and a second spline can control the point at which the camera is looking. The use of splines to set the positions of actors, camera and viewpoint is simple but needs careful thought, probably being best set up one at a time. Without experience it is easy for the spline combinations to produce overdramatic motion which can leave the viewer feeling seasick.

Any variable which changes during a sequence can be under the control of a spline, which does not need to be in 3D. A curve setting quantity against time is sufficient to control light intensity or the application of forces, for example, and constraints can be similarly controlled.

4.2 KINEMATICS

The kinematic method requires the specific positioning of the object's movements over time. It is necessary to first seek the "essential" element of the movement, the quality that makes the movement of that object characteristic or unique. In the case of an articulated figure, for example, this might be arrived at by direct observation, by rotascoping (digitising joint coordinates from film or video, requiring at least two orthogonal views), or by instrumentation. The real-time capture of live movement can be achieved by methods including the use of goniometers (which record position in 3-space), by making a film recording of LEDs (light emitting diodes) attached to the subject, or by using the DataGlove/DataSuit which will be described in Chapter 13.

4.3 PARAMETRICS

An alternative method of moving an object is to do so parametrically. After each frame, the parameters determining the position of the object are amended to move it to its next position, typically, being updated by a mathematical function on each pass through a program loop. For example, the variable denoting the X position of an object could be increased by 2 (i.e. $X=X+2$) each frame, and for a 20-frame sequence that segment of the program would be repeated 20 times. At the completion of 20 loops the object would have been moved 40 units along the X-axis. Key-frames are still likely to be used as points where the length and content of subsequent loops are changed, so that at frame 20 (a key-frame for our purposes) the loop controlling our object could be amended to $X=X+4, Y=Y+2$, and the loop length to 30. Over the 30 frames, therefore, the object would double the speed at which it was moving along the X-axis and start moving simultaneously along the Y-axis. (Cushioning could be implemented to smooth the transition occuring in our example at frame 20.)

4.4 DYNAMICS

Dynamics provides a further means of animating objects. By assigning an object a mass and a speed in a particular direction, its progress can be controlled by the application of forces such as gravity and friction. The trajectory of a projectile is thus easily calculated, with the option of setting forces to be natural or unnatural (i.e. no gravity or increased air friction). In fact this can be considered another form of parametric control, but using rules derived from physics rather than the animator's imagination (it has already been pointed out that the animator's imagination is primed by a natural awareness of physical laws). It is, of course, the way to drive a simulation, which will be looked at in Chapter 9. We will also consider the possibility of objects in a scene interacting spontaneously, such as in response to self-recognised collision.

4.5 INVERSE CONTROL

Though it will be mentioned again, we can acknowledge here that both dynamics and kinematics have a 'flip side'. Whilst kinematics deals with the shifts and rotations necessary to manoeuvre to a goal, it can prove easier to use inverse kinematics to start from the goal and work backwards to a starting position. This can be imagined from an example such as that of an articulated arm reaching out to grip a target object when it can be easier to calculate backwards from the successful grasp of the target to the starting position, since the two end states are known. Similarly, it can be useful to employ inverse dynamics to work backwards from the forces and torques existing in the end position, rather than to try and drive the object from the start position by the intuitive application of appropriate forces along the way.

4.6 HYBRID CONTROL

It is often convenient to be able to employ several different control methods in one animation. For example, a figure walking in a straight line might be controlled dynamically, whilst secondary movements of the figure, such as hand gestures, could be better controlled kinematically. In a scientific simulation it would be impossible to allow kinematic interference with the play of natural laws, but in other contexts it might be very convenient to let physically based controls drive primary movements, and leave details to the animator's kinematic control. Since an approximate application of natural laws often underpins an animation, it is convenient to let a dynamic system take care of that side of things and for the animator to be able to concentrate on details, subtleties and deviations from those natural laws by use of other means.

4.7 CONTROL LEVEL

As well as considering the method being used to move the actors, the animator will also be concerned with the level at which he has control. The level is a measure of the degree to which the animator is removed from the underlying mechanics of making things move. At a low level in a kinematic system he would have to specify the position of every part of every actor in each frame. At a higher level, a kinematic system might take responsibility for maintaining the correct relationships along the hierarchical chain of body parts of an articulated actor, and might support keyframing. That part of the animator's work is then reduced to positioning the actor in keyframes.

It can also enhance the total flexibility and extensibility of a system if it accepts input in the form of a computer language. Whilst this can allow very low level control, it can also constitute a script to drive any level of system with little, or no, subsequent user intervention. One particular virtue of a computer is its ability to iterate (to repeat instructions) and this can be employed to make workable, processes too tedious or time consuming to be practical if done by hand.

4.8 METAMORPHOSIS

Simple interpolation between coordinate positions in keyframes can sometimes be used to move objects, but we have already seen that it can prove problematic in 3D. It is best considered as being shape transformation. This carries with it the possibility of transforming one shape into an identical shape in another position, which will be visually synonymous with moving it. A particularly smooth shape metamorphosis can be achieved by interpolating between the control points in the start and finish frames of shapes defined by Bezier curves. It is not possible, however, to make a clean transformation between shapes (or, in 3-D, between objects) having different topologies, and an amount of engineering may be necessary to ensure the keyshapes have the necessary similar topologies.

To move from one keyshape to another using 'in-betweening' is straightforward. Each keyshape is decomposed into the separate line segments of which it is made, and the points defining each end of the line are moved from their position in the first keyframe to their position in the next keyframe in steps corresponding to the number of frames between the keyframes (i.e. if there are 10 frames to pass through, the point will be transposed one tenth of the way to its final position in each successive frame). The computer calculates the linear distance between points and divides it by the number of frames to arrive at the inbetween positions (Fig 4.8).

Fig 4.8
The metamorphosis
of a dragonfly into a
square

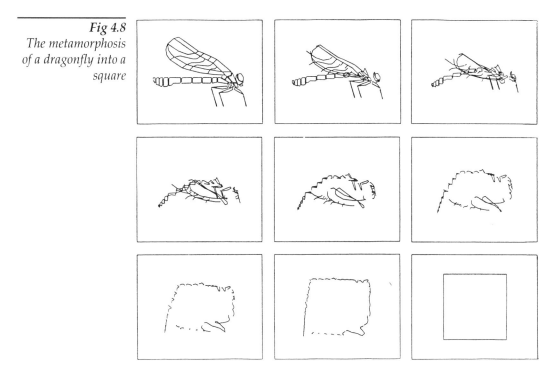

In order to accomplish a coherent transformation it is obviously necessary to ensure that each point is paired with the correct corresponding point in the next keyframe, and this is most easily achieved by creating the lines in each keyframe in the same order, so that the first point in keyframe 1 matches the first point in keyframe 2 and so on through all the points. This requires that the keyshapes are composed of the same number of lines, which is rarely the case, and a preprocessing step is, therefore, usually required. In this step the line-segments in the shape having the fewer line-segments, must be broken into smaller segments until the number matches that of the other keyshape. The interpolation need not be linear, and whilst the interpolation path is normally straight, it does not have to be so. To interpolate between complex images it can be simpler to derive simple skeletal elements for interpolation, and to add the detail subsequently. It is also possible to apply different interpolation rules to selected points or groups of points to create more satisfactory movement.

4.9 DISPLACEMENT ANIMATION

Displacement animation [Schafer 1989] allows the mixing of aspects of keyshapes without having to pass directly through them. The effect of the keyshapes on the transforming shape is in some ways similar to the influence of control points on a Bezier curve, controlling without necessarily being incorporated. It is suggested that this kind of animation is very good for simulating the movements involved in breathing or sitting down, for example, where rigid mathematics does not provide a sufficiently natural description. It is also suitable for in-betweening key-objects, Schafer's example being the use of a cube as an intermediate starting point in the transformation of an engine to a teddy bear. The cube can be turned into the two key-objects, but during the animation need not, itself, be passed through. He further points out that "as we test the animation we may discover an unappealing intermediate position. We can take this position, retouch it, and then have it influence the animation during the critical period. This direct interaction at the animation stage gives us tremendous flexibility and allows us to get the best results in the shortest time".

4.10 ROTATION

Although the complexity is likely to be hidden from us by the interface, to rotate an object in 3-space is not as intuitive as it might seem. Saying "rotate an object" suggests that the object rotates about its own centre, but as there are alternative centres of rotation, it is necessary to define which is to be used. Typically an object might rotate about its own centre, one of its own extremities, the centre of a group that it is in, or the centre of its universe. The default of an application is likely to be that it will rotate about the 'origin' at centre of the application's universe (where $X=Y=Z=0$). In order that it should rotate about any other centre, the object must be moved before the rotation is made, such that the required rotation point coincides with the origin, rotated, and then shifted back to its original position. These three transformations (translate, rotate, translate back) can be conveniently concatenated using matrix mathematics. It is also likely that an object will be made up of parts which have their own centres of rotation, for example, a car has a centre of rotation whilst each of its wheels has its own centre of rotation.

A further complication is that the required rotation is likely not to coincide with one of the three coordinate axes. Consider the illustration of the unpeeling sphere (Fig 4.10), where each facet hinges about the junction with its neighbouring facet, but where no two of the lines about which the facets rotate share the same axis alignment. It is therefore necessary, having translated the line so that it passes through the origin, to rotate about the X- and Y-axes until the Z-axis is aligned with the line, to make the required rotation, and then rotate back around X and Y and translate back to position. A well designed interface will hide these complications from the user.

Because the elements of a rotation matrix are not independent, a problem arises if you try to interpolate between the orientations of an object when such matrices are being used. There is the likelihood that the object will become deformed in the in-between frames. Several papers over the last few years have revived the idea from last century of using quaternions to specify rotation, a method already in use in the aviation industry (where the additional problem of 'gimbal lock' must be avoided). Euler has shown that any displacement of an object about a fixed point can be represented by a single rotation about some axis, and Shoemake [1985] suggests the use of quaternions for rotations in

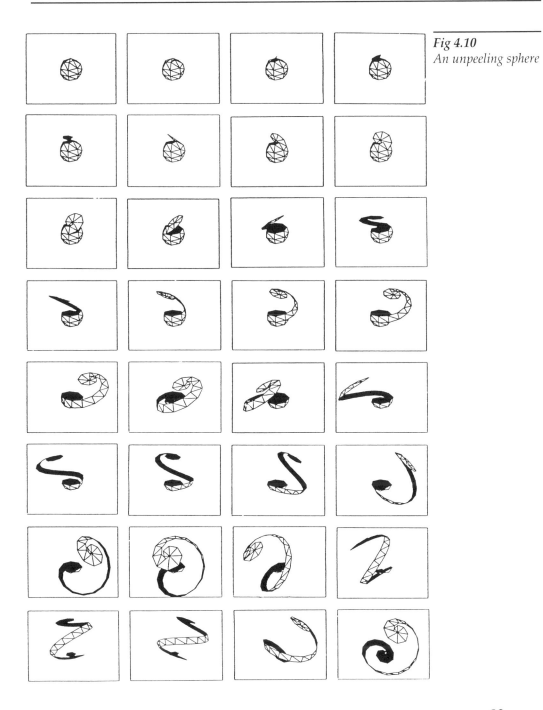

Fig 4.10
An unpeeling sphere

keyframe systems. They are economical in use and can be converted (internally) to and from a representation with which the animator may be more familiar.

4.11 MOTION BLUR

A computer animation will normally display a single, discrete image representing an infinitely small moment of time in each frame (unlike a camera shutter which will be open for a finite, even though short, moment of time). When we view a movement in real life it is continuous, rather than broken up into a number of separate moments, and the difference in quality between seeing real movement and viewing computer animated movement can prove obvious. Although it does not match the way we actually see things, the blurring of an object, which is caused by the object moving during the time a camera shutter is open, can help the impression of movement, particularly in a single image. It is consequently useful to be able to match the phenomenon in an animation. Other cartoon conventions, such as streaking lines from the rear of the moving object, can also aid the understanding of movement. (Since these streaks do not really exist, it is interesting to speculate about the extent to which the ability to understand them is learnt, rather than derived from real life observation.)

A number of methods have been developed for achieving the effect of motion blur, one of which uses an accumulation buffer [Haeberli 1990]. This buffer integrates a number of images that are then rendered into the frame buffer, the images having been created at a number of points in time between. It is, effectively, temporal super sampling, so that, if used in animation, each frame shows not only the state of movement at that moment in time, but this accumulation of images made at points in time much closer than the frame rate. If, for instance, the frame rate is 25fps and the movement is to be sampled 23 times between each frame point (their sample rate), then the image will be sampled 575 times each second, and the frame buffer will be fed the accumulation of 23 images to build up each single frame. The accumulation buffer was originally conceived of to deal with aliasing, but proves to deal effectively with depth of field, soft shadowing and motion blur as well. The number of samples per image determines the smoothness of the blurring.

Another method uses distributed ray tracing [Cook 1984], which also samples at a number of points in time for each image. Rather than take multiple time samples at every spatial location, the rays are distributed in time so that each location is sampled only once but locations are sampled at different times. This technique adds little to the complexity of the ray tracing process, and also has the ability to deal with depth of field, penumbras, translucency and fuzzy reflections. A delightful, overhead image of colliding pool balls is frequently used as an illustration of this process, evoking the sense of movement immediately but also offering, on closer observation, a more detailed history of the captured moment. The differing speeds of the balls, and in one case a change of direction following a collision, are clearly seen.

4.12 CONCLUSION

Although intrinsic to animation, movement on a computer screen is not difficult to achieve, and the principles are not basically complex. Moving a single rigid object is almost trivial, but complexity rapidly arises from the interaction of the parts of an articulated object, and from the interaction between actors and scene elements (including other actors). Some means for dealing with these interactions are described in later chapters and in the final chapter I propose the user friendly 'Eric' as an example of an actor of the future, who knows how to move himself.

CHAPTER 5

THE HUMAN/ COMPUTER INTERFACE

When someone uses a tool, an interface exists between the tool and the user. That interface is the common boundary between the two and determines how they communicate with one another; how the operator is able to control the tool and how the tool is able to feed back information about its state to the operator. The quality of the interface largely determines the efficiency with which that tool can be used, and thus the amount of benefit that can be gained from its use.

Even in a tool as simple as a pen, the size, weight, grip, nib type and ink all contribute to its ease of use, and the ease with which it can be used has a major effect on when and how it is used. There is no perfect pen, however, no single ergonomic and aesthetic solution to pen design which will be best for everyone. There are, nevertheless, parameters within which most functional pens are created, based on established hand proportions, writing surface requirements (the pen/ paper interface?) and general preferences. This means that most people can pick up most pens and write most things on most writing surfaces, though somewhere in the world there is probably a "jumbo" marker pen designed exclusively for left-handed people to write underwater.

A slightly more complicated tool, like a fighter aircraft, has a rather more complicated interface. It also carries more serious consequences if the interface is badly designed. The threshold at which an aircraft/pilot interface proves inadequate or inappropriate may be discovered when travelling at the speed of sound. Our concern is with a tool somewhere in complexity between a pen and a fighter aircraft, but sharing some requirements of each. I'm sure some computer animation companies would say that flying at the speed of sound is child's play compared with meeting their production deadlines.

5.1 REQUIREMENTS

It is tempting to launch straight into a discussion of the relative merits of various input devices, but let us first consider the animator's requirements and environment. In the broadest sense, the interface must be psychologically sound as well as ergonomically effective. It is not within the power of the system's designer to determine whether the animator works in monastic silence or with Wagner playing at full volume, nor whether the lighting is from soft uplighters or glaring spotlights, but these factors form part of the total interface. It is also the case that scientific visualisation, for instance, is likely to be carried out in a very different environment to that for the creation of a TV commercial, and that the personnel will have very different backgrounds. Someone with a scientific background, who has probably become familiar with computers and programming as a general purpose tool, is likely to be more comfortable inputting numbers through a keyboard than a graphic designer with, perhaps, no background in mathematics. The designer, on the other hand, will feel immediately comfortable holding a stylus that may be alien to the scientist, yet they may both need to use the same computer system. (By 'system' we mean the combination of the hardware and the applicatio or applications, it runs.)

Is a good interface one that is immediately comfortable or is it acceptable that the operator spends time adjusting to it? For someone who is to spend most of his working day at one machine, it may be that weeks can be allowed to get used to it, but if access is occasional or brief or shared by personnel with different levels of involvement, then a more immediate rapport may be preferable. "Friendly" is a word often used in value judgments about HCI (human/computer interface), probably because early computers were anything but friendly, and they are still treated with reserve by many. My first experience of them, 20 years ago, was of hours spent punching cards in a noisy, communal punch room, followed by the presentation of several boxes of cards to the computer operators through a mysterious hatch in the wall, and a day or two waiting for a print-out to be returned. If one hole was punched in the wrong place on one card then the program didn't run. Not the environment for which most designers would choose to abandon their drawing boards and putty rubbers.

First impressions of the friendliness of the interface are very important, both to a decision to buy the product, and to the level of ambition and confidence with which one starts to use it. In working with most art students it has proved important to produce the first images quickly, and with the minimum of "computing", in order to allay justifiable doubts about the degree of machine intervention in the creative process. Once a few clicks and sweeps with the mouse (or preferably the stylus on a graphics pad) have loaded a program, built a model, coloured it and spun it around on the screen, the audience is much more prepared to entertain the use of the keyboard as an alternative input device.

When a process such as drawing a freehand circle, with which we are all familiar using pencil and paper, is being undertaken on the machine, it is easiest to use an HCI that simulates the process with which we are familiar. In that instance using a stylus is manually identical to using a pencil, but with the initially disconcerting difference that you don't see the result of your drawing on the pad, but on the screen in front of you. A fresh coordination needs to be acquired between hand and eye. A mouse also requires the hand to be moved in a circle, but, being gripped differently, excludes the subtle finger control we would normally expect to exercise. Cursor keys present a further level of removal from the real-world experience and sitting down to write a program to draw the required circle is probably as far as you can get from using a pencil. (A screen cursor is a positional indicator, often a small arrow, which is displayed on the screen, and controlled by an input device.)

5.2 INPUT DEVICES

An input device is a piece of hardware which allows us to put data into the system. This input may be coded (such as a typed instruction) or positional (such as perhaps traced off a map). As animators we might often find ourselves concerned with inputting data in drawn form.

5.2.1 KEYBOARD

The ubiquitous keyboard is familiar from the typewriter, and usually conforms to the same layout of letters, figures and symbols (with some regional variations amongst the non-alphanumeric characters). It often has an additional numeric keypad to speed up numerical input, four cursor keys which move the screen cursor left, right, up and down, and 'function' keys which can be configured by the user (or the current application) to do prescribed jobs. Depression of a key, either on its own or in conjunction with another (e.g. SHIFT, CONTROL, ALTERNATE) generates a unique electronic digital code which is interpreted by the computer's CPU. The code is normally the international standard ASCII (pronounced "askey").

If a key is held down too long it will send its message more than onceeeeeeee. This is because the keyboard is checked by the CPU (or a delegated management chip) at regular intervals, which are set at 1/50 or 1/60 second by the 'interrupt clock'. Whilst the system may not respond to the repetition of messages from some keys, it is likely to do so with all the alpha-numeric keys, which can give rise to errors. Once a key has been recognised as having been pressed the significance of the code is considered according to an established priority, so that QUIT or BREAK, for example, may be given priority over everything else that is going on. An interrupt which is given priority over everything else is called an 'NMI' (non-maskable interrupt).

5.2.2 MOUSE

The mouse is a device that fits in the palm of the hand and is rolled over a smooth surface. A ball in the base of the mouse is rotated by the movement across a surface and these rotations are translated into data which moves a screen cursor on a corresponding path. This screen cursor is often not the same as the keyboard cursor, and may change its form according to the function it is currently fullfilling. The translation can be achieved mechanically or optically. Move the mouse to the right and the screen cursor moves a proportional distance to the right, move it forward (assuming a horizontal surface) and the cursor moves up the screen (assuming a vertical screen). The ratio of mouse movement to screen movement can often be set by the user. The mouse normally also has one, two or three buttons at the finger tip end, whose functions are set by the application, and is usually connected to the keyboard by a flexible lead. Some designers still make it difficult for mice to be used left handed, though cordless mice are now available, which are less restricting, more expensive and are ambidextrous. In general the mouse is cheap, simple and relatively low resolution. It is important to remember that the coordinates returned by the mouse are relative to the position on the last occasion that the ball was turned. If the mouse is taken off the surface its absolute position is lost.

5.2.3 TRACKER BALL

The 'tracker ball' is similar to an inverted mouse and is operated by turning the ball with the fingertips. It moves a screen cursor in the same way as a mouse but is slightly less intuitive to use. One of its advantages, however, is that it remains stationary and for this reason has become incorporated into some laptop computers. As the size of the ball is increased, so subtle movements become easier whilst big movements require the ball to be spun more. A giant tracker ball has been suggested as a control device for handicapped users who have difficulty making fine movements.

5.2.4 JOYSTICK

A 'joystick' controls the screen cursor by pressure on a small, vertical lever similar to an aircraft control column. Pressing to the right moves the cursor to the right, pressing forward moves it up the screen and so on, and sustained pressure allows continued movement of the cursor. It is commonly found in use with computer games, on control panels for 'caption generators' and some have been specially built for use with design programs.

One manufacturer has produced a control device which consists of a pressure sensitive ball, of gripable size, mounted on a plinth with buttons. The action of twisting the ball towards the direction required controls screen position and sustained pressure leads to sustained movement.

5.2.4 DIGITISING PAD

'Digitisers' have a pad, normally between A4 and A0 size, on which the position of a hand held sighting device called a 'puck' can be detected with great accuracy. They can also be used with digitising tables of much greater size for higher levels of precision, though not typically in the context of animation. The puck has a small window showing cross hairs, which are to be aligned with the current data point, and buttons to determine the use that is to be made of that data. Either the pad or the puck transmits continuous signals which the other receives, and can be electromagnetic, electrostatic, ultrasonic or infrared. The signals translate into X,Y positions with an accuracy of up to 0.001 of an inch, and the pads are widely used as a means of transferring data from a drawing on paper to the computer. Before starting work the digitiser must be orientated to the sheet of paper, so that verticals remain vertical and the origin is correctly located.

If the puck is replaced by a stylus (a pen-like device) then the same principles allow freehand drawing, such as might be useful in a paint program. In this context the digitising pad is often referred to as a 'graphics tablet'. Whilst the puck is often used to input data without reference to a display monitor, the stylus operator normally uses the monitor for positional feedback. The use of the stylus is associated more with continuous movement and the puck with the input of discrete points. Some styluses are pressure sensitive, which is a great advantage in trying to match the subtlety of normal hand media. Both puck and stylus are normally connected to the pad with a flexible lead though cordless versions are now available, with the disadvantage that they are easier to mislay.

The digitising pad can often be configured by the user, allowing the relationship between its drawing area, and the screen area it maps, to be flexible. Some applications cover part of the pad with menu overlays relating to program functions, and when the stylus or puck is used to select from this menu it is said to be used as a 'pick'. The same applies to the use of pick or stylus to move the screen cursor in order to select from any screen menu displayed. The stylus, in particular, is often used to select data from the current screen image for further treatment, for example in a paint program to select one colour from the screen image for use elsewhere.

5.2.5 OTHER DEVICES

Light sensitive pens can be used to interact directly with the screen, though this is now rarely found to be convenient or accurate. Touch sensitive screens share the same limitations but can be useful when an interface is required with the general public.

Analogue devices, such as simple knobs connected to potentiometers, can also be usefully employed as input devices. When working on a 3-D scene it can be much clearer to allocate separate knobs to rotations around each axis, and to functions such as 'zooming', than to have them all operated by a single device such as a mouse. If the control knobs are geared down, it also allows very fine tuning of parameters. Buttons and switches are further simple input devices, and can have their functions defined either by the user or the application, thus comprising a PFK (programmed function keyboard). The means for inputting complex images, such as photographs, are described in Chapter 6.8.

The systems described so far have been used for inputting 2-D information, and this may, of course, provide the basis for building a 3-D model. It is, however, possible to input 3-D information directly, though the equipment for doing so is not yet widely found. The position of a stylus tip, moving in 3-space, can be tracked using acoustic, mechanical, optical or electromagnetic means. An object can thus be traced over with the stylus, but care must be taken to select logically suitable points on its surface for digitising. (From the June 1990 *Design* magazine's report of the *National Computer Graphics Association* conference and exhibition comes word of a new device for the input of 3-D information into a computer. A sonic digitiser uses four microphone sensors to calculate distance from a stylus tip emitting an ultrasonic signal at a rate of up to 60 times per second.) Commonly, the object would have a mesh grid drawn over its surface, and the intersection points would be those digitised. The process is time-consuming and painstaking. Laser scanning provides an alternative method, but all systems have problems with objects containing inaccessible areas.

Three forms of input which are in their infancy are 'OCR' (optical character recognition), in which an intelligent system reads printed (or sometimes even handwritten) text; direct speech, in which a system understands human speech (in a currently limited vocabulary); and the 'DataGlove' which translates movements of the operator's hand (encased in the DataGlove) into comparable movements in the 3-space of a robotic hand which might exist or merely be a computer model. The DataGlove is one tool of 'virtual reality' in which the operator is able to enter into a 3-D computer-generated space, and the potential and implications of virtual reality are so great that it will be dealt with at length later in the book. A directional hand tool (a palm-held ball shape, tapering to a pointer, with input buttons) has been developed to allow someone in a virtual environment to 'fly' through the virtual space that surrounds him.

5.3 FEEDBACK

When an input device is used it is usual to expect some sort of feedback to confirm its satisfactory operation. It would be difficult to input the data for our freehand circle, using a stylus and graphics tablet, if the VDU (visual display unit) screen did not demonstrate our progress. Input from a drawing, using the puck, might only produce the numerical coordinates on screen, but in this case we have visual coordination between the source drawing and the puck, which the numerical coordinates can be used to double check. If an image is produced by a written program, there might be a long delay between writing the program and producing the image, possibly days or weeks so that direct visual feedback is impossible. Some rendering techniques might also produce a delay of hours or even days.

Since the essence of animation is visual, this could be a major problem. An artist relies on instantaneous feedback in order to be able to produce a drawing, if even a small delay is introduced between making a mark and seeing it appear it is likely to prove impossible to continue coherently. Interruptions to this flow of consciousness are impossible to avoid at all points in the production of animation, but are less critical at some times than at others. In a process requiring hand/eye skills their avoidance is essential. When building a model,

104

the decision to create a cube, for example, has a completeness which will not be corrupted by a short delay. A subsequent decision (based on its appearance on screen) to change its scale, is similarly amenable to a short delay. If, however, its scale or position needs to be subjectively modified relative to another object on screen, then it is necessary to be able to see the changes to the cube appear as they occur, or the process will deteriorate into one of successively refined error correction. I specify "subjective" to distinguish the example from one where the cube's required transformations could be described mathematically.

Rendering delays have become accepted as normal, but this has merely served to modify the way in which rendering decisions are made. The incentive is to set a complete global model in a single action, rather than to build one up light source by light source, changing lighting positions, intensities and colours in response to their effect, as would be the case if it could be achieved interactively in real-time. This results in a strong sense, in much computer imagery, of rendering by formula (which relies on the experience of the operator), though increases in rendering speed in the next few years will remove the need for this shortcut. The incentive may be even stronger if the images are produced by a program custom-written for the task, in which case the whole cycle of editing and compilation adds further to the delay, and to further removal from the direct experience.

Possibly the most problematic area is that of movement, for the ability to evaluate the quality of a movement requires that it should be viewed at real speed. If that can only be done by slowly generating individual frames and then dumping them one at a time to video, then the delay between initiating and seeing the movement can be enormous. This problem is usually minimised by previewing a reduced, possibly wireframe, version of the final scene, which can be generated and replayed quickly within the memory of the computer. It still invites major surprises in the final rendered version, however, when unforeseen elements effect the expected result. Again, experience proves to be the main judgmental tool.

5.4 THE SCREEN ENVIRONMENT

The computer's operating system (OS) protects the user from

the need to become too intimate with the low level requirements of the system. (The 'level' of operation refers to the closeness of the user to the machine workings of the computer, 'low' being close, 'high' being removed from the need to know how the machine performs required tasks.) Amongst other things, the OS translates high level user input (such as typing in a command word, or hitting the BREAK key) into instructions to which the machine can respond. The application, sits 'above' the operating system, and is likely to share the same interface, possibly providing alternative levels of control and alternative input and output devices. Our main interest is likely to be in the VDU screen, in what it tells us and in how we can communicate through it. Some form of graphical user interface ('GUI', pronounced "gooey") is now almost standard.

The word processor application, with which I am working, uses a WIMP environment but is not fully WYSIWYG (pronounced whizywig)! WIMP is an acronym for "windows, icons, menus and pointers", WYSIWYG stands for "what you see is what you get". The term WYSIWYG is most often applied to DTP (desktop publishing) applications, where the means of mapping fonts to the screen could be different from that used on a laser printer, for example, and consequently would effect the precise appearance of the layout. It is possible to employ the same means to ensure that the screen and printer images are the same (within the limits of the resolution of the two devices), and the 'PostScript' language is one which is currently being employed to drive both devices. In a broader sense, it is possible for screen information not to be updated immediately, in which case the screen fails to give an accurate description of the state of the application, and impairs the ability of the user to make sound judgments.

The WIMP environment is analogous to a desktop, with sheets of paper laid on its surface, the sheets corresponding to the 'windows' which contain views of the application. These windows may contain text or images, and can be moved around the screen (which has become the 'desktop') and overlapped just as papers can be organised on a desk (Fig 5.4a). Current papers can be moved to the top of the pile and documents can be laid side by side for cross-referencing, the maximum number of windows available at any one time being determined by the system. The windows can also be 'sized' (interactively reproportioned) which accounts for their name, since rather than actually "being" the document or image itself, the window

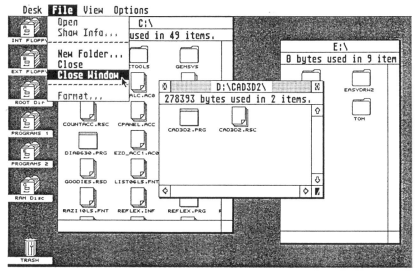

Fig 5.4a
A simple WIMP
desktop

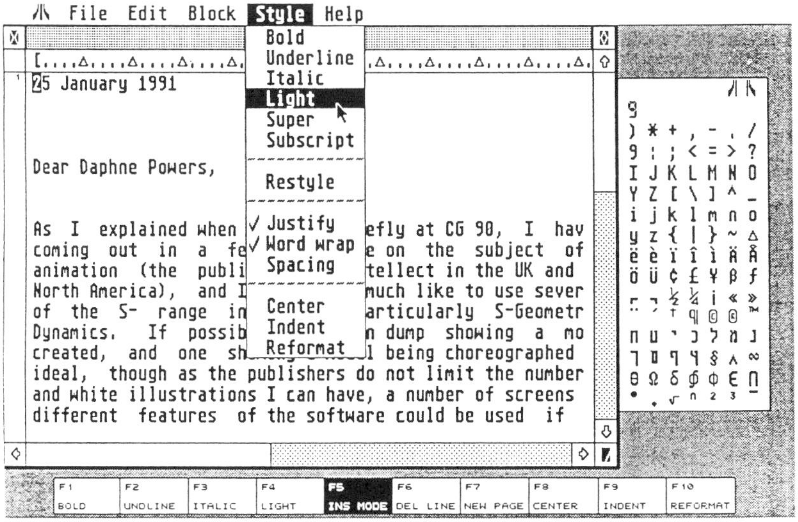

Fig 5.4b
A wordprocessor
screen

107

offers a view onto the document or image. As I write this, my growing document scrolls past the currently live window, which overlaps a window containing my bibliography document, and in some more powerful systems, the various windows can even be running animations or live video.

At the top of my screen are several words: File, Edit, Block, Style and Help. Each one is a menu heading, and if I move the screen cursor over one of those words then a list, or 'menu', of related functions appears on screen (Fig 5.4b). For instance, if I 'pull down' the "style" menu I am offered a choice of typeface styles that I can use in my document, such as: Bold, Underline and Italic. I select the style I want by moving the cursor over the appropriate selection and 'clicking' the mouse button. The menu thus allows easy access to a wide range of facilities that are available in the application, without the clutter of having them all on screen at once. In more complex applications menus may be 'nested' hierarchically in order to arrange logically a large number of options. In that case the selection of a menu item causes a sub-menu to be written on screen, and possibly the selection of an item on the sub-menu will reveal a further sub-menu. The choice of wording in a menu needs to be clear, but in its attempt to be brief may use jargon which will need to be learnt. Icons are graphical symbols designed to be identified with particular functions that are available, and may be used in conjunction with menus, or may replace them in simple situations. They are selected by the screen cursor. Standardisation of icons is poor between applications, though there are some familiar ones on most desktops, for instance a dustbin (trashcan) icon for removing redundant files when they are dragged to the icon. A problem with icons is the need to visually evoke a particular function, which may be complex and esoteric, within the confines of a grid (perhaps 10 pixels square), in such a way that its meaning is instantly apparent to the operator. In fact this is rarely possible, and the icons will need to be learnt, but they should provide a visual shorthand for a function. A further complication is that the icon may need to describe a function which is completely new to the operator, in terms of imagery which is already understood by him, and should also be international (do all cultures have dustbins that look the same?). It is an interesting problem to create a universal icon to stand for an obscure process or function, and one which has led to some magnificently confusing failures. A recent research project on computer-based iconic language has led to the development of hierarchical icons which can be interrogated to give static or animated iconic explanations of themselves [Mealing 1990].

The use of static icons is being supplemented by MICONS (motion icons) in which the iconic image was originally a repeating morsel of live video. Whilst these have the potential for fuller description they also have the potential for turning the desktop into an animated theatre of confusion, and should be used sparingly. As well as effectively being a mini video, a typical, stylised icon can be animated. An icon can also be a photographic quality image, and as such is referred to as a PICON (picture icon) and can have sound associated with its operation, such as a suitable noise to accompany 'dragging' a file to the trashcan.

Some functions (such as for the volume of sound) require graduated control and this is often achieved by using a variable screen device imitating a mechanical one. For instance, a virtual 'slider' on screen can be dragged by a mouse to match the effect of a mechanical slider on a hi-fi set. Alternatively a numerical display (such as of volume on a scale from 0 to 10) can be controlled by 'plus' and 'minus' buttons, or, of course, by keyboard. One function which has led to a number of control solutions is that of colour mixing, where the type of intuition that can be brought to bear depends on the operator's background. An artist and a physicist might be expected to feel comfortable with different analogies. Colour is often set by three sliders corresponding to the numerical balance of the three primary colours (in this context) of red, green and blue, but can also be set by the separate selection of hue and intensity from graded 2-D charts. In the case of a limited computer palette, direct selection is an option, but in some paintbox applications the manual mixing of colours on a real palette is effectively simulated, using a stylus. Since mixing red and green paint produces khaki, whilst mixing red and green light produces yellow, the computer is required to convert internally between different colour systems. One other option is to select from a 3-D colour model, but this presents problems since it is displayed in 2-D on screen.

'Pointers' are the mechanism for selecting an icon, selecting from a menu, or determining the screen location for a prescribed event to occur (such as my now using the mouse to locate the screen cursor at the location where I want the text cursor to allow me to insert a missing letter). The pointer can be controlled by a range of input devices, and can change its visual form as a reminder of the function it is currently fulfilling. In conjunction with the rest of the WIMP environment, it allows the operator to entirely control much of the current application through a simple device like a mouse. Our animator's screen could then, at any one moment, contain wireframe and rendered views of the 3-D model he is working on, a text window at which he edits the program that is producing the model, a window in which his model is animated, and menus and icons for controlling the application.

Familiarity contributes to the apparent friendliness of the interface and many "traditional" computer operators prefer the 'command line' control which was universal before WIMP arrived. This requires that commands are typed in at the keyboard, from a repertoire of often many hundreds, with a syntax which takes the uninitiated time to acquire. Whilst not seeming a convenient system to many users, it sometimes offers the opportunity to briefly express a wider range of options. It might not seem obvious that the screen image is much different from the final image produced by another output device, but in some cases the difference is significant.

5.5 THE 3-D ENVIRONMENT

Is it possible to navigate a 3-D environment when viewed "through" a 2-D screen? Whilst perspective and hidden-line removal give us a lot of assistance, real world depth clues are often much more subtle. We have mentioned that texture can help to evoke spatial depth by diminishing in scale with distance, but aerial perspective is more difficult. This change in the apparent colour and clarity of distant objects, due to atmospheric influences, can be simulated, but only at the expense of computing time. Both texture and aerial perspective are also mainly relevant when the space in question is great.

Most 3-D modelling packages offer three or four views of the current scene on screen at once in separate windows. Top view (plan), front view (front elevation) and side view (side elevation) offer three coordinated diagrams which allow positions in 3-space to be evaluated accurately but not intuitively. All the windows are updated as close to simultaneously as the application will allow, but inevitable delays can make interactive navigation tedious, and it is common to use wireframe views when possible for the sake of speed. The choice of views can usually be set to determine whether the view is of top or bottom, front or back, left or right, and additionally a 'camera' view gives a perspectival view from a defined point in 3-space corresponding to the viewer's imagined position.

The need to position objects in space by rotating them around X-,Y- and Z-axes has found different solutions. Sometimes the three axes are controlled similarly but separately, perhaps by knobs or by mouse after the appropriate axis icon is selected, but more often rotation about the axis orthogonal to the screen plane (i.e. the Z-axis) has a different control. Rotations around the X- and Y-axes are typically controlled by virtual sliders aligned along the X- and Y-axes, or by horizontal and vertical movements of the mouse (because horizontal movements to left and right can be seen as analogous to turning a freely held object around the Y-axis, and vertical movements around the X-axis). It is less easy to find a method of mimicking rotation around the Z-axis which is consistent with those of X and Y, and a less intuitive use of the same devices is often implemented. Research on the problem has produced a number of inventive solutions which represent the movements in terms of circles or spheres, and different manufacturers have their own preferences. The movement of the object might be made in real time, in which case control of positioning can be interactive, and it is likely that numerical positioning will be available for greater accuracy. The axes around which the object rotates by default are normally the world axes, which are unlikely to coincide with any of the object's axes (except when the object is in its canonical position or has been shifted without rotation). The pressure sensitive ball device, that has already been mentioned, represents one mechanical solution to the problem.

None of these methods matches our own use of binocular vision to interpret spatial position. Our brain uses the difference in information received from our two eyes to understand depth, and even slight head movements can be enough to clarify spatial ambiguities. Stereoscopic viewing is available for use in conjunction with computers, but tends to be used for viewing the final result rather than for interactive creation and manipulation. The method used involves replacing the single screen image viewed by both eyes, with separate images for each eye. Spectacles can hold separate mini-screens in front of each eye, or can be used to filter separate information for each eye from a single screen by the familiar red/green lenses, or by polarising lenses at right angles to one another. Alternatively the screen information intended for each eye can be presented in turn whilst the lens covering the opposite eye is blacked out electronically, the synchronisation being controlled by the computer presenting the images. If the information for both eyes is shown on a single screen, then the display can be confusing for a viewer without the appropriate spectacles.

An additional complication with a 3-D environment is that you can only see all of the scene if you are outside of it. Once you have moved your viewpoint into the scene you may find that objects lie behind you, and if you have stayed outside the scene but magnified your view by 'zooming in', your reduced field of view may have cut off your sight of all objects. Most interface tools are not expressive enough to deal with these problems in an intuitive way. VDUs don't have wing mirrors and it becomes a little like negotiating the room you are in whilst looking through a cardboard tube. Perhaps a stylus that operates in 3-D, instead of being confined to rest on a 2-D pad, might evolve, rather like the input device for a 3-D digitiser. A veritable magic wand to fly the operator through space, and indeed I have just read (in *Design* magazine, June 1990) that the 'Flying Mouse' from Simgraphics performs like a standard three-button mouse until it is lifted from the pad, at which time it moves into 3-D mode and can be used to manipulate objects with six degrees of freedom of movement.

Alternatively, virtual reality tools will allow you to enter into the same space as your objects, and manipulate them from there, though this may not always prove preferable to viewing the scene from the outside.

Another spatial problem arises in setting the position and direction of light sources in the scene and there have been a number of very different methods employed by various applications. If the light source is not directional then only the position of the light itself has to be established, and methods vary from placement in top/side/front windows to dragging a patch which represents the light around the surface of a sphere which stands for the boundary of the objects' world. It is also possible to position the light, not by setting its position in space, but by demonstrating its effect on a symbolic object in the scene, as seen from the current viewpoint. A directional light has to be similarly positioned in space but also has to have the direction of its beam established, and probably the angle of the beam as well. This is quite effectively done in some applications by siting the light in the 3-D environment and dragging out a line representing the beam direction vector from the light to another point in 3-space. If the beam angle is variable then lines can be used to represent the edges of the beam instead of the beam's central direction, which has the advantage of increasing the accuracy with which a beam can be positioned.

5.6 HCI FOR ANIMATORS

Does animation make any special demands of the human/ computer interface? One consideration which has already been mentioned, is the potential variety of backgrounds which users may bring to the system. Because, as we have shown in an earlier chapter, computer animation is being created within disciplines throughout the spectrum from pure science to pure art, it is difficult to make assumptions about the user preferences which will be brought to the system. In many instances it will be appropriate to "remove" the animator as far as possible from the "computing", whilst in others the animator may need to operate at a low level, perhaps writing code in assembly language. The most versatile system would incorporate a high-level interface yet still allow the animator to "get his hands dirty" with low-level operations. There are a number of reasons why this is not always the case, and, it must be acknowledged, a number of situations in which the double facility would prove superfluous.

It is not easy to specify an ideal interface for an animator, given the many intentions and disciplines using the medium. It is only a little easier to define the exact functions that the animator should have control over, but the chapter on software will give an idea of what is currently available. Facilities will be required, however, for modelling (either in 2, 21/2, or 3 dimensions), for controlling colour and texture and (in 3D) lighting and rendering, and for choreographing movement.

CHAPTER 6

HARDWARE CONSIDERATIONS

'Hardware' describes the physical components of a computer system, the machinery itself, as opposed to 'software', which refers to the programs that control the hardware and the applications that run on the hardware. Your paint program is a piece of software, the box which sits on your desk and runs the paint program is hardware, together with its monitor and peripherals. The same terms apply in other areas, and we will also look here at relevant video hardware. Since most computers can be persuaded to do most general purpose tasks at some level, it could be said that too many people get too involved with the subtle distinctions between different machines (encouraged, of course, by sales hype). Similarly, any car is likely to get you from A to B, but if you want to complete the journey fast or in great comfort then a more particular vehicle might be required. Also if you wish to take a dozen passengers, cross a river en route, tow a caravan or impress your friends, then a more specific choice is needed. This chapter will give a brief overview of the types of hardware that get mentioned in the context of computer animation.

As with all things, there is a hierarchy in computers which stretches, in this case, from the humble home micro up to the super-computer. Starting with the last generation of micros, the 8-bit machine, which is now largely superseded (though still in many homes and schools), as you move up the list, machines get 'bigger', 'faster', 'more powerful' and more expensive, but only the meaning of the last term is self-evident. We need to know what 'bigger' and 'faster' mean, whether machines can be meaningfully compared, what the extra size and speed will do for our animation, and if the improvements justify any extra expense, (we will discover that speed is important for graphics applications and for animation in particular). A computer is made up of five basic units, the features of which determine the limits of its performance, and they are: the central processing unit (CPU), the memory associated with the CPU, the secondary storage and the input and output devices. The last chapter looked at input devices, and this chapter will briefly consider each of the others in turn, and consider their significance to animation.

6.1 BITS AND CHIPS

The CPU is the heart of the computer, where the instructions specified by the program are carried out, and where the operation of all other elements of the computing process is coordinated. It is built as a tiny integrated circuit (IC), often referred to as a chip, and has shrunk so much in the last 30 years that a computer as powerful as the basic machine sitting on my desk would then have filled a room. There are several families of chips which are commonly used, and each has particular features which cause manufacturers to build machines around it. For instance the Motorola 68000 chip is a 16-bit chip which has provided the basis for several graphics orientated computers: the Apple Mac, the Atari ST and the Commodore Amiga. As the chip has developed its added capabilities are indicated by a higher reference number, so that the the Motorola 68020 is a full 32-bit device, the 68030 adds technical enhancements (like multi-tasking) and the 68040 develops further still (incorporating a high degree of parallelism). The three machines mentioned have all provided the foundation for more advanced models based around the improved chips, and computers often find themselves referred to by their chip number as it gives a general indication of their performance. It is interesting to note that the 68000 chip incorporates 68,000 transistors (guess where it got its name from) but the 68040 builds in a massive 1.2 million transistors. VLSI technology (Very Large Scale Integration) permits the fabrication of this number of transistors on a single chip.

'Bit' is short for 'BInary digiT', and is the smallest unit of storage in the computer. Groups of bits are classified as 'nibbles', 'bytes' and 'words', and a 16-bit machine is one that uses a word size of 16 bits, (a byte is normally 8 bits, and can conveniently be thought of as the amount of memory required to hold a single character such as 'S', '?' or '5'). The size of the word determines how much information can be handled at any one moment, and the bigger the word size the faster an amount of information can be processed. Home machines are now commonly 16-bit, with 32-bit machines just starting to come close to a 'home budget' price, but the current speed of development of computer hardware suggests that 32-bit machines will soon be 'bottom of the range' and 64-bit machines more commonplace. The word size is determined by the architecture of the chip, and is sometimes confused by the description of a chip as being, for example, '16/32 bit'. This distinguishes between the word size that can be handled internally by the chip, and the word size which it can handle when communicating externally.

The speed at which operations are carried out by the CPU is determined by the 'clock rate', measured in megahertz (MHz), a megahertz representing one million cycles per second (the 68000 chip typically being run at 8 MHz).The faster the clock rate the faster information is processed, but since different machines do a different amount of work in one cycle it is not sufficient merely to compare clock rates. Bench marks are used to compare the speed of different machines, and time each machine as it completes the same tasks, but whilst these tests are accurate they are not necessarily helpful. It might be that the tasks accomplished in the bench test are not relevant to the application in mind, that the machine is optimised to produce good bench test results, or even that the machine is too clever for the tests. (Some of the tests require the computer to perform large numbers of unproductive loops, where it repeats part of a program without doing anything, and good optimising compilers can spot this wasted energy and bypass the loop.)

The speed of operation is now popularly described in 'mips' (millions of instructions per second) and 'mega-flops' (millions of floating point operations per second), with alternative prefixes 'giga-' (one billion) and 'tera-' (one trillion) increasingly being used to whet the appetite. A new machine from Hewlett-Packard (the HP 9000 Series 400), for example, is described as running a Motorola 68040 chip at 25 MHz to do 20 mips and 3.5 mega-flops, with 26 mips and 4.5 mega-flops possible at 33 MHz, whilst the older 68030 chip will deliver 12 mips at 50 MHz. For graphics applications it is often more useful to know how many polygon fills it can achieve in a second, or how many vectors it can draw in a second, a calculation directly related to the end product and which takes into account any special graphics hardware aboard.

The basic chip is often supplemented by others which do specialised jobs and take part of the workload from the CPU. The most common is the maths co-processor, which relieves the CPU of much of the burden of mathematical calculation, and is often available as an optional extra. Sometimes an I/O processor handles input and output, and we will be interested in graphics co-processors which take over graphics chores. These supplementary chips are optimised to undertake their limited functions more efficiently than any general purpose chip, and allow the whole process to be markedly speeded up.

6.2 ARCHITECTURE

The traditional arrangement of elements in a computer is the von Neumann architecture, in which the memory and processor are separated by a databus, an organisation designed to make best use of the components originally available. A consequence of this arrangement is that most computer time is spent moving words up and down the databus which creates a bottleneck, and none of the improvements that have been made can avoid the problem. This architecture is 'sequential'. The real world is concurrent, however, which means that lots of things happen at the same time, and this is reflected in parallel architecture computers. By connecting memory and processor directly in a single unit which can be used in quantity, it is practical to build a concurrent machine. These units are assigned tasks which can be carried out simultaneously, and the topology of their connection is variable. Whilst it has been shown that increasing the size of a von Neumann machine does not greatly increase its processing power, this is not the case with a parallel machine. The idea of parallel computers has been around for at least forty years [Watts 1989] but technological changes have only recently made it viable, and it is suggested that this new direction may prove to be particularly useful for graphics.

RISC chips and transputers are the processors currently associated with parallel machines. 'RISC' stands for Reduced Instruction Set Computer and is a development arising from the observation that most processors spend most of their time working on only a few instructions out of the many of which they are capable. A RISC chip is therefore optimised to do the few most common instructions extremely fast, and to construct the rarer ones from the reduced set when needed. A transputer is a chip with its own memory that effectively constitutes a complete processor, and is intended to be used in conjunction with other transputers (a 'farm' of transputers) to co-operate on processing, each transputer completing its delegated part of a calculation.

Transputers are commonly arranged in a 2-D grid or in a cubic configuration known as a hypercube, and there are two main types of parallel computer. One is the SIMD (single- instruction multiple-data) computer, where the processors carry out the same operations on many pieces of data at the same time. They are particularly good at image processing, for instance, where fragments of picture are analysed in the same way simultaneously. In MIMD (multiple-instruction multiple-data) computers, however, processors carry out different operations at the same time. They are better at solving problems that require each processor to execute its own program on its own data, communicating periodically with its neighbours [Watts 1989].

At the moment the performance limits of the various technologies are leapfrogging one another, but parallelism is favoured to increase in importance. The obvious attraction of a machine that can do many things at the same time, is currently offset by the problem of distributing a problem efficiently between the processing elements, and by bottlenecks elsewhere in the system. Certain graphics algorithms have been highlighted as potentially able to exploit parallelism, one example being raytracing, where each ray could ultimately have its own processor.

Machines are often described as 'multi-tasking', meaning that they can be doing several jobs at once, but this is not a strictly accurate definition and should be distinguished from true parallel processing. A multi-tasking system gives the appearance of doing more than one thing at once by switching its CPU time between several jobs in progress. Since many applications will leave the CPU relatively idle (a good example being the word processing I am currently engaged upon) the spare time can be usefully employed to do something else in the background. Partitioning the memory and allocating parts to several applications, which can then be switched between, is also now common. It requires the complete state of each application to be frozen when it is switched from, and then restored when it is switched to, and does not mean that any application but the current one is active. Mainframes are often required to switch their time between different users and different applications, often using a predetermined priority of allocation. The unpredictability of time allocation makes real-time animation on such a system impossible, and the potential delays in polling users rules out the use of an interactive device like a mouse.

6.3 MEMORY

Computer memory is where data is stored, either permanently, or while calculations are carried out with it. It size is usually described in kilobytes and megabytes ('k' and 'meg'), which stand respectively for thousands and millions of bytes, though sometimes it is described in words rather than bytes, which renders the description machine specific. (Strictly the value of a kilobyte is 2^{10} or 1,024 bytes and of a megabyte is 2^{20} or 1,084,576 bytes.) Most memory is random access memory (RAM) in which memory locations can be written to and read from without having to work through a sequence of storage locations, and its contents are normally volatile (disappearing when the machine is switched off). Read only memory (ROM) is non-volatile, can only be read from (as a protection from being overwritten), and is therefore typically used to hold information such as the operating system.

Mainframes swap chunks ('pages') of memory between RAM and secondary storage, so when a program is running it might not all be in main memory at once, but will be called up in sections as needed. This requires very fast secondary storage and efficient paging techniques. 'Virtual memory' describes the use of secondary storage as if it were RAM, by use of paging techniques. 'Caching' can be used to improve on access times to secondary storage by holding in RAM the data which an algorithm deems most likely to be required next.

Secondary storage is most commonly provided by disc drives

which hold information on magnetic 'floppy' discs loaded into the drive (currently having about 1 megabyte of storage capacity), and hard drives which use permanently mounted discs with very fast access times (typically holding 20 - 120 megabytes). Of these two, only the hard drive is suitable for the creation of virtual memory. Tape provides an alternative magnetic storage medium (one use being in 'tapestreamers' which can be used for backing-up hard discs), and graphics applications can benefit from specialised storage, such as the frame store, which will be mentioned later. Laser technology can dramatically increase memory storage capacity and improve access times, but is only just starting to become commonly available for computers, having already established itself in CD players for hi-fi systems. Fast solid state secondary storage is also becoming used and its progressive availability is likely to be inversely proportional to the price of the material. The CPU can handle information faster than it can take it from secondary storage, and, therefore, slow access times can cause severe processing bottlenecks, which becomes a very real concern for animation. A machine's memory can be extended since secondary storage can be bought 'off the shelf' and plugged in externally, and additional RAM chips can often be added to increase internal memory. New operating systems and applications increasingly allow secondary storage to be treated as 'virtual' memory so that a hard drive can effectively be used as if it was RAM, though access times are slightly slower than true RAM.

It is possible to maximise the use of storage space by compressing information when it is stored and then decompressing it when it is retrieved. For graphics applications, one commonly used compaction technique is 'run-length' encoding. Rather than separately store the actual intensity of every pixel, run-length encoding stores the intensity of a pixel and the number of following pixels with that same intensity. Imagine a single pixel being ON at the centre of a 640 x 400 pixel display. Instead of individually recording the state of all 256,000 pixels, it would be sufficient to record that the first 127,999 pixels were OFF, the next one was ON, and the remaining 128,000 were OFF. The efficiency of the technique is greatest in images with blocks of similarly set pixels and would become inefficient in the rare case that no pixel was the same intensity as its neighbour. A number of other methods for compression are available, and some applications can select from a library of different techniques after assessing which is most efficient for each given image. The encoding and decoding can sometimes be achieved in real time using either software or dedicated hardware methods.

If you consider the amount of storage required to store one second of high-resolution, 24-bit colour animation, it is clear that efficient compression algorithms are essential if we are to be able to develop the medium. Even at 640x480 pixels, one second of 24-bit, 30 fps video requires 30 MB of memory, and one minute needs 1.8 gigabytes. Assuming the storage is available there remains the problem of getting that much data to the screen fast enough for real-time display. Another problem arises if that information is to be sent over a phone line, since it will take about 15 minutes per MB using a 9600-bps (baud per second) modem. A single, full-colour, A4 size image, scanned at 300 dpi (dots per inch) and 24-bits per dot would take about 6 hours to transmit [Baran 1990].

A common method of compacting animation is to store the first frame in its entirety and, thereafter, to store only the changes between subsequent frames. This is extremely efficient when few pixels have changed between frames, which may often be the case in computer generated sequences. It is likely to be far less efficient in handling sequences from a video source, since random changes are likely to be occurring to pixels throughout every frame, even in areas of apparently unchanging colour. Two standard algorithms are emerging: the Joint Photographics Experts Group (JPEG) algorithm for still images, and the Motion Picture Experts Group (MPEG) algorithm for motion picture images [Calvigioli 1990,1991]. The JPEG algorithm can compress an image by 25 to 1 with minimal loss of quality, but can take 15 minutes to compress a 25MB image in software (on a 25-MHz 68030 machine). Built into hardware, however, specialised compression processors have the performance to sustain video rates. The algorithms must, of course, be able to decompress as efficiently as they compress, and the JPEG algorithm is an example of a symmetrical algorithm which uses the same number of operations for both processes, and hence the same time [Baran 1990].

6.4 TYPES OF COMPUTER

Computers are often categorised with rather vague labels that imply some position in a performance hierarchy. Amongst the terms used are: 'home micro', 'micro', 'PC', 'workstation', 'mini', 'mainframe' and 'super-computer', which might variously be qualified with 'humble', 'low-end', 'high-end' or 'turbo'. As performance has increased across-the-board, any valid distinctions that existed between these different types have become blurred, and the middle ground occupied by the workstation has become one of the most competitive areas. 'Micro' loosely refers to unspecialised 8,16 and 32-bit machines, small enough to sit on a table top and sold in the general marketplace. 'Home micro' qualifies a micro as being one that can be expected to be commonly found at home, I tend to use that term, in a rather vague fashion, when indicating that a technique under discussion does not require any specialist hardware. 'PC' stands for Personal Computer and is associated with IBM desk top business machines and their numerous imitators. A 'workstation' is likely to be a fast 32-bit machine with good resolution and graphics capability, in which the main computer is housed in a small 'tower unit' beside the desk. The performance standard defining a high-end workstation (according to *'Managing Automation'*, April 1989) has evolved from 1 MIPS in 1984 to 50 MIPS in 1989, during which period the ability to create 3-D vectors has risen from 20,000 to 1 million per second, and the ability to draw Gouraud polygons has risen from 0 to 100,000 per second.

A 'mainframe' is a big machine, housed in an air-conditioned room, usually used where large volumes of data are processed, accessed by a number of users on separate terminals, and named because its component parts were originally racked up on frames. There is a movement away from mainframes towards individual machines, sometimes 'networked' together in order to share resources. When computing is distributed, mainframes are often used now as fileservers, giving access to files and applications which no longer need to be separately held by each machine. 'Minis' have the power previously attributed to mainframes but may be only be the size of a large suitcase, and in their most powerful incarnations are referred to as 'super-minis'. 'Supercomputers' are big, massively powerful machines exploiting the latest technologies and accessible by few people. The much vaunted 'Cray' supercomputers are often used as a yardstick against which other machines are measured, and they look the part when seen in photographs, standing in spotlight isolation with glowing liquid coolant flowing through their veins.

The physical size required to house a particular level of machine performance is shrinking fast, and in some markets portables are outselling desktop machines. The descriptions given for machines that can be moved around easily range from 'luggable' (describing an over-optimistically named portable) through 'portable' and 'laptop' to 'pocketable'. Screen technology has already enabled a number of machines to offer flat monochrome screens with 640 x 400 resolution and better, and higher resolutions with full colour will arrive before too long. An important requirement of the screen, and of other components, in a portable machine is that they do not use too much electrical power, since battery technology is responding more slowly than hoped to the challenge. A high specification machine which can run off its batteries for only 20 minutes is of limited use. Portables often manage to include hard discs as well as external drives, and will be amongst the first machines to avail themselves of solid-state storage when available. Their ultimate size seems controlled by the keyboard, which has an ergonomic minimum size, but alternative future input devices, and also screen replacements (electric glasses?), suggest that workstation power will be pocketable in the foreseeable future.

A number of input devices have already been described in the chapter on HCI, examples of output devices being printers, plotters, video recorders and VDUs. It is important to recognise that the display shown by any output device can only be faithful to an image held in the memory of the computer within its own device limitations. It is often thought that the image seen on a computer monitor IS the image held in the computer, but it is merely a representation of that internal image, displayed to the best ability of the monitor hardware. The same internal image, displayed by a different monitor, or produced by a printer, will show changes in colour and resolution, for example, that are specific to the output device alone. A perfect circle can be stored in the computer's memory by three numbers, the X,Y coordinates of its centre and its radius, but when it is displayed on a VDU it will become a ragged approximation of a true circle, the 'staircasing' of the line becoming less noticeable as the resolution increases (Fig 6.4). A plotter, however, may produce a true circle. The primary output device to which the operator will refer is normally a VDU screen, the maximum resolution and maximum colour range which it can display being determined by its hardware, and the actual resolution and

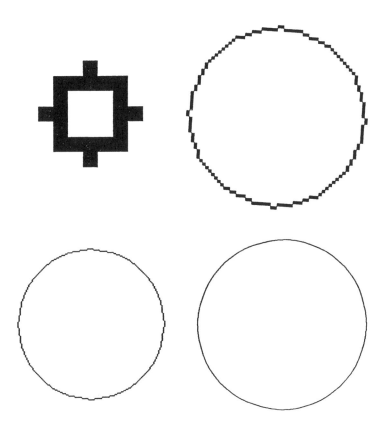

Fig 6.4
The relative
smoothness of circles
shown at different
screen resolutions

colour range displayed being determined by the hardware of the computer and the application that is running.

6.5 DISPLAY

The technicalities of different screen technologies are beyond the scope of this book, but we can make several pragmatic distinctions. Most displays use cathode ray tubes (CRTs) which are flexible and relatively inexpensive emitter displays (discussed clearly in Salmon [1987]). Another type usefully mentioned here is the liquid crystal display, which is currently used in 'laptop' computer screens, and is set for much wider use as the technology develops. The CRT screen is incorporated, with its associated electronics, into a monitor. For our purposes this can be expected to be a 'raster scanned' monitor, in which an electron beam systematically scans the whole screen area in horizontal lines from top to bottom. American TV has 525 raster scan lines, European TV uses 625 lines, but new standards for high definition television (HDTV) are being proposed, of 1125 lines at 60Hz and 1250 lines at 50Hz, and programmes are already being produced to these standards. The alternative, a 'vector refresh' monitor, steers the beam around the screen along vectors, and its high resolution is typically used in cockpit instrument displays and sometimes in computer aided design.

The raster scan sets the pixel intensities, and the speed at which the scan is repeated is the 'scan rate'. The higher the scan rate, the less 'flicker' the display exhibits, and the less strain is experienced in its use, (flicker can also be reduced by the use of longer persistence phosphors in the screen manufacture). Animation flicker is avoided by synchronising the moment at which each new frame is displayed to the screen's vertical retrace. My black and white monitor refreshes the whole image 70 times a second (70 Hz) and produces a very stable picture, which is particularly desirable when it is being closely observed, as in word processing. A colour monitor would typically run at 50 Hz, which is the television broadcasting standard in the UK (60 Hz in the USA), and be acceptably stable when broadcast because the moving image is not scrutinised minutely, but more tiring to work with closely. The capability of a monitor is often described by its 'bandwidth' which is calculated from the scan rate and number of pixels in the display, a high bandwidth (typically 88 MHz) indicating a high performance, and likely to be reflected in a high price. Television is broadcast using interlaced raster scanning, in which alternate raster lines are scanned in each pass, first odd lines then even lines, etc. (Fig 6.5). This means that the rate at which the complete screen is refreshed is 25 Hz (30 Hz in the USA) and leads to economies in the design of the electronics with subsequent cost savings. TV sets are often used as monitors for home micros but are not satisfactory for demanding work.

Monitors usually have an external control for roughly adjusting the colour balance and internal controls for fine adjustment, together with control over screen brightness. This should be limited in order

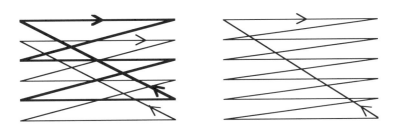

Fig 6.5
Raster scanning.
Non-interlaced
(left), interlaced
(right)

to reduce eyestrain and screen radiation (which is easier to do if the room is not brightly lit). If images are to be broadcast then the monitor may be supplemented by a small waveform monitor which is used to check for 'illegal' colours that can be created on the main monitor but not broadcast satisfactorily. It is also common to have a second monitor to show the image as it would appear when broadcast, since edges of the image can come to be cut off, and perhaps a monochrome monitor may be added to display menus and commands used by the application.

In order to display an image the monitor needs to receive an input signal which will control the electron beam that scans the screen. This signal synchronises the horizontal scans, the vertical moves between the scans and the intensity at which each pixel is set. To display colour it additionally requires information in the form of the red, green and blue components of each colour, and it also needs sound information if present. (The monochrome component of a colour television signal is the 'luminance', the colour part of the signal, relating to the hue and saturation, but not brightness, is the 'chrominance'.) Broadcast television supplies all this information combined into one signal known as 'composite video', which is fed into the TV aerial socket. If the signal components are kept separate it is 'component video'. Since the signals suffer a reduced bandwidth by being encoded into one and cannot then be perfectly decoded on reception, it is desirable to use component video between machines up until the final moment of broadcast. A composite signal is used by the main broadcast systems of PAL and SECAM in Europe and NTSC in the USA, but new transmission proposals are for component systems.

Describing and transmitting colour is dealt with in a number of ways, and the area has given rise to a minefield of abbreviations. It is not necessary to deal with them in detail here, but the main ones that may be come across are -

Transmission standards:

PAL	Phase Alternation Line - (much of Europe)
SECAM	Sequentiel Couleur a Memoire - (France and USSR)
NTSC	National Television System Committee - (USA and Japan) (also, allegedly "Never Twice the Same Colour")
MAC	Multiplexed Analogue Components - (proposed new standard)
CCIR	Comite Consultatif International des Radio-communications (UN regulatory body for communications)

Colour description systems:

RGB	Red, Green, Blue - (used for screen display)
CMY	Cyan, Magenta, Yellow - (used for hardcopy)
HSI	Hue, Saturation (chroma), Intensity - (or 'HIS')
HSV	Hue, Saturation, Value
HSB	Hue, Saturation, Brightness
HLS	Hue, Lightness, Saturation
DLP	Dominant wavelength, Luminance, Purity
YIQ	Intensity, flesh tone, other colour info - (used by NTSC)
YUV	Intensity, mixture of RGB info - (used by PAL)
CIE	Commission Internationale L'Eclairage - (based on a 2D colour diagram)

6.6 FRAME BUFFERS

The size of the palette that can be represented depends on the number of bits allocated to each pixel in memory. One bit can have the binary value 0 or 1, which means the pixel can be shown either off or on. Two bits can have the values 00, 01, 10 and 11 which allows us to show four ($=2^2$) different brightness levels. Three bits allows eight ($=2^3$) levels, eight bits allows 256 ($=2^8$) levels, twelve bits allows 4096 ($=2^{12}$) levels etc. If eight bits were to be allocated to each of the three component colours, red, green and blue, then 256 x 256 x 256 = 16,777,216 different colours could be represented using a total of

24 bits. A special area of memory is usually allocated to hold this screen information, either a reserved area of RAM in a machine with a limited palette or an external 'frame buffer' when a large palette is to be available. A frame buffer which is 24 bits 'deep' will allocate 24 bits to each pixel over its whole area, which might typically be 1024 x 1024 pixels (some frame buffers are dimensioned with respect to screen ratio, i.e. 640 x 400). The bits are allocated to planes which would typically be three 8-bit planes in a 24-bit buffer, one for each colour, although other permutations may be chosen if different information is needed about each pixel. A 32-bit buffer will typically hold 24-bit colour information, and have a further 8 bits available for describing transparency, or other pixel information.

'Lookup tables' provide an alternative way of storing pixel information which is memory efficient for limited palettes. Instead of storing the RGB values for each individual pixel, a table of colours values is created and the pixel colour is referred to by the location in the table of its colour value. This has the advantage that in order to change a colour throughout the image, it is only necessary to change the values at one place in the lookup table, rather than at every frame buffer location where it occurs. Obviously if the lookup table was to contain more colours than there are pixels, it would use more memory than a frame buffer, and carries the added memory burden of storing the pointers. This colour mapping with lookup tables also permits a limited form of animation, where sequential changes of the colour table can can suggest movement. For example if the colours of pixels describing water are set in a range between blue and white and then cycled through a blue/white palette, there can be a suggestion of movement in the water. Alternatively colour cycling can have the same effect of movement as advertising hoardings made up of light bulbs, such as are regularly filmed outside Las Vegas casinos.

6.7 SAVING THE IMAGE

It would be very limiting if images generated by the computer could not be saved. The best medium for saving them depends on their intended use, and the most usual would be in secondary storage (for future recall by a computer), on video tape (for broadcast or local use), on film (either still or cine-film) and on paper (as an end product or to be used as part of a longer process). To save to tape, film or paper requires an output device and the needs of animation prove more particular than those for saving single images. Although animation consists of a series of single images, the accuracy with which they must be located in time and space is crucial to the credibility of the animation.

6.7.1 HARD COPY

The most obvious output device is the printer, of which there are several types. The cheapest and most popular is the 'dot matrix' printer, which strikes the paper through an inked ribbon with a number of fine pins. The pins are carried in a moving head and the image is made up of a number of small dots, the resolution of which is determined by the number of pins in the head, and the subtlety of the software driving it. A basic printer has nine pins, twenty-four pin machines are now common and higher pin numbers have recently become available. Many dot matrix printers can be equipped with colour ribbons (comprising bands of magenta, cyan, yellow and black) through which the pins selectively strike, but the results are not very convincing and are liable to be inconsistent as the ribbon fades. Laser printers employ electrophotographic technology (first developed in photocopiers), are more expensive but produce very good quality results in black and white, typically with a resolution of 300 dots per inch (dpi), and will soon be available with higher resolutions and with colour. (The human eye can distinguish separate dots up to about 1000 dpi.)

Several technologies have been employed to produce better colour reproduction, and inkjet machines (which shoot precise jets of coloured ink onto the paper) are reasonably priced, quiet, and give clean colour, whilst thermal transfer printers (which use special paper) are effective but relatively expensive. It will always be the case (with foreseeable technology), that screen colour will fail to match printed output accurately, due to the different ways in which the images are formed. The additive colour (RGB) of screens is fundamentally different from the subtractive colour (CYM) of printing, which requires an additional true black (K), and mapping RGB to CYMK is not easy. Pantone have produced a set of matches between printing colours and screen colours, which is important in areas such as DTP, but an accurate match requires particular combinations of screen and video card under controlled conditions.

Plotters produce hardcopy by drawing on paper with pens which can move along the X-axis and be raised from, or lowered to, the surface of the paper. Either the pens can also move along the Y-axis or the paper can be moved along that axis past the pens. 'Flatbed' plotters hold the paper flat in either horizontal or vertical plane and can vary from A4 size to 10 ft long. 'Drum' plotters take less floor space to produce large plots on cut, or continuous roll, paper, by wrapping the paper over a drum roller, or by moving it from one roller to another. The plotter usually has between 4 and 10 pens, selected under software control. Since the pen can produce only lines and dots, and must combine these styles to produce shading, it is best suited to linear or diagrammatic images only. The software that drives the plotter cannot convert raster images to plotable form.

Whilst printing or plotting onto paper does not, of itself, produce animation, it can provide a useful record of a stage in the process, perhaps feeding back into the storyboard. It is often possible to send a sequential file of a wireframe animation to a plotter, which will intelligently organise the images on the sheet of paper into a storyboard. This can again provide a useful reference, or can be cut up and made into a flicker book animation. Up until a few years ago, many computer animations were made by filming individually plotted images, but the fashion for glowing, linear images (produced by backlighting negatives made from the plots) passed and technology has moved on to make rendering easier. Images from the plotter or printer can also find subsequent use as material for traditional animation.

6.7.2 FILM

Saving a single image to film from the screen is simple provided care is taken. The camera must be set up on a tripod, daylight balanced film used, a shutter speed slower than the screen refresh rate used, and ambient light must be prevented from falling on the screen and causing reflections (usually by improvising a hood to enclose screen and camera). It is also desirable to run tests to find the ideal exposure and best screen contrast to set, the maximum contrast available on the screen being outside the range of film to record accurately (colour prints having a lower contrast ratio than transparencies). The maximum resolution will be that of the screen, however, and the scan lines may be more obvious in the photograph than on the screen itself. There is also likely to be some distortion of the image due to the curvature of the screen. In order to guarantee the highest possible quality images, special film recorders have been developed. These contain a very high resolution black and white monitor with a flat screen and three coloured filters, to which the camera must be accurately aligned. The three colour planes in the frame buffer are separately displayed through the appropriate filter, and recorded onto the same piece of film. The resultant resolution is far greater than on a colour monitor since the black and white screen is not restricted by the shadow mask required by the former. It is also possible to bypass the frame buffer and send the image to the recorder as a sequence of single scan lines which can result in a resolution higher than even the film can resolve. Bureaux are available to produce slides at a resolution of 4000 to 8000 lines. The same principles apply to recording sequential images on cine film, with the added problem that the camera must be capable of reliable single framing, preferably under the control of the computer. It is not practical to film animation of any quality from screen in real time because synchronisation problems between the shutter and the scanning are added to those described for still images.

6.7.3 VIDEO

Video tape is the most commonly used medium for recording animation today. A large number of formats are already available, and more are developing, with great increases in quality. Whilst it is still generally true that the larger the tape width, the greater the potential quality, improvements in tape technology mean that excellent results are now practical on narrower tapes which are associated with smaller (often cheaper) machines, though not necessarily to broadcast standard. Traditionally tape has been used for analogue recording, but increasingly digital technology is invading the market place, and can be expected to grow in influence over the next few years. Digital storage allows images to be subject to manipulation without loss of quality, and is in the form needed to be handled by computers.

There are many video formats, as one might expect of a (relatively) newly popular medium, which reflect the range of qualities, sizes and prices of systems available for use from home to professional broadcast standard. A significant distinction is between those that store either the Red, Green and Blue signals or the Luminence and Chroma information separately (component) and those that merge them together (composite). The highest standard professional formats are component, but broadcast transmissions are currently composite. The most commonly encountered formats are:

Domestic and semi-pro -

Video8 (V8)	Aprox 250 lines horizontal resolution
VHS	"
VHS-C	Compact size VHS
Betamax	Less common than VHS
Hi-8	Aprox 400 lines horizontal resolution
Super VHS (S-VHS)	"
S-VHS-C	Compact size S-VHS

Professional only -

U-Matic lowband	Aprox 450 lines resolution
U-Matic highband	Aprox 550 lines resolution + timecode
Umatic SP	Superior U-matic
Betacam	High quality, component
Betacam SP	Superior Betacam
DI	Digital, component

It is often possible to plug a home micro into a domestic video tape recorder (VTR) and record live animation without further complication, many computers offering composite and RGB outputs. Sometimes an external modulator is needed, or an internal video card, but the main restriction is that domestic VTRs are not able to record single frames, and can rarely be controlled by the computer. Since most animation is not generated in real time, and only a limited amount can be saved in RAM for replay in real time, it is necessary to move up to High-band U-Matic standard before a timecode can be added to the tape to achieve this. As well as being relatively expensive, there is also the need for additional hardware to allow the machine to be controlled by the computer, which can then generate a frame, 'drop' it to tape, and move the tape on one frame to await the next frame. In fact the High-band U-Matic machine winds the tape back to a 'parking' place beyond the limits of the recording, and then runs the tape through to build up to the correct speed before a frame is dropped, exact synchronisation being possible due to a time code on the tape. It is also unacceptable to leave the tape heads at one point on the tape for too long, and machines will normally cut out after seven minutes, which might prove insufficient time to generate each frame. VITC (Vertical Interval Time Code) is a relatively new development which permits frame-accurate editing on low-cost formats, and may be adopted for use with desk-top animation.

Other pieces of electronic hardware are necessary for different video related chores. If there is more than one video signal a 'genlock' is needed to synchronise and lock them together, a common requirement being the superimposition of a computer generated sequence onto a sequence from another source, known as an 'overlay'. (One hindrance to the development of multimedia is the fact that owning video and computer equipment does not guarantee that they can be used together easily.) For the less frequent requirement of converting material between broadcasting standards, sophisticated equipment is needed, and is usually found only in specialist bureaux.

Having recorded animation to tape it is often necessary to edit the material, and the minimum requirement for this is two VTRs and an edit controller (though modern portable video cameras can sometimes be used as source machine and controller). Since it is likely that frame accurate editing will be required, the minimum standard is again High-band U-Matic, and you can see that the computer can often prove to be the cheapest part of an animation set-up. Professional edit suites can be hired by the hour, and major animation companies may have their own in-house. A major problem with video is that every time it is transferred to a another tape, such as when editing, is suffers 'generation loss' which lowers the quality. The degree of loss is determined by the format used and the quality of equipment, but it precludes sequences being built up by successively adding layers of images. New digital technology, however, preserves the quality intact through any number of processes if a solid state device is used (and with very limited loss if digital tape is used), and has allowed video 'collages' to become commonplace (notably in pop music videos).

Desktop video (DTV) is heralded as opening up a whole new

video world accessible to everyone. At the moment the "everyone" needs to be able to spend quite a lot of money, and is, therefore, likely to be a professional video worker, but DTV is already cost-effective and due to become a lot cheaper. It is suggested that a Macintosh based system, for instance, can already offer 75 per cent of the effects and quality of a top-level system costing more than three times as much, and can cut production costs to a tenth. The compromises involved in the cheaper system are quite acceptable in many contexts, and a few more price reductions will put DTV within reach of a big, new market. The future development of DTV is compared with the growth of desktop publishing (DTP), which has never threatened the high-end publishing systems but has led to much publishing being done in-house, and many more people becoming layout-literate. The memory taken up by a frame of 24-bit colour video is 1.2Mb and an obvious problem of a DTV system is finding sufficient storage for a worthwhile amount of video. For this reason data compression, described in Chapter 6.3, is important and chips are available that offer compression of up to 150:1 [Hodgson 1990].

6.8 IMAGE INPUT DEVICES

Manual input devices were considered in the last chapter on human/computer interfaces, but we are likely to need to import complete images intact from a range of sources, as well as to create them by hand. Flat art work can be imported using a 'scanner', in which the material is placed face down on a glass plate, and scanned using similar technology to a photocopier, producing a file in a common format. Until recently they were only available for black and white reproduction, but are now available for use with colour. Their usual image size is about A4, and small hand scanners are available which cover a width of about four inches, whilst being dragged manually down the image. Problems can arise if the copy is slightly misaligned, or, in the case of the hand scanner, the dragging is not even, but the latest software improvements have largely overcome these faults. When text is imported, the use of OCR software can produce a portable ASCII file (ASCII, pronounced "askey", forms an internationally used character set). For example newspaper page could be scanned and converted to a standard ASCII file which could then be reset using a typographic package.

It is also common to import material from a video source, which might be either direct through a video camera, or using prerecorded material through a VCR. A vertically mounted camera is usually to be found in the corner of computer graphics studios standing ready to import flat art work, which might, of course, be in the form of traditional animation cels. It is equally possible to import live video sequences, even simple equipment being able to digitise (black and white images at least) at the video rate of 25/30 frames per second. A problem, however, is storage, since ten seconds of video requires the storage of 250 images (at UK standards). A versatile solution is found in the digital editor 'Harry' from Quantel, which saves over 3000 frames on Winchester Disk Drives on-line, and can swap any part of this material with that held on VTRs under its control.

6.9 STANDARDS

Hardware standards appear to be honoured more in the breach than in the observation. Whilst many attempts have been made to standardise aspects of computing hardware, the interests of the consumer and the manufacturers are not the same. It is likely, and desirable, that designers will seek to improve on existing products, but if it is seen as commercially advantageous to create a captive market by introducing an element which is incompatible with other manufacturers' systems, then that is likely to happen (try and fit a VW exhaust pipe to a Ford). Some things appear similar on different pieces of equipment, such as RS232 sockets, but the fact that one plug fits another socket does not guarantee that they are wired the same way internally. The whole area of interfacing is a potential minefield, and whilst organisations of any size will have experts to deal with such problems, the individual may experience difficulty.

It is not even necessarily safe to stick with a single manufacturer, since it is common for updated models to prove incompatible, or only partially compatible, with the previous range. The humble disc drive might appear to accept your size discs (3.5 inch and 5.25 inch being the most common), but is it single sided, double sided, single density, double density or high density? If your disc is taken from a different make of computer it is likely that the new machine will require it to be formatted differently, and there is no certainty that the drive will even access the disc at a constant speed (whilst drive units themselves are often interchangeable, they can be controlled differently by various operating systems). Output devices such as monitors, printers and plotters are more likely to prove easily compatible with a range of machines, and it is in the interest of third party manufacturers to ensure as big a market for their product as possible.

6.10 HARDWARE FOR ANIMATION

Whilst the animator's aim will be to generate real-time material directly on the computer, he must currently be resigned to the fact that even the fastest of hardware will not be able to generate complex images at video rates. The two obvious alternatives are either to wait (for minutes, hours, or days) for the sequence to be generated frame by frame and saved on a medium which can be replayed at the correct speed, or to settle for a simple display which it is within the power of the available hardware to generate in real-time. A compromise is the most likely solution, with a simplified image being animated as close to real time as practical (8 fps might be acceptable), in order to check the quality of movement, a few keyframes being fully rendered to check the image quality, and then the image in its full, technicolour, ray-traced complexity, being produced in the computer's own best time. Specific production requirements might effect the balance of the compromise. In the event that it is chosen to animate a simplified image, the level of simplification will again be determined by the power of the computer. The system might be able to substitute a Lambert shaded model, a wireframe model or just a wireframe of the convex hulls in order to get the complexity of the object down within its limits for acceptable speed of animation.

When talking about a 'system' we are describing the entire hardware and software package. The best hardware in the world will not produce any animation at all without suitable software to drive it, and that will be the subject of the next chapter. It serves as a reminder, however, that the suitability of the hardware for animation cannot be considered alone, and a machine with a marvellous internal specification might be totally unsuitable for your particular purposes. Until recently, business machines paid little attention to their graphics capability, and even though paint and animation packages were available for them, their performance was markedly inferior to some much less powerful machines which had been designed with graphics in mind. Similarly, when a new machine comes onto the market it is likely to have a better specification than existing machines in its class, but until it has sold well enough to create a sizeable user base software houses might be reluctant to write applications for it. It is an anomaly, therefore, that the biggest range of software is likely to be available for the outdated machine. It should go without saying that a system must have 'extensibility' to deal with future needs.

CHAPTER 7

SOFTWARE

An application is a program designed to do a specific job. Its expression in computer-readable form constitutes a piece of software, and the two words often prove interchangeable. It is the software that instructs the hardware to operate to our ends, whether interactively (at a high, visible level) as in a paint package or, unseen in the background, controlling the operating system. Animation is one of the few areas in computing where software development is ahead of the available hardware. The computational expense of graphics and animation algorithms requires extremely powerful hardware, and developments in areas such as rendering, coupled with the desire to improve resolution, constantly stretch hardware to its absolute limits. Since effective animation can be produced on the simplest of computers, however, this chapter will look at the facilities that software can be expected to provide at the bottom as well as at the top of the range.

7.1 CHOICE

It is the case that software prices will be conditioned by the size of the user base, because the expectation of few sales for a package which might represent several year's work will force high prices to justify the effort, and because a bigger user base leads to more software competition which, in turn, keeps prices down. It will also be affected by the cost of the machine (if you can afford an expensive machine you can expect to have to afford expensive software), and by the market at which the machine is aimed (business users are led to expect to pay more for software than home users will for similar packages). There is even a credibility factor: "if the software is a lot less than the competition it can't be any good". I have found that software for some popular micros can be only one-tenth the price of inferior software for more 'prestigious' machines.

Higher up the market, the software might cost as much as the machine, and you are then effectively choosing the software first and then finding a machine to run it. If the machine is to be dedicated to one purpose, in our case producing animation, it makes sense to consider the availability of suitable software as part of any decision on the best hardware for your particular use. It is not much use having the latest machine with its superb specification if no-one has yet written the software that you need to run on it. Whilst this must seem obvious, I know people who have bought state-of-the-art micros and have been waiting 2 years for the software they need to appear, by which time their machine is starting to look dated. It is worth noting that software which proves successful on one machine is sometimes rewritten for other machines, but that its performance is likely to be modified by the requirements of the new host architecture.

It is often difficult to get competent demonstrations of cheaper software, particularly in such a specialised area as ours, since salesmen cannot be expected to be familiar with the vast number of packages available. When buying expensive packages (£10,000 plus) which are dedicated for use on particular machines, then the pricing should include an allowance for an experienced demonstrator and after sales training. It is obviously necessary to approach any purchase with a clear idea of the features required both now and in the foreseeable future. Whilst I would happily recommend machine/software combinations to anyone purchasing today (for those situations with which I am familiar) those recommendations are sure to be superseded in a year's time. Also, as this book hopes to be relevant to people working in a wide range of areas, with an equally wide range of different priorities, it is not practical to try and make generalised suggestions.

140

7.2 EXAMPLES

As a means of explaining the capabilities of current software, I will start by describing, in some detail, an inexpensive 16-bit package, and then see what changes and improvements are added to packages as we move 'up market' from there. Figs 7.2 show screen interfaces from the software mentioned. The functionality of the software will be considered in each of the three stages of creating a computer animation: building the objects, choreographing their movement and rendering.

The software described first is the 'Cyber Studio' series for the Atari ST from Antic Publishing Inc., which is now several years old but still very powerful, (it is interesting to discover that Tom Hudson, the creator of its central program, made a point of finding out what was possible on workstations at that time, and then trying to fit the same features into his 16-bit program, with some success). Examples of the features available in programs for more powerful machines are taken from 'Swivel 3D' from Paracomp, which can run on a basic 16-bit Apple Macintosh, but can also take advantage of the added power of 32-bit Macintosh machines, the 'Explore' range from TDI for Silicon Graphics workstations, and the 'S-' range from Symbolics for their own workstations. The packages from Antic, TDI and Symbolics comprise a suite of programs designed to be used together, whilst Swivel 3D is a single program which can be used alone, or in conjunction with software from other manufacturers to increase its versatility. It is not intended to give thorough descriptions of any of the packages, but to draw from them examples of the sort of facilities currently on offer. As good software is subject to regular updating, it can be expected that the packages described will offer more advanced features by the time this is read.

7.2.1 MODELLING

The basic model building tools in the Cyber Studio package are the fairly standard ones of extruding and spinning objects (from 2-D templates usually drawn with a mouse) and using readymade, scalable primitives (cube, wedge, cylinder, sphere, toroid, cone, prism). Additionally objects can be created from 2-D cross-sections

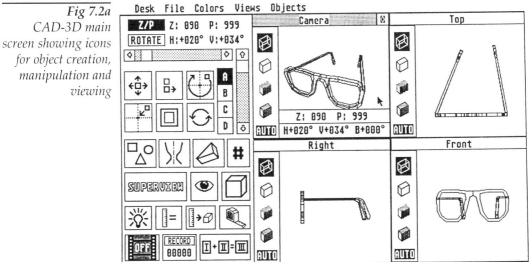

Fig 7.2a
CAD-3D main screen showing icons for object creation, manipulation and viewing

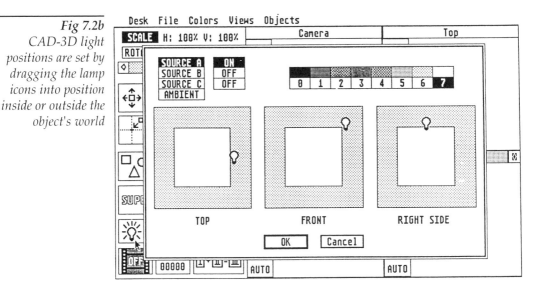

Fig 7.2b
CAD-3D light positions are set by dragging the lamp icons into position inside or outside the object's world

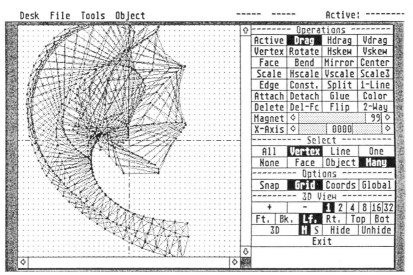

Fig 7.2c
Cybersculpt model
manipulation
interface

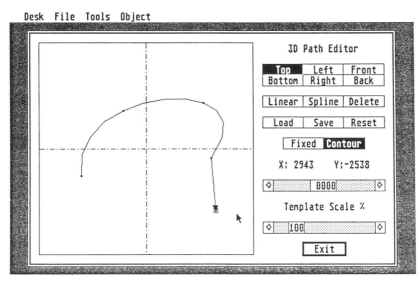

Fig 7.2d
Cybersculpt 3-D
path editor. The path
can be used in the
creation of an object
by extrusion or by
spinning

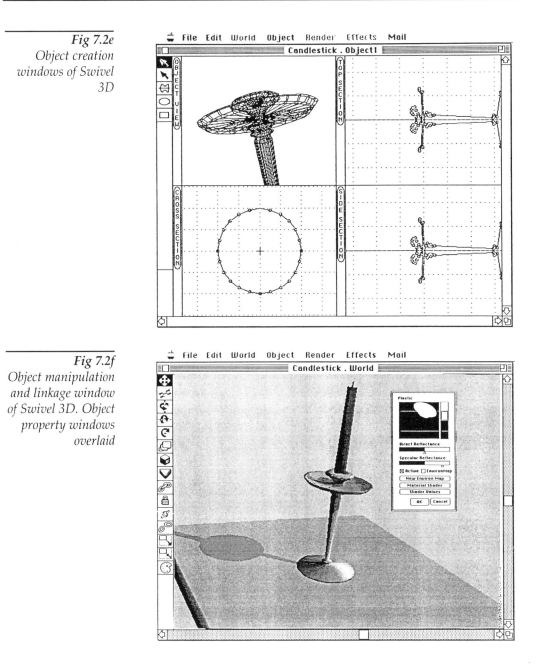

Fig 7.2e
Object creation windows of Swivel 3D

Fig 7.2f
Object manipulation and linkage window of Swivel 3D. Object property windows overlaid

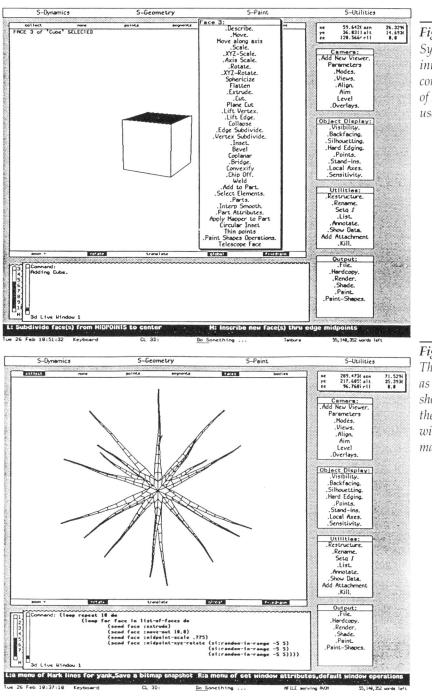

Fig 7.2g
Symbolics modelling
interface showing a
comprehensive menu
of actions that can be
used

Fig 7.2h
The same interface
as above but
showing the use of
the command
window to program
manipulations

145

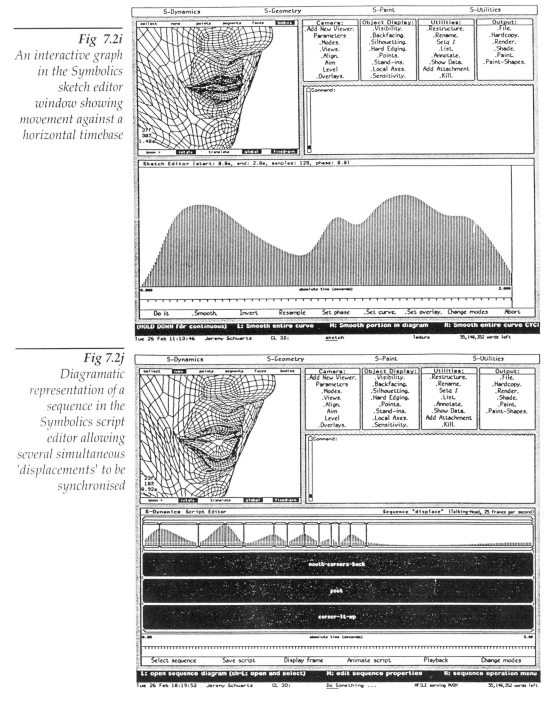

Fig 7.2i
An interactive graph in the Symbolics sketch editor window showing movement against a horizontal timebase

Fig 7.2j
Diagramatic representation of a sequence in the Symbolics script editor allowing several simultaneous 'displacements' to be synchronised

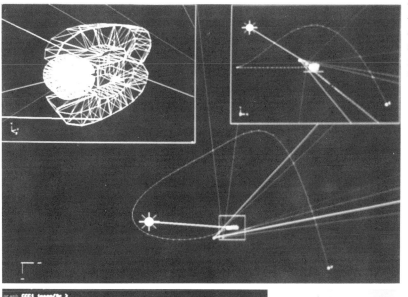

Fig 7.2k
*Animating a logo
along a spline path
using 'Explore' from
TDI*

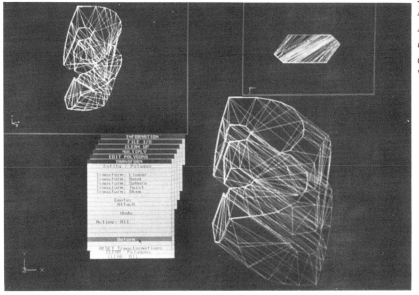

Fig 7.2l
*Applying a
deformation to an
object in a TDI
'Explore' modeller*

147

positioned along the object's length (a ship's hull could thus be built from sections through the hull). Objects of any complexity are made by combining basic shapes, created with one of the above methods, and by using Boolean functions to add, subtract, 'difference' and stamp the parts (as described under CSG modelling). The objects are seen in three views (normally top, right and front view) and in a 'camera' view which enables you to move your viewpoint around the object. Using these tools, parts of the object can be created, aligned (by dragging with the mouse and by rotating around any axis), scaled (in any or all dimensions) and cloned (exactly duplicated). Simultaneous viewing of the object along three axes facilitates creation, whilst interactive movement of the viewpoint allows the object to pictured 'in the round'.

    The scaling of objects can be achieved by percentage changes (either positive or negative) achieved by dragging 'virtual' sliders using mouse or keys, or by entering numerical data. It is thus possible to 'spin' a bottle, build a table from 'extrusions', and then by keying in their required dimensions, arrive at exactly the right relative proportions. Any of the viewing windows can be enlarged to enable detailed alignment to be made. Distances within the object's world can be measured with a 'virtual' tape measure. Objects can be manipulated individually or in defined groups and the ability to define arbitrary centres of rotation enables hinging to be accomplished.

    Within the package a more sophisticated modelling tool allows models to be modified vertex by vertex, line by line and face by face, either singly or in selected groups. The chosen element(s) can be dragged, bent, rotated, skewed, mirrored and scaled relative to the rest of the object, or the object as a whole can be similarly manipulated. Any of these elements can also be detached, attached or deleted, and new facets can be 'hand built' or redefined. A 'magnet' tool allows selected elements to be moved proportionally towards (or away from) the cursor, and this comprehensive range of tools allows sophisticated tuning of models made from basic shapes.

    Objects can not only be created by sweeping templates along a straight path in the extrude tool, but can be extruded along other user-defined, three dimensional paths, and can be twisted during the extrusion (either evenly or with uneven twist). These paths are created by laying down control points in 3-space which are connected by either straight line sections, splines or combinations of the two. The template can be rotated a specified amount during its extrusion, and the ends of the extruded object can be left open or capped. Polygon creation and spline tools simplify template construction, and the number of sections created by the extrusion is definable (the more sections created, the smoother the passage around a curve, but the added complexity of the object carries with it computational overheads).

Similar paths can be defined for the creation of sectional objects, so that a teapot spout, for example, could be created by connecting reducing cross-sections along a curved path. Objects created by sweeping a template around an axis can be 'spun' by a defined number of turns or degrees, and the template can be moved along a path as previously described. This enables corkscrew shapes to be made, for instance, the smoothness again being subject to the number of sections defined. At all stages of the modelling process, grids and viewing scale changes are available to make manipulation more accurate, and input is usually available either from mouse or keyboard. It is usually possible to 'undo' the last action though prior stages will be 'fixed', and it is, therefore, wise to save a copy of the object at each stage of the construction in case it becomes necessary to return to an earlier stage.

Swivel 3D approaches object creation somewhat differently, and the program is likely to be used in conjunction with a more sophisticated modelling package for the construction of complex objects. Objects are created using four view windows, by dragging points on a default object (a cube), or by use of a freehand polygon-creation tool. Each part of the object is, therefore, built from a 3-D block rather than 2-D templates, though this can leads to similar objects to those made with spin and extrude tools. Objects can be rotated by selecting the appropriate axis icon and then positioning with the mouse, during which movement the object is replaced by a cuboid convex hull to facilitate real-time action.

Whilst less sophisticated in its modelling tools, the package has an impressive joint definition facility, from which it presumably gets its name. Parent/child relationships are easily defined by dragging the mouse from one object to another, the relationship locked to form a joint (e.g. hinge, ball and socket) or left free, and the degree of permitted movement around each axis ('yaw', 'pitch' and 'roll') entered numerically. For this reason the package is very good for the simple creation of hierarchical animation.

Moving up to top commercial software, a host of additional sophisticated features appear. Edges can be bevelled, non-linear transformations (such as twisting) can be effected on objects, and free-form deformation is possible. Much larger and more complex objects and scenes can be manipulated at an acceptable speed and features such as multiple windowing allow the screen to be customised (these features resulting from the power of the hardware required to run this level of software). Object information (such as surface normals and bounding box centres) can be handled, and non-polygonal modelling is available. The ability, for instance, to use particle systems is now built into some packages.

One of the biggest improvements in modelling at this level comes with the ability to generate curved surfaces. Interactive manipulation of lines, profiles, networks and surfaces, and software exploiting NURBS to simplify curve creation, provides a rich vocabulary of shape generation. 'Skinning' (creating a skin around a skeletal object) and the automatic, smooth connection of surface patches extends the range of object types which can be simply built. A high level of interaction can be expected throughout the modelling process to help foster a friendly creation environment, but the greatly increased range of facilities now available leads to a more complex interface. Menus are likely to be longer and hierarchical, and designed in the expectation that more time will be devoted to familiarisation with the system. User intuition now requires more support from training, though if the system has the ability to keep a full history of the construction process it becomes possible to undo previous actions.

7.2.2 RENDERING

One of the most obvious differences between the Cyber Studio package and those for more powerful machines lies in the rendering facilities available. Very fast hardware, large amounts of storage and high resolution are usually required of the host machine before a package offers sophisticated rendering. It is also common in more advanced packages, for one application to be used to build the models and for a second to accept the model files for subsequent rendering. The Atari ST has a resolution in black and white of 640x400, and offers 16 colours (from a palette of 512) at a resolution of 320x200, which is not sufficient to make good use of anti-aliasing, for example. It would also take a long time to raytrace a simple image, and cannot be expected to produce smooth gradations of a range of colours within a scene.

Objects can be displayed in four forms: as wireframe images (in which mode the viewpoint can be moved interactively using the mouse), as images with hidden lines removed, as solid, shaded images and as solid images with edges drawn ('outlined'). There are two hidden line routines available, the 'draft' routine being quick but subject to mild errors, and the 'final' routine being slower but accurate. The shading routine uses the cosine method, and three light sources can be defined in addition to ambient light. The light sources can be positioned within the object's world, in which case they function as spotlights (with diverging beams), or outside the world, in which case they have a parallel beam (effectively like the sun). Lights are positioned using three view windows separate from the object view windows, which makes their relationship to the objects less intuitive than with some other methods. The intensity of each light source can be set separately. Once hidden line and shading are in use, the viewpoint can no longer be moved interactively using the mouse, the new position is set and then enacted by clicking within the 'camera' viewing frame.

In black and white, each object is assigned a position on a 15-point tonal scale. In lower resolutions colours can be assigned to objects in several ways. Either each object can have a single colour (the maximum colours available being 14, plus two for background and outline), or fewer colours can be used to achieve a tonal range within each colour (the maximum tonal range being 14 tones of one colour). Texture mapping of primitive shapes is possible.

Swivel 3D offers fairly similar rendering options, but is able to make use of a much larger palette when running on suitable hardware. It also permits texture mapping of objects created in the program, and special effects, such as antialiasing, are available.

At the highest level - texture mapping, 3-D texturing, bump mapping, reflection mapping, transparency mapping, full anti-aliasing, shadows (with variable softness), fog and textured light sources become available. Ray tracing also becomes a realistic option.

151

7.2.3 CHOREOGRAPHY

The central application in the Cyber Studio package allows animation of the models to be carried out 'manually', each movement in each frame being made individually, and then the frame saved in an animation file. The full range of rotations, shifts, scalings, creations and removals can be enacted on the object(s), which can have individual rotation points set to facilitate articulated movement. Viewpoint, lights and colour can also be controlled. It is very trying and time consuming to create any but the simplest animation this way, however, and it is also very easy to make an irrevocable slip in frame 199 out of 250 which will ruin the sequence. The program Cybercontrol, which loads as a desk accessory, makes life much easier by allowing all the operations to be put under the control of a BASIC-like program.

In Cybercontrol other camera types become available, allowing fly-throughs by the definition of camera coordinates plus either the coordinates of the point viewed or heading/pitch/bank (plus focus in stereo mode). Motion paths for objects, lights and camera can be controlled by B-splines, by splines which pass through the control points and by 'linear splines' (which are not true splines but connect control points with straight lines). Support for the definition of parent/child relationships (in conjunction with defined centres of rotation and joint limitation) makes hierarchical movement much easier to carry out, and other minor features make the whole animation process far smoother. The ease of having an animation create itself while you take a teabreak, makes the whole process less precious and therefore encourages changes to be made and variations to be tried.

Swivel 3D animates by tweening, the first and last frames being set manually, and the specified number of inbetween frames being calculated by the program. These frames can be saved in a suitable form for playing back in another application if rendered, and can be previewed within Swivel 3D in wireframe form. Linked or separate objects can be animated, and multiple keyframes can be used for more complex motions. Paths can be smoothed with Bezier curves and cushioning is available.

The top systems offer a range of methods for animating objects. Traditional keyframe control is available together with keyframe control offering position or temporal priority, inverse kinematics helps in the animation of articulated structures, and control can be by data from an external program or script. Object metamorphosis allows real-time transformations, and hierarchical articulation is strongly supported. The establishment and manipulation of paths is interactive, and real-time line testing is immediate.

7.2.4 2D

The emphasis in this book is on 3-D rather than on 2-D. This is partly because the principles of 2-D are similar to (though simpler than) 3-D, but mainly because whilst 2-D work follows on quite closely from traditional animation, in the area of 3-D the medium offers completely new horizons and insights and is therefore the focus of most current research and development. Following the initial surge of interest in 3-D, however, there has been a renewed recognition of the role that two dimensional animation can play, not least by way of economy. A 3-D sequence may cost from 5 to 50 times as much as a 2-D sequence of similar length, and consequently rule itself out on budgetary grounds. Even when a budget can cover the cost of 3-D, the money is wasted if a 2-D sequence could be produced to do as effective a job. Paint systems can be central to the creation of 2-D animation and a useful tool in 3-D animation.

Cyberpaint is a 2-D paint and animation program that will accept animation files created in Cyber Studio and can therefore be used for 'post-production'. It can also accept digitised video sequences and be used to create cel animation, allowing material from a range of sources to be collaged together. Facilities such as 'blueing' (a term coming from printing) are incorporated, to allow information from the previous frame to be overlaid on the current frame for registration purposes. The animation can be built up in superimposed layers, and cut and pasting is available for both single images and sequences. A range of 'effects' such as anti-aliasing, 'tiling' and 'dissolves' is incorporated, and a powerful feature which allows the enlarging, shrinking, shifting and rotation in three dimensions of single frames or animated sequences. Tweening is also available in conjunction with many of the operations. Output from the Cyberstudio programs can be routed to one of the standard formats accepted by other packages on the Atari, though this is likely to mean dealing with sequences frame by frame.

Swivel 3D does not include specifically 2-D features but its output can be saved in a format which is accessible to the many paint and 2-D animation packages available for the Apple Macintosh. Indeed it is intended that other packages will be used for the display of Swivel 3D animation, and this compatibility is part of the Mac philosophy.

Images from high-end machines may be output to specialist paint systems such as the Quantel *Paintbox*, but are increasingly likely to offer their own integrated, top specification paint package, with 2-D animation options. The specification for S-Paint includes, for example, unlimited brushes, including specialist brushes such as airbrush, blend, diffuse, speckle, scatter, tile, rubber, stamp and wash (the brush names referring to the traditional tools and processes they emulate and extend). Subpixel positioning and small anti-aliased brushes make it easier to draw fine lines in detailed work. 'Scatter' and 'randomise' features allow you to break up images into fragments and disperse them across the canvas. Gradients for any shape can be created, using multiple colours and/or opacities, whilst operations such as copying, squeezing, stretching, canvas scaling, mirroring and applying digital optical effects are available. Digital image manipulation features permit the use of image processing techniques, including adjustments to luminance, colour balance and contrast of images. 'Unpainting' and 'repainting' facilities are not only convenient but can provide the basis for real-time animation of simple imagery, the powerful ability to generate versatile mattes is supported, stencils can be animated and digital compositing allows infinite layering of images.

7.3 CUSTOMISED

Production houses often choose to write some of their own software. This might be because of a specialist requirement, such as the need for a particle system, in order to update or improve existing software, such as a renderer, or to enable the interfacing of miscellaneous equipment. Similarly, in a research situation, it is likely that the research process will require specialised software to be written. It is also possible that existing software may need to be customised to meet the particular requirements of the current user or his system. At the simplest level this might involve amending the assign system (which tells the program where to find all the files it needs), loading appropriate device drivers or setting up macros to be associated with function keys. At a more fundamental level it might be necessary to insert, delete or change code in the program itself, in order to fulfil a particular objective, although applications are often not amenable to this sort of interference. My personal preference would always be for an application to include the ability to accept user generated code.

7.4 COMPATIBILITY

Since no single piece of software includes every feature you might desire, it is convenient to be able to move between applications and take full advantage of all their features. Many applications are written with the intention of providing solutions to just one part of a process, providing just modelling facilities or just rendering perhaps. In the case of these specialist programs it is reasonable to expect greater sophistication than in a single program trying to deal with everything. Several of the packages already referred to divide the total process into separate, compatible pieces of software. The crucial word, of course, is 'compatible', describing the ability of individual applications to create files which can be read by other applications, and to read files created by other applications (in addition, of course, to being machine compatible). It is noticeable that this compatibility is now strongly emphasised in the promotion of applications, the advertising material including an increasingly long list of file types that can be read and written. Although this serves to confirm the lack of universal file standards, it does allow the user the opportunity to assemble a package of software components to suit his own particular requirements. There is also increased development of file conversion software to allow portability between different hardware bases.

Whilst the packages from Symbolics and TDI aim to be very comprehensive, providing everything necessary to produce superb broadcast quality animation (possibly with the addition of some post production work), the current version of Swivel 3D is normally described as being used in conjunction with other software for the most comprehensive results. As part of the pattern of Macintosh development, its large user base has encouraged the development of separate applications at a range of levels to match its range of hardware, from basic home machine to the latest Macintosh hardware which has workstation performance. This means that anyone with a 'Mac', and the curiosity to look at animation, is catered for, whilst the cost of top-end systems rules out all but the really serious. Although it is impractical to be specific about the cost of complete top-level systems, a rough indication would be to expect to pay as much as for a house (systems ranging from modest to grand, just like houses).

7.4.1 STANDARDS

A number of attempts have been made, and are continuing to be made, to develop standards for computer graphics systems. These efforts are coordinated by the ISO (International Standards Organisation). Unfortunately the timescales and requirements for the functioning of a committee and for development in the marketplace are not closely matched, but the evolution of even an imperfect standard does offer a starting point for greater compatibility. The standards require the definition of graphics functions as a set of abstract specifications, together with a language binding which defines how the functions are to be accessed from a particular programming language.

Of the suggestions put forward, the ISO chose to develop GKS (Graphical Kernel System) which is a purely two-dimensional system, and has developed GKS-3D to extend the current standard into three dimensions. Many graphics functions are defined, their specification being in English rather than directly in any computer language, in order that maximum independence should be maintained, and the standard covers not only image manipulation, but also device handling, and, therefore, deals with input, storage and display. A more powerful system called PHIGS (Programmers' Hierarchical Interactive Graphics System) has been developed by ANSI (American National Standards Institute) but neither PHIGS nor GKS covers lighting and shading, and PHIGS+ has evolved to include these controls and others. In the area of image transfer and exchange, the CGM (Computer Graphics Metafile) is often used on hardware from micro level up to workstations, as are file formats such as GIF and TIFF.

7.4.2 POSTSCRIPT

PostScript is a page description language which is normally invisible to the user. It describes to an output device exactly how to present either text or images at the best resolution of which the device is capable. An application will generate the PostScript code from the page(s) created by the user, and this can then be read by any device with a PostScript interpreter, whether it is a laser printer at 300 dpi or a Linotronic printer with a resolution of 2,400 dpi. Since the output device can also be a monitor, it is possible to have an accurate screen representation of a page as it is developed, true 'WYSIWYG'. PostScript can also be handwritten and sent to an output device and , as such, has been used to create simple animations, but this is not its most usual role.

7.4.3 RENDERMAN

Whilst formats exist for transferring 3-D object information between different hardware bases, the same has not been true of scene descriptions, each package having its own method for specifying surface, lighting and camera parameters. Pixar has now come out with a very comprehensive package called 'RenderMan' which accepts files using RIP (RenderMan Interface Protocol) commands to describe a scene, and offers high level rendering. It hopes to establish RIP as a standard for the exchange of files, and may prove more successful than previous attempts since it is already being taken up by some major companies. It is also possible to import RIP files into a device, such as a film printer, which has its own RenderMan interpreter and can translate the file contents for its own use. The RenderMan features are summarised in promotional literature as:

1. Primitive surfaces
   Quadratic surfaces (surfaces of revolution)
       Disk
       Sphere
       Cone
       Hyperboloid

Paraboloid
Torus
Polygons
Parametric surfaces
Uniform surfaces
Bilinear
Bicubic
Non-Uniform Rational B-Splines (NURBS)
2. Hierarchical modeling
3. Motion blur
4. Depth of Field
5. Filter Mechanisms
6. Extensive I/O Capabilities
(RenderMan will read and write a ranges of files)

The files describe the geometry of objects and attributes of objects, light sources and ambient conditions using what Pixar calls 'shaders'. For example, an object can thus be defined as being of wood, marble or perhaps a 'home made' material, with a specific degree of specularity, transparency or reflectance, having an image-mapped or distorted surface, lighted by a particular combination of light sources, and immersed in a fog of defined density. It is anticipated that customised shaders will be marketed in the same way as fonts for DTP use. The quality and level of detail of the resultant RenderMan image is very impressive, though current examples tend towards the 'photographic realism' school which is prevalent.

7.5 DEVICE CONTROL

As well as being used to produce images, software often needs to control external devices such as printers and VTRs. If your application doesn't have the correct printer driver, it can't send anything to your printer. If your application can't control your VTR then dropping single frames to tape is going to be either tedious or impossible. A further area which can give rise to compatibility issues, therefore, is that of input and output devices, which the software must be able to 'talk' to. It is not sufficient that the software can accept input from a digitising pad, it must be able to accept it from the particular type of pad that you are going to connected it to (and with the right cable).

7.5.1 MULTIMEDIA

A critical part of the development of multimedia is the software. It must not only be able to communicate with a range of different devices but must also ensure a smooth interaction between them. A sophisticated interface becomes necessary to enable the operator to handle text, graphics, animation, live video and sound. At the same time, of course, a suitable hardware base is needed. Apple is having a big hand in establishing multimedia as a viable resource, by developing (and encouraging the development of) the appropriate applications for its Macintosh range. Their 'HyperCard' application, sets the tone for multimedia with its interactive access to databases of potentially different media, and by packaging it with all new Macs since late 1987, Apple has ensured that a growing userbase is familiar with its concepts. Underlying the functioning of HyperCard is the object-orientated language 'HyperTalk', which normally remains invisible to the user but can be used fairly simply to program the environment and to control devices.

The predicted boom in multimedia will increase demand for animation, and it is sure to become an accepted and expected part of presentations and publications. It remains to be seen whether multimedia authors will recognise the need to acquire design and animation skills, but the pattern of competence will probably be similar to that of DTP. The cost of investing in professional systems will not encourage the unskilled.

7.6 CONCLUSION

The capability of the software that is available (at every level of hardware) is increasing very fast. Every time I returned to the draft of this chapter it seemed necessary to add more features in order to keep up to date, but the best that can be expected is that the state of the area is described at one moment in time, and that the relativity of performance at different levels will remain. Improvements are not just being made in the available hardware and in the algorithms used, but also in the expectation of the user. Increased exposure to sophisticated, high quality animation has led to greater demands from the user, and in a market driven economy this demand is likely to be met.

Whilst low resolutions and limited palattes are not satisfactory for convincing ray-tracing or anti-aliasing, both these features are now becoming available as standard in rendering packages for all machines. However, machines with the resolution, palette size and speed to use such features to good purpose are now available at reasonable prices, and there is a rush by all manufacturers to provide competitive graphics performance. New versions of machines which have usually been thought of as predominently for business use, such as those in the PC range, and which were notoriously difficult to program for effective graphics, have now been updated to produce good quality images. It is now realistic to expect to have available Lambert, Gouraud and Phong shading models together with ray-tracing, image and texture mapping and anti-aliasing.

It is noticeable that many packages for modelling and rendering now include animation facilities, but that these are mainly limited to basic keyframe systems. Whilst these might be adequate for simple presentation graphics they have obvious limitations for more ambitious work. It is likely that the market is too new for it to be clear what level of facilities is going to be required, but that the more people who have the opportunity to become involved with animation the more sophisticated will become the demand. It is also likely that this demand will be encouraged by a reduction in the cost of saving the animation to a suitable secondary medium, and that the development of digital technologies will enable this to happen.

CHAPTER 8

LANGUAGE CONSIDERATIONS

It is not the intention, in this book, to discuss programming in any depth. The subject deserves a shelf of books to itself, and many have already been written, but it is worth considering the relationship of the program to the end result. The choice between, on the one hand, taking a programming route to building an animation and, on the other, exploiting a fully written application, has implications for the final product. In the case of the first route, the choice of language used also has an effect, as its structure and peculiarities can steer the user in particular directions. Having said that, it is possible to do most things with most languages, and our brief summary will merely aim to familiarise the reader with the most common options available.

The computer program is a medium through which to instruct the computer to do something (hopefully something useful) and a range of languages exists for writing computer programs which may, or may not, be transparent to the user. It is increasingly possible to use a computer without any knowledge of, or interest in, programming, but it is equally possible to communicate with the machine only through writing programs. Both approaches can be appropriate in the field of computer animation but a middle course often proves most fruitful. Without access to programming skills you are resigned to work within the limitations of the available applications and there is always a point where the software won't do quite what you want. On the other hand, many applications are not written with the intention of their being open to addition or amendment. Some of the most versatile packages allow both. It should be noted that 'debugging' a program (tracing and correcting errors and removing unwanted side effects) is usually a much longer task than writing the initial program code, and that many professional programmers spend their time updating and improving existing code, rather than writing fresh programs.

Important properties of a language are the ability to carry out 'assignment' (attributing numerical values) and 'iteration' (repeating pieces of program many times), selection using 'conditionals' (making choices based on the current state of the program) and 'modularity' (breaking down the program into reusable units called 'subroutines', 'procedures' or 'functions').

8.1 LANGUAGE TYPES

There are a large number of computer languages in existence, some outdated, some still waiting to reach fruition, some widely used, and some esoteric. All have been created to address specific needs that existed at specific moments in time, either designed to work efficiently with a particular hardware configuration or to satisfy the demands of a particular task (such as animation). They can be classified in a number of ways.

8.1.1 LOW LEVEL/HIGH LEVEL

The "height" of a language describes how far it distances itself from the innermost workings of the computer, low level languages are computer orientated whilst high level languages are problem orientated. The only true low-level language is machine code which is a binary notation directly translated into computer operations by the electronic circuits. It would, however, take a strange and very particular mentality to choose to create an animation by sending individual numbers to specific computer memory locations and registers.

Whilst early computers could only be programmed in that way, it did not take long before languages evolved which were more comprehensible to their users, and which allowed programmers to instruct their machines in a form more easily identified with each instruction's actual function. This development was not only for the sanity of the programmer but was also the only realistic way in which long programs could be written and maintained without error. These 'high level' programming languages use commands close to written English but are converted by the computer into machine code, the conversion being transparent to the programmer. This enhanced 'readability' is vital to the sure comprehension of a program, particularly when worked on by numbers of people, as is usually the case.

It is sometimes necessary to resort to low-level programming in the search for maximum efficiency and speed, but this is considered the province of the hardened programmer rather than the animator. Modern high-level languages are getting much closer to the speed of lower ones, and are able to remove the user still further from the machine workings, to the extent that the user need have little or no understanding of how his instructions produce the results he gets. This is not always a good thing, particularly if the results prove not to be what was expected, but, with the advent of increasingly intelligent interfaces, it is the way the art will progress.

8.1.2 INTERPRETED/COMPILED

A program written in a high-level language has to be translated into machine instructions that can be acted on by the hardware. This can be done line by line as the program is running ('interpreted') or the whole program can be converted in advance of being run ('compiled'). A compiler may first translate the source program into an assembly language program, and then use its own assembler to complete the translation to machine code. An 'optimising' compiler will attempt to improve the efficiency of the code produced, the use of optimisation being an option set by the user.

Languages are normally either interpreted or compiled, but some versions of a few languages (e.g. BASIC) allow you to use either method. The advantage of interpreters is that they can provide a friendly development environment, easing debugging by running the program up to the point where an error is encountered and then halting, usually returning to the source code at the point the error was discovered. A disadvantage is that the program running speed is compromised by the need to undertake translation into machine language whilst running, and that repeated parts of the program (loops etc.) have to be freshly translated each time they are used. Modern interpreters are much quicker, relative to compilers, than in the past, but the speed required for animation would seem to favour compilers.

Compiled programs are often a lot faster, and the 'object' code produced can be run without the presence of the application that produced it (interpreter applications sometimes include a run-time package which allows a stripped-down version of the translator to be attached to the source code, so that it can be run on its own). Compilers are generally less friendly towards the inexperienced programmer, though more versatile, and a bigger part of the development cycle seems to be spent in frustrating delays while the source code is compiled yet again. Compilers thus encourage a different working method for debugging and a convenient combination can be to use the interpreted method at this stage, and then to compile before final use. Compiled programs can take advantage of other already-compiled programs, so that it is possible to compile just the current part of a larger program and 'link' it to completed parts.

8.1.3 PROCEDURAL/DECLARATIVE

Procedural languages (e.g. FORTRAN, BASIC and C) tell the computer what to do, declarative languages (e.g. Lisp and Prolog) tell it what you want to accomplish and things it should know, and are hence good for dealing with knowledge and facts.

8.1.4 OBJECT-ORIENTATED

Object-orientated languages ("object-oriented" in the USA), known as 'OOPS' languages, are finding great favour at the moment, and it has been suggested that they present the form of the next generation of computing languages. Simula, Smalltalk, Object Pascal and C++ are examples of OOPS languages and they operate by passing messages between active objects which are analogues of things which exist in the real world. These objects (in some languages called 'classes') are self-reliant, combining their own data with the functions that operate on them. Sub-classes can be inherited from existing classes, and the model OOPS presents is often much closer to the way the real world works than traditional languages.

Object-orientation encourages the production of efficient, self-contained units of code which can be easily employed by a number of programmers, and are therefore particularly useful on large projects. It provides a highly extensible programming environment, and has an intuitive affinity with graphics and animation. Computer Graphics conferences are currently including a growing number of papers on the advantages of OOPs for CG.

(It is worth noting that the term 'oject-orientated' is also used in other contexts, notably to distinguish vector graphics from raster based (or 'bit-mapped') graphics in contexts such as fonts for DTP systems.)

8.1.5 PARALLEL/SEQUENTIAL

The architecture of a computer is reflected in the structure of its language. Most procedural languages are associated with traditional von Neumann computers, and are structured in a way that mirrors their sequential operation. They require each operation in a series to be carried out before the next can be attempted. Languages for parallel use allow different operations to be carried out at the same time, and must have the ability to provide the correct sequencing for the enactment of tasks which depend on one another. They must allocate tasks to different processors when appropriate, and ensure efficient 'housekeeping'. At the time of writing, occam is the only language specifically designed for parallel use, but parallel versions of existing languages are becoming available.

8.1.6 DEDICATED LANGUAGES

A number of packages have been written especially for animation, or for graphics with an animation facility included, three examples of which are given. PICASO is graphics library written at Middlesex Polytechnic, England [Vince 1986] (initially in FORTRAN), which provides a large number of graphics routines that can be called from a host language. MIRA-3D is a graphical extension to PASCAL developed by Magnanet-Thalmann [1983] which has led on to the animation language CINEMIRA, and MIRANIM system [Magnenat-Thalmann 1985]. The Clockworks is an object oriented test-bed animation system implemented in C, developed at Rensselaer Polytechnic Institute, New York [Getto 1987].

Such packages are normally extensions to existing languages rather than new languages in their own right. They do, however, provide a fresh range of commands relevant to the graphics/animation discipline, and sometimes their own syntax, so can reasonably be considered alongside languages. Such packages are often developed for a particular context or project and rarely have more than a small user-base. Watt [1989] suggests that an animation language will reduce the conceptual distance between a program and script and its effect, and should be accessible to animators who are not necessarily skilled programmers.

8.1.7 HYBRID LANGUAGES

Many language applications allow the linking of compiled code written in different languages, thus permitting the various advantages of more than one language to be incorporated into a single program. This might be useful, for instance, if an expert system, typically written in PROLOG, was to be used within a program written in C. A number of hybrid languages exist which have been developed to combine procedural and declarative modes, such as ORIENT 84/K offering features of Smalltalk and PROLOG [Tokoro 1984], and EXPERTMIRA combining Mira with PROLOG [Thalmann 1986].

8.2 RELEVANT LANGUAGES

Of the many languages available, those most likely to be met in the course of reading about computer animation are listed below in alphabetical order. Of these, BASIC is common in books at an introductory level, and PASCAL and C are most used at a higher level.

Pseudocode is often used as an explanatory medium which can be converted into a range of high level languages.

8.2.1 ALGOL

A procedure orientated programming language, whose name derives from ALGOrithmic Language, ALGOL exists in many variations and is internationally used by the scientific community. It is only mentioned here because a number of books on computer graphics describe the programming of algorithms using an ALGOL-like pseudo code.

8.2.2 ASSEMBLER

Assembler developed in the 1950s as a sort of machine code shorthand, using a series of very basic instructions that correspond to the architecture of the processor, and which are then translated into the binary code which the computer understands. Given that machine code is too problematic for normal use, assembler produces the fastest, most compact code and allows programmers the greatest access and control over the machine's inner workings. Its use requires an understanding of computers at a low level, its superficial form reflects how the computer works rather than what the program is meant to do, it often takes a number of assembler statements to achieve the same result as one high-level language statement, and it is unforgiving. In order to get the best of all worlds, it is common for programs to be written in a high level language which will then call in pieces of assembler at points where fast code is particularly important. Assembler is also needed sometimes in device drivers (programs which assist the operating system in working with external hardware, such as a plotter).

8.2.3 BASIC

The name is an acronym for Beginner's All-purpose Symbolic Instruction Code, and it was designed in 1964 as an easy-to-use language for non-computer scientists. It is usually interpreted, although compiled versions are now available, and has often been criticised for slow speed and the encouragement of poor programming style. Its ease of use has led to it being packaged with many machines, which has guaranteed a big user-base, and it has provided many people's introduction to programming. It handles text better than some other popular languages, but is rarely chosen for serious graphics use, and comes in a wide range of dialects which inhibits its portability. Recent versions show major speed improvements.

8.2.4 C

The C language was developed in the early seventies by Dennis Ritchie at Bell Laboratories, and the standard text on the language is by Kernhigan and Ritchie. Apparently APL (A Programming Language !) begat BCPL begat the language B begat C, and its development is intertwined with that of the UNIX operating system. The widespread use of UNIX guarantees a long life for C and it is often described as the most popular language today, currently seeming fashionable to the point of being a cult. Its popularity derives from the way it manages to combine aspects of high- and low-level programming in a general purpose language "which features economy of expression, modern control flow and data structures and a rich set of operators...its absence of restrictions and its generality make it more convenient and effective for many tasks than supposedly more powerful languages" [Kernighan 1988].

It has a small vocabulary of key words, 32 in the approved ANSI standard version (compared with over 400 in some BASICS), an economy which is achieved through the addition of a standard library using 15 headers to provide various functions and definitions. Being independent of the architecture of any particular machine, it is possible to write programs which will run on a variety of machines, though the highest level of portability requires taking some care in the writing of the program. Its economy allows you to write code which can be almost impenetrable to an outsider, and sometimes to the programmer himself after a week's absence, so full accompanying comments become essential.

It has been suggested that if computer languages were bicycles,

BASIC would be a pushbike, PASCAL would be a motorbike with a sidecar and C would be a motorbike with no sidecar and no brakes.

8.2.5 C++

An object-orientated superset of C, C++ was developed in the eighties by Bjorn Stroustrup at AT&T Bell Laboratories. It incorporates all of standard and ANSI C, enhances C with a number of small, helpful improvements, and adds support for object-orientation. Weiner [1988] describes the additions as including: data abstraction (the association of a data type with the operations available to it), encapsulation (the process of defining an object which includes the definition of how it interacts with other objects), inheritance (the ability to create a subclass of objects which inherits characteristics from a 'parent' class) and polymorphism (the ability of an object and its subclasses to respond to the same message in their individually defined ways). It has considerable potential for use with graphics and is likely to find widespread use. Apple has just written the new operating system (System 7) for its Macintosh range in the language, and a number of manufacturers have extended their C languages to include support for object orientation. In some cases these extensions are described as supersets of C and subsets of C++ rather than as being full C++, but there is not, at the time of writing, an ANSI standard for C++.

8.2.6 FORTH

Not a commonly used language in our context, the name FORTH comes from FOuRTH generation language (4GL), and it was developed in 1970 for the direct control of equipment (initially in the observatory of its astronomer creator, Charles Moore). It is mentioned here because it can be used for robotics and arcade games [Pfaffenberger 1990], and can be good for controlling external devices.

8.2.7 FORTRAN

The name is an acronym for FORmula TRANslation and the

language is primarily used in scientific and technical contexts for handling mathematical formulae and expressions. It is one of the earliest high level computer languages and is still quite widely used because of its compact notation, and the problem of replacing the large quantity of existing code. It also has a considerable history in computer graphics because many graphics libraries were, and still are, FORTRAN callable. Being highly portable from machine to machine it can also survive the replacement of its host hardware. There are a number of versions of FORTRAN, with variations of features and syntax, but it tends not to be used in our context except when a base of FORTRAN code already exists to be exploited. The latest version is FORTRAN 8X which includes specific parallel facilities.

8.2.8 LISP

Lisp was designed in the mid-1950s by John McCarthy who wanted a list processing language for artificial intelligence work on the IBM 704. It is potentially useful for graphics because lists of items are commonly found here (e.g. lists of vertices and facets) and a number of drafting systems have LISP interpreters (e.g. AUTOCAD). Some graphics workstations have been designed to work directly on LISP but there is no ANSI standard yet, 'common LISP' being the closest to a standard. To programmers brought up on traditional procedural languages a conceptual adjustment is required, though it has been argued that the principles of LISP are, in fact, more intuitive.

8.2.9 LOGO

Designed by Seymour Papert to help teach children about computing, LOGO is based on LISP and has commands built into the language which are very suitable for basic animation. A key feature of the language is 'turtle graphics', in which a wheeled 'turtle' supporting a pen is directed across a drawing surface by the computer, under instruction as simple as to 'go forward', 'turn right' and so on. Recursion is made simple. LOGO provides the basis for the animation language DIRECTOR (by Kahn) and ASAS (by Reynolds) which develops the former into 3-D [Magnenat-Thalmann 1985].

8.2.10 OCCAM

Created for programming on parallel architecture machines, OCCAM is not used yet in mainstream animation. It seems to have met some resistance from programmers new to parallel systems, who prefer to carry on with more familiar languages. Makers of parallel machines usually indulge this inclination by permitting the use of traditional languages, although they might not yet have the efficiency of OCCAM in this context. It is listed here, solely because the reader is likely to come across reference to it when parallelism is mentioned.

8.2.11 PASCAL

Pascal was named after Blaise Pascal, the french mathematician, by its creator Niklaus Wirth and was written primarily as a teaching language designed to support the concepts of structured programming. It is straightforward to learn since a formal language like Pascal is essentially similar to a sentence, can have a syntax diagram, and even ends with a full-stop. Many books on computer graphics give coding examples in Pascal, and since many programmers will have passed through Pascal in their training it is a convenient language for this job.

It is a heavily 'typed' language, which means that everything has to be explicitly defined, and this makes it intolerant of errors and forces discipline on the user's programming style. This intolerance is a virtue as some other languages allow you to write very confused code which does not lend itself to error checking. An object orientated version called 'Object Pascal' has recently emerged, and 'Modula-2' (created by Wirth) has been described as a Pascal that lets you get your hands dirty (i.e. lets you deal directly with things at a lower level than Pascal itself). Some recent versions of the language have improved graphics capability.

8.2.12 PROLOG

Prolog is a 'descriptive' language used for solving problems which involve 'objects' and the relationships between them, and was to be the language of the much vaunted Japanese "fifth generation" of computers (of which little is currently heard) which were to make heavy use of artificial intelligence. It is made up of a number of 'clauses' containing either a fact about the data or a rule about how the solution may relate to, or be inferred from, the given facts. A Prolog program is a collection of facts and rules which establish a knowledge base, used to answer questions about the objects and their relationships using a formal system of logic. Its name comes from PROgramming LOGic.

8.2.13 PSEUDOCODE

Pseudocode is not an authentic programming language, but is mentioned here for the sake of completeness. It is often desirable to explain the general principle of the construction of a piece of code, without giving an example which is language specific (even within a single language it can be necessary to avoid being dialect specific). Pseudocode presents a generalised version of the way in which a real language would be written, and should be able to be readily coded into any chosen language using the same structures. It is not standardised, though usually procedural, and is often reinvented by each author as required.

8.2.14 SMALLTALK

The first object orientated language, and often claimed to be the purest. Every operation is carried out by an object, even the function of a mathematical operand such as an addition sign. The language itself includes a large number of readymade objects and includes its own graphical user interface. Although it has not become a mainstream language it has been very influential in the development of others, notably HyperTalk (the programming language for HyperCard from Macintosh, itself an influential application). Some versions of SMALLTALK include graphical abilities which can be used for animation [Magnenat-Thalmann 1985].

172

8.3 CHOICE OF LANGUAGE

In practice, the choice of a suitable computer language is often inhibited by pragmatic constraints. The decision may be influenced by the architecture of the available hardware (e.g. parallel or sequential), the language used by the favoured application (e.g. LISP is used by graphics applications running on Symbolics hardware), compatibility with existing software (e.g. if millions of lines of FORTRAN have accumulated over a number of years there might be a strong incentive to continue with it), the languages available (it is no small matter to add another language to a mainframe, for instance), and the existing skills of the programming team. It is also worth bearing in mind that the most difficult part of writing a graphics program is often the part which fits it to display its images on your particular hardware.

C is almost certainly the most popular language in use for animation and graphics today, but my own prediction is that the rapid growth of interest in object-orientation will continue, and that C++ is the natural choice of language to use by those already working with C since it can work with all the existing code. The natural tendencies to (a) stick with a language that works, or (b) use the latest language because it 'must' be better, can be reconciled in C++, where the new conceptual simplicity can be implemented with relatively few additions to the old language.

It is interesting to note the comments of Simon Ritchie [1989] who suggests that C is, in fact, particularly unsuitable for graphics. Although it is inappropriate to get into much depth on the subject, for the programmers who are reading this book I list his main reservations, which are (a) that its untyped argument passing mechanism is inadequate, (b) that arguments are always passed 'by value' (rather than optionally 'called by reference'), and (c) that it shares the typical inability of high-level languages to handle objects other than numbers (e.g. matrices and points) pleasantly by permitting operator overloading. He also suggests that some features of C make it a puzzling first programming language, particularly for teaching Graphic Design students for instance, and it is hard to disagree with this.

The example that (Simon) Ritchie gives using C++ to build a simple graphics library, employs Stroustrup's 'programming with data abstraction' through the use of classes, but does not fully exploit

173

object-orientation he says, suggesting it is more appropriate for a more complex piece of software. This serves as a warning that the use of the tools of object-orientated programming is not the same as programming with object-orientation. In fact it is equally possible to use the object-orientated paradigm with ordinary C, it is just less convenient to do so than with the additional tools offered by C++. At the same time C++ offers improved handling in the context of graphics than C without it being necessary to resort to OOPS.

In the final analysis, of course, what matters is that the chosen language does the required job for the current user. The corners of a facet are no sharper, and the reds no warmer, in a program written in C++ rather than BASIC. It is sensible, however, to be aware of the potential advantages and disadvantages of the languages available to you, in order to work effectively and efficiently in your particular environment.

PART TWO

CHAPTER 9

STATE-OF-THE-ART:
SIMULATION

In the context of this book, simulation is taken to be a special case of computer animation in which the aim is to model an occurrence dynamically using physical laws. (Dynamics being the branch of mechanics concerned with the forces that change or produce the motion of bodies, and the occurrence being either of the real world, for instance a car crash, or of a hypothetical world where forces and masses can be defined arbitrarily.) A simulation is a scientific experiment and is solved incrementally, each successive frame being dependent upon the calculation of the previous frame. Simulation is an empirical method used where it is necessary to evaluate the circumstances in order to determine the result, rather than simply to draw the result [Reynolds 1986].

9.1 DYNAMICS

Dynamics deals with the way masses move under the influence of forces and torques (unlike kinematics which studies the movement of objects without regard to cause). The application of basic physical laws enables the realistic simulation of the motion of bodies, and cannot only be applied to separate complex bodies, but can automatically describe the conduct of bodies in collision. It therefore takes little effort to simulate a raindrop falling or a ball being thrown, by specifying mass, starting velocity and direction to a system that knows what gravity is, perhaps that there is a cross-wind and how to apply the rules. A little more information is needed to cope with friction and bouncing, and more again if the object is articulated, flexible or asymmetrical, but although the number and length of the required equations grows, the governing rules remain clear. The body of literature on the subject is considerable and the papers by Jane Wilhelms[1987a,b,c] are particularly clear and explicit.

The simplest object to deal with is a particle. This is a single point in 3-space, fully describable by its X,Y,Z coordinates and with three degrees of freedom of movement (Fig 9.1a) i.e. it can move in any direction, but since the rotation of a point is meaningless it is denied the further three degrees of freedom available to a 3-D body which can be translated and rotated relative to each of the three axes. As a particle is, in theory, infinitely small, it could be said not to have a mass but it often proves convenient to attribute it with one. This equates with the fact that it needs to have a physical display size in order to be visible to us.

Fig 9.1a
Degrees of freedom
of movement

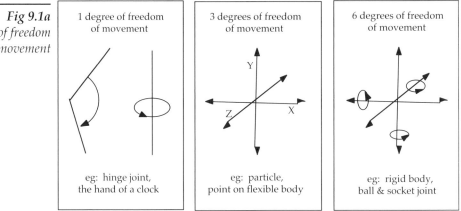

| 1 degree of freedom of movement | 3 degrees of freedom of movement | 6 degrees of freedom of movement |
| eg: hinge joint, the hand of a clock | eg: particle, point on flexible body | eg: rigid body, ball & socket joint |

We can describe the movement of a particle under the control of forces, such as gravity, by the application of Newton's three laws of motion which he formulated in 1687 (Appendix B). If you know the original position and velocity of the particle and how the force varies with time, you can write an equation which will tell you its position at any time in the future (Fig 9.1b).

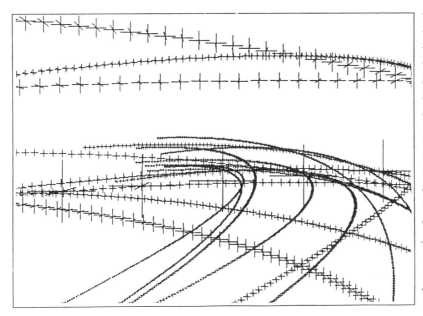

Fig 9.1b
A dynamic particle system. The top picture shows the paths of 3-D particles propelled into space against a vector wind'. The lower picture shows the paths of particles attempting to use their randomly assigned forces to follow a circling target, whilst resisting the force of gravity. (Particles 'die' on collision)

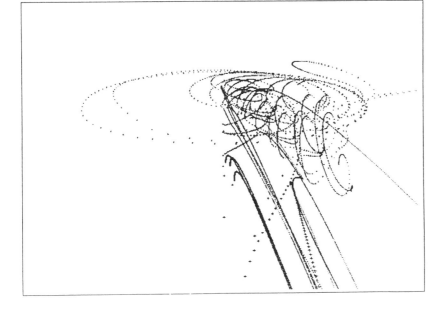

From the force on the particle you can find its acceleration. You integrate the acceleration with respect to time to get the velocity and you integrate the velocity to get the position [Balch 1989b]. Fortunately, for anyone with a non-mathematical background, it is possible to apply the formulae without understanding them! Since even the simplest dynamic simulation can prove totally engrossing, an appendix gives basic information for the reader who might like to experiment with the area.

A simple method is provided by combining the formulations of Newton and the 18th century Swiss mathematician Euler (Appendix B). A limitation of the Newton/Euler method of numerical integration is that inaccuracies arise if the time-step used is not relatively small (Fig 9.1c). This means that it might well be necessary to make all the calculations several times for each frame, but the simplicity of the method often outweighs the requirement to keep increments small. It is beyond the scope of this book to describe the rival merits of different dynamic formulations, but papers on the subject most commonly refer to those of Newton, Euler, Lagrange, Runge-Kutta, Gibbs-Appell, Armstrong and Featherstone. Some of them benefit from recursion and all of them are appropriate in different situations when it may be necessary to trade off cost against ease of use or generality.

Most objects in the real world have the additional ability to spin and are therefore no longer point masses but are extended masses. In order to manipulate the extended mass it becomes necessary to know the centre of mass of the object and how the mass is distributed about the centre. For symmetrical objects the mass distribution requires the calculation of three moments of inertia, one about each axis, though it is often sufficient for the calculations of a 'shaped' object to be made on its bounding box (Fig 9.1d). (A bounding box is a simple space-frame, typically cuboid, which closely contains a more complex form. It can be substituted for the form it contains in order to simplify calculations when absolute accuracy is not essential.) A non-symmetrical object requires the additional calculation of three products of inertia. The extra three (rotational) degrees of freedom of an extended mass mean that turning forces (torques) as well as straight, directional forces can be applied. Forces applied other than at the centre of mass also produce torque.

It will often be the case that a single rigid body does not

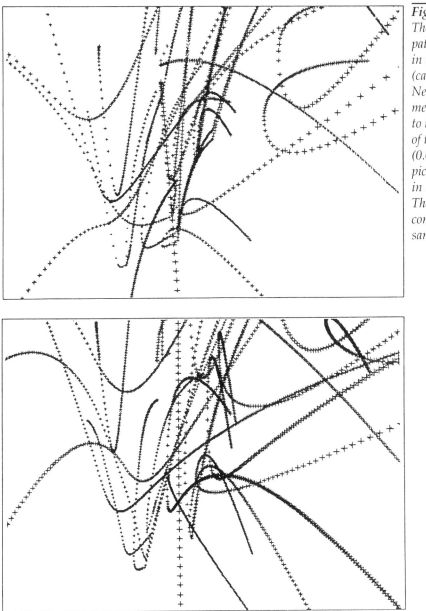

Fig 9.1c
The difference in the paths of the particles in the two pictures (calculated using the Newton/Euler method) is due soley to the different size of the time step used (0.02 seconds in top picture, 0.04 seconds in lower picture). Their starting conditions were the same

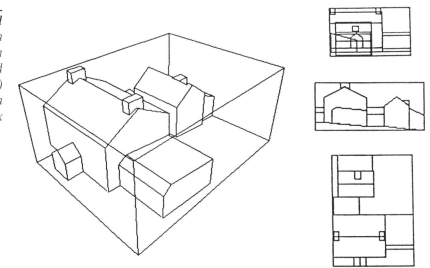

Fig 9.1d
*A model of a
building (shown in
front, side, top and
three-quarter views)
contained in a
bounding box*

provide a sufficiently sophisticated representation of the object to be manipulated. A skeleton and an anglepoise ('Luxo') lamp, for example, are constructed of rigid elements which hinge about one another, each element subject individually to internal and external forces and to the effect of similar forces on its connective neighbours. The cumulative effect of all these forces determines the global movement of the object.

Dynamic analysis continues to offer a prediction of realistic movement, and as the complexity of kinematic specification becomes too great, becomes a more amenable method, even given its high computational cost. Many types of motion, such as falling or reacting to collisions, can be found automatically and the description of the object can readily incorporate appropriate limitations to the freedom of movement of each joint. It is possible to specify motion at a limited subset of body joints and have the dynamics calculate motion at the rest, i.e. the movement of a hand can be specified and the movements of the wrist, lower arm and upper arm can be calculated. This broaches the problem of inverse kinematics (working backwards from the desired end position to find acceptable joint positions) as the hand can reach its target equally well by realistic and unrealistic routes, i.e. it might be possible for the arm to remain bent and for the legs and body to manoeuvre the hand, which would not normally be considered realistic movement. The problem will be discussed in a later chapter.

9.2 PHYSICALLY BASED MODELLING

"A physically based model is a mathematical representation of an object (or its behaviour) which incorporates forces, torques, energies, and other attributes of Newtonian physics. With this approach, it is possible to simulate realistic behaviour of flexible and rigid objects, and cause objects to do what we wish them to do (without specifying unnecessary details)" [Barr 1989a].

So having defined a ball and a surface we can 'drop' the ball and watch it bounce around until coming to rest. If we care to drop a properly defined cup onto a properly defined pillow we can witness its progress at a level of accuracy prescribed by our definitions. Snooker balls can interact realistically, articulated figures can trampoline and leaves can gently flutter down in a breeze. Not surprisingly, some things are easier to define than others and many things are too complex for it to be practical to attempt a definition. Nevertheless there is always an addictive magic about witnessing even a simple occurrence unfolding under its own (apparent) initiative.

Having set the starting conditions for an incident, the animator (or should it be simulator?) can take a lunch break whilst his machine works through the calculations, creating and storing each frame, and return to watch, as a spectator, the event running in real-time. For a complex simulation he may currently need to take a vacation rather than a lunch break, but hardware progress is moving us towards calculation and display happening in real-time. This state would then have the exciting potential for real-time interaction with the model, tweaking parameters as the incident unfolds, perhaps changing forces and constraints to exactly meet production requirements.

A crucial difference between a kinematic animation and a simulation is that the first is storyboarded and the second open-ended. In the first case specified things must happen in a specified sequence and take a specified time (a 'two-point boundary problem'), in the second case (an 'initial value problem' of forward simulation) once the incident has been set in motion there is no external control over when it stops (if ever). This can prove an impossible production constraint if, for instance, an object is required to come to rest at point xyz in frame 150. Inverse dynamics can help to work backwards from an end state to calculate the required initialising forces.

9.3 CONSTRAINTS

It is often desirable, and sometimes essential, in the course of animating an object, to observe certain limitations to its movement. This might be as simple as requiring objects not to pass through the plane of the floor on which they are resting, or as complex as requiring the bones of a skeleton to retain the correct connections and appropriate degrees of freedom of movement at all joints. These limitations to the uninhibited movement of an object are 'constraints' upon it. Kinematically, the object need never be placed below the floor plane, but in a dynamic simulation the constraints may be enforced by the physics built into the scene i.e. the object may be prevented from passing through the floor because it recognises an upward force offered by the floor, equal to its own mass.

If your shoe is fixed to the floor with a single nail then your foot is constrained to stay on the ground, though able to rotate about the nail in the plane of the floor, and the rest of your body is constrained by its natural joint linkages, with their various degrees of freedom of movement. If your shoe is glued to the floor then the constraint on your foot is total (as long as the floor stays put!) and the rest of your body movements limited accordingly. A rubber band connecting your shoe to a nail in the floor restricts the amount of movement you can take away from that point, and increases the force on your foot to return to that spot in proportion to the amount you try to move away. The limit of your movement in the latter case is determined either by the maximum stretch of the rubber band or your ability to pass the band's breaking point. Extending this bondage analogy: handcuffs constrain your wrists to remain within a limited distance of one another, though not to any particular spatial point, with consequent limitations along your hierarchical links. A room constrains your spatial freedom, an appointment constrains your temporal freedom, a lack of clothes (usually) constrains your behavioural freedom, and your physical condition constrains the height you can jump in the air to protest at all these other constraints. In real life there are always some limitations to movement, and it is desirable in an animation, and essential in a simulation, that they can be incurred automatically. A number of papers [Barzel 1988, Isaacs 1987, Witkin 1987,1988, Platt 1989] deal with the problem at some length, and it is an area of much current interest.

Barzel and Barr [1988] say that their modelling system, based on dynamic constraints, consists of instantiating primitive bodies, connecting and controlling them with constraints, and influencing their behaviour by explicitly applying external forces. The geometric constraints are implemented by solving an inverse dynamics problem which requires the determination of forces needed to meet and maintain a constraint (unlike forward dynamics which determines an object's behaviour given the forces acting upon it). Their constraint library includes:

'Point-to-nail' constraint, which fixes a point on a body to a user-specified location in space and allows the body to swivel and swing about the point.

'Point-to-point' constraint, which forms a joint between two bodies (the bodies remaining free to move).

'Point-to-path' constraint, with which a point can be required to follow a user-specified path.

'Orientation' constraint, which aligns objects by rotating them.

Other constraints include those to restrict a point to lie on a given line, and those to require two spheres to touch (whilst allowing them to slide along each other).

As well as creating and maintaining the constraints it is necessary to decide how the constraint should be met: along what path the object should move to meet the constraint, and at what speed. If the constraints are being used to initialise positions in a scene then these issues are not important, but if they are being enacted during an animation then they must be considered (in the Barzel/Barr system a user-specified time constant controls the exponential rate of decay of deviation of the constrained point).

Each constraint force is supposed to produce its desired behaviour taking into account all other forces in the system,

185

producing a linear system of simultaneous equations describing the constraint forces and their relationship to each other. Constraint-force equations can be under-constrained, in which case they can have many solutions which will produce the desired result, or over-constrained, in which case the constraint can not be fully met. In both cases it is necessary to make an additional judgment about the desired result either explicitly or by embedding rules in the system (e.g. 'use the solution with the smallest magnitude' or 'get as close as possible'). At an early stage in the development of their system, Barzel and Barr acknowledged that it was necessary to have a good physical intuition in order to apply constraints effectively (though this reservation appears not to have been repeated in later papers).

It has been suggested [Kass 1989] that Aristotelian dynamics, which is intuitively good though strictly inaccurate, works well for constraints and is automatically critically damped. (Newton said Force=mass*acceleration, Aristotle said Force=mass*velocity.)

9.4 COLLISIONS

When objects are in motion in a dynamic animation, it is likely that collisions will occur between them (and between them and their environment, if defined). It is necessary, therefore, to check for collisions and to implement an appropriate response once detected. (The former is fundamentally a kinematic problem involving the positional relationship of objects in the world. The latter is a dynamic problem, in that it involves predicting behaviour according to physical laws [Moore 1988].) An unsophisticated detection algorithm may be sufficiently visually convincing when dealing with simple interactions of rigid masses. However, in a true simulation there are complex issues to consider with a proportional expense in computation time, further complicated if articulation and flexibility are involved.

9.4.1 COLLISION DETECTION

A detection check which is simple to implement uses a spherical bounding box and computes the distance of each object from each of the others in turn. If the distance is less than the sum of the radii of the two bounding spheres, then the spheres intersect and a collision has been detected. It is sometimes only necessary to know that an object has been in a collision, without the need for information on further collisions which might effect the response. In that case the response can be speeded up by removing all objects found to have been in collision from the calculation at the moment the collision is detected. The time step at which the collision check is made must be small enough to exclude the possibility of an object passing through another within the period chosen, or other tests implemented.

Though possibly adequate for production purposes, the bounding box test provides only a crude judgment about the relative positions of complex objects. To determine the moment and point of collision between two chairs, for example, it would be necessary to check all surfaces of one chair for intersection with all points on the other chair at each moment in time. It would be sensible, however, to use the quick bounding box test to see whether the chairs were within touching distance, and only then to implement the more sophisticated tests. Similarly it would be possible to use relatively large time steps until a collision had been found to have occurred and then to work back and forth with reducing time steps to calculate more accurately the moment of collision. (The Cyrus-Beck algorithm [Rogers 1985] includes an example of a simple 2-D test to tell whether a point is inside a convex polygon.)

A number of interpenetration algorithms, more subtle than our spherical bounding box, have been proposed [Moore 1988, Uchiki 1983] particularly in the field of CAD/CAM and robotics, but the necessity of checking for penetration of each facet (in a B-rep model) can be expensive. Methods for dealing with CSG and voxel-based models are also available.

Further economy would be possible by reducing the indiscriminate collision checking of every object (or vertex) against every other, using a method such as a space-occupancy check with an octree search. In this case divisions of space would be examined to see if they contained more than one object, and if they did would be sub-divided and re-examined until a suitably small area was found to contain more than one object. At this point suitable collision tests would be introduced. The efficiency of this procedure would depend on the population of objects and its distribution at the time.

9.4.2 COLLISION RESPONSE

Having detected a collision it is necessary to initiate a response. Response to non-anticipatory detection can be dealt with by physical laws. This would be more straightforward in the case of colliding snooker balls than in the case of a boomerang hitting a doughnut or a cow falling downstairs, but the laws to deal with all cases exist. The response can be calculated analytically by considering the linear velocity, angular velocity, mass, centre of mass and inertial tensor of the colliding masses. This is computationally expensive but usually applied only once for each collision (linear and angular momentum must be preserved and a new direction vector sought). It would lend itself readily to a simulation of gas molecules in an enclosed space, for example, when (if the coefficient of restitution is one) the molecules would ricochet off the walls and off one another indefinitely.

Alternatively, a more intuitive method is to temporarily insert a stiff spring between the points of closest approach (or deepest interpenetration) of the two objects. The spring force is applied equally and in opposite directions to the two objects, and the direction of force is such as to push them apart (or reduce their depth of interpenetration). Whilst this is simple to implement, it will generally have to be applied over a large number of small time steps. Friction between colliding surfaces should also be considered (if they are infinitely rough the objects will come to rest!) but a simple approximation will often suffice. It might also, in some situations, be useful to have a merely didactic response such as 'if in collision, turn red', so that the status of objects in a simulation can be more clearly followed.

9.4.3 COLLISION AVOIDANCE

Collision detection is normally implemented in order that a response can be made, but the types of response can be varied. If the collision can be anticipated then feedback may be provided which can prevent the collision taking place, either by activating immediate behavioural rules on the part of the object, or by causing the path-planning procedures to back-step and recalculate. (A physically based object is, of course, resigned to collisions unless credited with foresight.)

Back-stepping and replanning is probably inappropriate in a simulation unless it is assuming the role of long range vision, as it implies a static path through a dynamic world. It could readily form part of the learning process of a sophisticated object, however, where success and failure at navigating an environment lead to an improved (= collision free) path. Jane Wilhelms [1987a] suggests that collision avoidance done "on the fly" is better described under the heading of stimulus-response control, which involves the two steps of: (a) recognising the state of the environment, and (b) developing a response to it.

Another method of preventing collisions in a scene is to build force fields around the objects to repel contact. These fields (which can be recognised using the bounding box method) can be graduated according to the distance from interception, in order to produce gentle deceleration or diversion. A problem arises, however, when an object is travelling straight down a 'force beam', because a standoff results unless some rules have been added to deal with this special case. It is analogous to the rejection forces of opposing magnetic poles and could, perhaps, be used as the method for enacting a behavioural response.

The Lozano-Perez [1979] algorithm provides an alternative to iterative collision detection (repeatedly checking for collisions at each timestep) by specifying constraints on the vertices of the moving object, and solving for a path that obeys constraints simultaneously.

9.5 BEHAVIOUR

An actor may display intentioned behaviour which could be set to include goal seeking. It is likely that spatial goal-seeking will require the ability to avoid obstacles, possibly through simulating vision, and, as such, is relevant to us here. The area of behavioural animation, however, is sufficiently important to have earned a chapter to itself, and these issues are discussed there.

9.6 TELEOLOGICAL MODELLING

A term recently imported to computer graphics (from the fields of philosophy and biology) is that of teleological modelling. Derived from the Greek word 'teleos', meaning end or goal, it provides an extension of the current definitions of modelling to include a number of recent developments, and provide a model which is goal-orientated. It is a mathematical representation which calculates the object's behaviour from what the object is 'supposed' to do. Alan Barr [1989b] suggests that it has the potential to extend the scientific foundation of computer graphics and to vastly extend the state-of-the-art for computer graphics modelling. He says that teleological methods can create mechanistic mathematical models with predictive capability, and produce compact formal descriptions of complex physical states and systems.

It seems that teleological modelling does not offer new methods, but provides a conceptual framework within which recent (and future) methods governing an object's purpose, can be related to existing modelling methods. The teleological model of an object includes time-dependent behavioural goals as part of the object's fundamental representation.

Barr [1989b] presents a hierarchy of abstractions for objects:

1. An object is a timeline of 'goals': Teleological modelling primitives

2. An object is its Newtonian behaviour: 3-D physical modelling primitives

3. An object is its shape: 3-D kinematic primitives

4. An object is an image: 2-D modelling primitives

Quoting directly from that SIGGRAPH paper: "Perhaps the simplest abstraction of an object is its graphical appearance (4). The 'object-as-image' is represented by two dimensional primitives, primarily consisting of pixel images and vector drawings.

The next abstraction is that of shape (3). The Greeks created the polyhedra and the conic sections; graphics has not progressed significantly beyond this modelling approach (certainly there has been some progress - the Greeks did not invent bicubic patches!). The 'object-as-shape' is represented with polygons, patches and the like. The next abstraction is that an object is represented through its physical behaviour (2). Isaac Newton's physics was founded very much on the same principles derived by the Greeks, although it was derived nearly two millennia afterwards. 'Objects-as-behaviour' are represented as rigid and flexible physical bodies.

The final abstraction is teleological(1). A teleological model incorporates time-dependent 'goals of behaviour' or 'purpose' as the fundamental representation of what the object is. Just as physics incorporates 'geometry' as an integral part of its world view, the teleological approach incorporates physics. Examples of teleological objects are 'objects-as-timelines' or 'objects-as- set-of-goals'.

The teleological approach makes possible a new graphics pipeline. The user gives the teleological system a timeline of motion and position goals; inverse dynamics and other teleological techniques are used to produce a physics of interaction of the objects; physical simulation then produces the positions and orientations of the objects, via polygons, bicubic patches, and other kinematic modelling elements. Finally, rendering techniques such as ray tracing and depth buffering techniques are used to convert the shape of the object into an image."

Applied in animation, a teleologically modelled object will do what you want it to (or, at least, do what you say you want it to), the object 'being' its physical behaviour. It could be said to consist of physics + 'what you want'. The links of a chain created by Barzel and Barr [1988] leap to join one another, and span the gap between two supports, because the knowledge of their role in the chain is a part of their model definition. In doing so, they avoid one of the main problems in animation by dynamics, that of attaining time/space goals.

CHAPTER 10

STATE-OF-THE-ART:
SOFT MODELLING

Computer modelling has always lent itself to building mathematically defined shapes. Architecture, machinery and letterforms can be usually built from cubes, cylinders and other regular primitives; most designs that are created with drawing boards, parallel rules and set squares can readily be converted into data on which the computer can act. Consider how much of the real world these methods will enable us to satisfactorily model.

If I glance aside from my VDU, and look towards the window, little of what I see could be constructed from geometric shapes. The window frame is made of regular mouldings and the window catches are regularly defined shapes, but surrounding them are draped curtains and beyond them are bushes, trees, grass, clouds and my wife talking to a neighbour. A nearby wall appears to be a regular grid of similar, rectangular bricks, but my own front wall is a clumsy construction of old, battered bricks of visibly different sizes. No part of my wife seems easily described by formulae. I know that her head of hair is a collection of simple filaments, but cutting, styling and standing in the wind has transformed it into a far more complex object. Similarly, her clothes are constructed from clearly defined pieces of planar fabric, joined with simple, repetitive stitching but this knowledge seems of minimal help in understanding the folds and creases wrought by fashion, gravity and wind around her 'convex hull'.

The natural world rarely, if ever, matches the geometric predictability that is the result of man-made mass production in the Western world, yet it is unlikely that animators would be willing to restrict their subject matter to cars driving through cities or to telephones in office interiors. Whilst the future might conveniently be pictured as formally more regular, our pre-machine past (or the present of a jungle tribe) is clearly not so. It is therefore necessary to find ways of dealing with more informal structures, and this pursuit is often referred to as 'soft modelling'. It will be found that soft modelling often aims to match the appearance of an object or phenomenon without plagiarising its actual construction, whilst 'traditional' modelling often uses that construction as its starting point.

Over the last few years great interest has been shown in the area, partly enabled by dramatic hardware improvements which have facilitated previously impractical methods. This interest in things which are not clearly defined finds parallels in other disciplines, such as artificial intelligence, where 'fuzzy' logic [Zadeh 1965,1983] contributes to a more realistic model of knowledge representation and decision making than 'crisp' formal logic. A technique which is often employed at some stage in the soft modelling process, in order to allow departure from certainty (in time or space), is the use of stochastics. Controlled stochastics employs randomness within prescribed limits to automatically produce variations on a theme.

10.1 PARTICLE SYSTEMS

A particle has already been identified as a single point in 3-space. A particle system is a collection of these particles, normally in large quantity (between 10^4 and 10^6). Typically, each particle will be created with a position, lifespan, and velocity (probably randomly determined between fixed limits), will change its position according to algorithmic rules, may change its colour or transparency, and will age and 'die'. The simple 'typhoon' animation illustrated (Fig 10.1a) uses eleven parameters (including four which establish the span of the random numbers) to sweep particles up a spiral path, changing them during their lifespan from white to red.

Particle systems have, in recent years, been used to represent fuzzy objects such as cloud, smoke, fire and spray in either dynamic

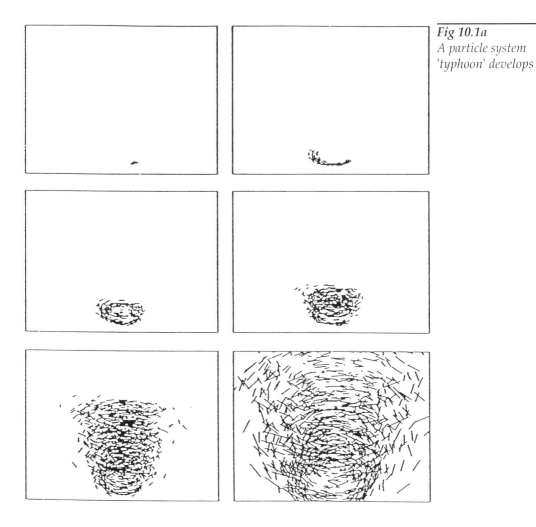

Fig 10.1a
A particle system
'typhoon' develops

or static states, and to grow hair and grass, and they have the potential for doing much more. When used to describe a fuzzy form, the boundary of the object is not defined by surface primitives, but by a cloud of particles defining its volume. As its attributes are normally defined by a set of constrained stochastic processes, the surface is not cleanly defined (though there is no reason why the position should not be defined by a mathematical description of the object, in which case the particles could offer a 'clean' description). It is obviously appropriate that a cloud should not have a precisely defined edge, but there may be a situation where a cube of particles is called for. The particles are also not normally static in space or time, so the appearance of the object changes with time (though, again, there is no reason why it should not be deterministic).

Reeves [1983], who has been credited with coining the term 'particle system', describes several advantages of his systems over classical surface-orientated techniques. The most obvious is that a particle is much simpler to define than a polygon, to create and to move, so it demands less computing time. He also points out that its simplicity makes it easy to simulate the blurring associated with movement, by extending the point into a line tracing its recent path (and optionally reducing its intensity or changing its colour along that path). The second advantage is that it is procedurally defined, which means that a highly detailed model does not necessarily require more time to build than a simple one. It can also adapt its level of detail to the viewing parameters, so that detail can increase as you get closer (as with fractals). Thirdly, the collection of particles changes form over a period of time, which can be difficult to duplicate using surface modelling techniques. He also cites a number of examples of their use in video games, flight simulators, smoke models, for star creation and death in a galaxy, and for producing images of the rings of Saturn. It can readily be seen to be appropriate for dust, cloud and spray, since these natural phenomena are made up of particles (of water, for example, or dust particles in suspension).

A system need not be a constant size but can grow or shrink by changing the particle birth and/or death rate, death being controlled by age, position, intensity level, colour or other parameter. It is also possible for each particle to be the parent of another particle system, up to a theoretically unlimited level of hierarchy, with the parent having global control over its children. This method was used in the much quoted 'Genesis Demo' sequence from the movie 'Star Trek II': The Wrath of Khan' [Reeves 1983], where an expanding wall of fire is made to spread across a planet's surface. Reeves describes a two-level hierarchy, where the top-level system was centred at the impact point of the 'Genesis' bomb (which caused the fire) and generated child systems randomly on concentric rings spreading from the impact point, at times related to their distance from the impact. The second-level systems were modelled to look like explosions on the surface of the planet, with particles flying up at a random ejection angle and falling on a parabolic path under the influence of gravity. Other parameters, such as colour, were inherited from the parent system but varied with the same constrained stochastics. These features have also been used to model fireworks [Reeves 1983].

Grass and hair could be 'grown' by 'seeding' the surface with particles (which will represent the tip of the filament), ejected outwards with random variations from a perpendicular to the surface. If the particles are dynamic (responsive to gravity, etc.), or at least obey rules approximating response to appropriate forces, they will define a suitable parabola, and by connecting each point passed through by the particle, a filament is created. The process can be halted when the length is satisfactory and 'frozen' as a model of a lawn or head of hair, or the filaments can be allowed to continue growing. If each filament is allowed to articulate at each of the points defining its length, and the dynamics is continued down the hierarchical chain, then the filament can flow and bounce in response to outside forces such as wind or surface movement. It would require some subtlety in the definition of the hair's structure (straight, curly, permed ?), in the subsequent collision responses and in the usual range of constrained stochastics, but it is all possible. Unfortunately it would be practical to deal dynamically with little more than a small moustache using current hardware, but the principles are sound.

A particularly effective and attractive animation of a waterfall (see back cover) was constructed by Karl Simms [1989a] in "Particle Dreams". He applied gravity to blue particles which flowed over a 'cliff' and bounced off spherical 'rocks', exhibiting friction and resilience, turning white on bouncing and fading back to blue. The 'camera' tracked over the scene, and the sparkling splashes remarkably evoked similar emotions to viewing a real waterfall.

A mildly 'intelligent' particle system of my own [Mealing 1989] was able to make decisions on matters such as goal seeking and grouping as well as being dynamic, and evolved as a test-bed for motion control algorithms (Fig 10.1b). It soon became clear that the interaction of simple behavioural rules created complex motion patterns from which those same rules could not be deduced. It also seemed that the particle system could provide the heart of a more complex movement control system, able to handle actors more

Fig 10.1b
The patterns of three versions of a particle system (each given different starting conditions) attempting to make optimal use of available forces to follow a moving target. In the bottom picture, particles can be seen bouncing off a horizontal plane

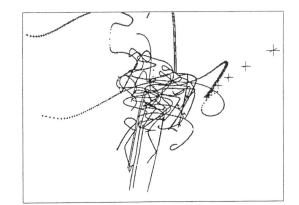

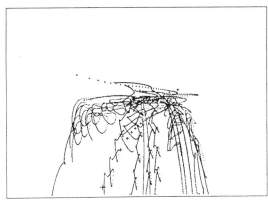

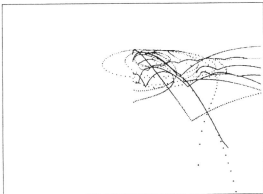

sophisticated than point masses by using the particle as a reference point in the local coordinate system of the new actor. The definition of the new actor would include the additional mathematics that its sophistication required, a property made easy by the use of C++ as the programming language. In this way the simplicity and elegance of particle systems could be employed to 'drive' more complex animations. The system's knowledge, experience and intelligence could be local to the individual particles or communal, allowing the particle cloud to maintain a single identity if required, and this area (distributed artificial intelligence) is fruitfully explored by Reynolds[1987] with his flocking birds, which are described later.

Computer memory is quickly eaten up as a particle system grows, and if the particles are to interact then very efficient algorithms are needed to keep calculation times within acceptable limits. The definition of a particle system seems to lend itself to parallelisation, and the question has been addressed by Simms [1989a], but again, interaction causes problems by creating potential bottlenecks. It seems likely, however, that new computer architectures will be particularly amenable to the problems of particle systems, and their potential is not yet realised.

Several papers address the question of how to render particle systems [Reeves 1983,1985, Glazzard 1987, Inakage 1988] and the subject will not be dealt with here. It is, however, of interest to mention Inakage's [1988] emphasis on the aesthetic virtues of using particle systems to model fuzzy objects and also to create 3-D textures, and Reeves' [1983] use of the systems in tree simulations by rule based construction (i.e. not surface modelled). His algorithm starts with the main trunk and constructs the tree by recursively generating sub-branches, having stochastically assigned a set of initial characteristics and dimensions randomly drawn from distributions associated with the type of tree. The regularity of the trees' structure is modified to simulate the effects of natural forces by post-processing their 3-D descriptions using various bending and warping algorithms. The elements generated with particle systems were combined with elements computed using other techniques, such as texture- mapped truncated cones.

10.1.1 GLOBULAR DYNAMICS

It is relevant, whilst considering particle systems, to look briefly at 'globular dynamics', described by Miller and Pearce [1989]. They present a connected particle system for modelling viscous fluids which allows for dynamic collision detection between particles and obstacles, both stationary and mobile, and allows solid objects to break and melt (temperature being a potential parameter). The elements of the connected particle system are called 'globules', and have radial force fields which lead to a 'dynamically changing topology of interactions'. 'Soft' collisions are permitted between globules (avoiding the rigid stacking exhibited by marbles) in which the rejection forces between globules are proportional, in strength and damping, to their depth of interpenetration. Globules are thus allowed to cluster or break off, either individually or in clusters, and are covered with a (virtual) isosurface for rendering.

The method is described as using a coarse approximation of the molecular movement within the fluid, and by tuning the damping and radial forces, can be used to simulate materials of different viscosity (powder has a short range repulsion and limited damping, liquid has damping forces of twice the repulsion term, and foams have medium term attraction). For more accurate simulation it will be necessary to use density distributions in real fluids to compute pressures, and hence forces, on particles. It offers the advantage that, compared with particles, relatively few globules are needed in a typical simulation as they are much bigger, but up to 30 time-steps per frame are required by the dynamics calculations, corresponding to movements of a small fraction of the globules' radius. it is suggested that the method lends itself to parallel processing.

10.2 PARAMETRIC MODELLING

Many objects have smoothly curved surfaces and blended edges which are not readily represented by conventional methods such as polygon meshes or CSG models. Parametric modelling provides a compact and easily manipulated representation in which the need to store the large numbers of coordinates otherwise required is avoided. Instead of considering a curve in its analytic form (as the relationship between X, Y and Z coordinate values) in its parametric form it is specified in terms of other variables or parameters.

10.2.1 CLOUDS

A relatively simple representation is often desirable, as in a flight simulator, where real-time updating of the scene is computationally heavy and the production of clouds presents an interesting problem. They have been created using particle systems and by other methods based on the accurate modelling of cloud physics, but the mathematics involved has a high computational cost.

Gardner [1985] describes a method from a study at the Grumman Corporate Research Center to develop cost-effective scene simulation technology, which constructs the visual appearance of clouds parametrically. Note that this models only the appearance of clouds, and as such need only be a 2-D representation, unlike the fully 3-D model which might be constructed with a particle system model, for instance. The technique, however, can model different cloud types viewed from a range of angles and distances. He identifies three basic cloud types: cirrus (wispy, high altitude clouds), stratus (low, layered clouds without distinct detail) and cumulus (low, heaped clouds). Clouds which combine these basic characteristics are described with combinations of the basic names (e.g. stratocumulus). Cloud formations can develop horizontally (layers) or vertically (cumuliform). A cloud layer can be modelled by a single textured plane in the sky with the solidity and density of the layer defined by functions governing translucence and spectral content. This plane can be viewed satisfactorily from a distance and can be combined with 3-D cloud models. It can be animated by changing the texturing function parameters with time, and by moving the entire texture pattern.

His 3-D model uses ellipsoids as building blocks and modifies surface shading intensity and translucence using sine wave functions. "This approach results in a very compact data base because the same texture pattern can be used for any number of ellipsoids". Ellipsoids can be used singly or linked to build complex cloud forms, though this involves additional work to avoid unnatural boundaries. Horizontal and vertical cloud formations are achieved by variously modifying the size, orientation and position of the ellipsoids, by creating hierarchical levels of clusters of ellipsoids, and even by using a dummy terrain map to set cloud heights to simulate updrafts.

10.2.2 WAVES

Waves have also been effectively modelled parametrically [Fournier 1986], in this case in conjunction with particle systems. Fournier describes the most common waves as resulting from the disturbing force of wind and the restoring force of gravity and bases his model on water particles describing circular or elliptical stationary orbits effected by the topology of the ocean floor. From these mechanical principals a parametric surface is derived, modified with our now familiar stochastics, and enhanced with foam and spray generated with particle systems. At the rendering stage a moving bump map simplifies the representation of the surface perturbations which give rise to shimmering. As a further reminder of how far we are from real time simulation, note that a short animation using this method took 10 hours and 21 minutes per frame to compute on their computer.

10.2.3 PLANT MODELS

One of the subjects which has received much research attention within the area of modelling natural forms, is that of plant image synthesis. Many of these models start with an analysis of the plant's architecture and build the plants by repetitively applying a few rules thus derived. Some recent attempts use a developmental model with which it is possible to animate the growth and ageing of herbaceous plants [Prusinkiewicz 1988] and trees and herbs [de Reffye 1988]. This has the added advantage that, as well as being able to produce a single model of a particular plant, a range of models of the same plant can be created at different stages in its development, allowing botanists and agronomists to study environmental and other effects (which can be introduced as parameters). Their models incorporate the botanical laws which determine the architecture and growth of plants and include tropisms (the tendency to develop in response to stimuli such as light and gravity), external forces (such as wind) and knowledge about growing conditions. Note that here is a rich literature illustrating a range of other methods of building plants, including the use of fractals [Oppenheimer 1986].

10.3 VOXELS

An interesting plant modelling method using a voxel data base is described by Greene [89]. "Models are 'grown' from predefined geometric elements according to rules based on simple relationships like intersection, proximity, and occlusion which can be evaluated more quickly and easily in voxel space than with analytic geometry." (Voxels, you will remember, are the cubic volume elements into which 3-space can be divided.) Greene suggests that this method simplifies sensing of the environment by the growth process and he calls the growth processes that sense and react to the voxel environment 'voxel space automata'. Being affected by local conditions and environment, the growth pattern mimics natural growth processes, the growth rules are based on simple spatial relationships like intersection, proximity and obstruction avoidance, and by response to light.

The method involves checking randomly propagated growth against the rules and selecting the best fit. It is a method which represents a generalised developmental model and is not designed for realistic plant simulation. It does, however, create some very usable images, particularly interesting for the manner in which they can be 'grown' around objects in a visually similar manner to clinging ivy. The growing model is described as feeling its way through voxel space by sensing the voxel representation of objects in its environment.

10.4 FRACTALS

The word 'fractal' was coined by Benoit Mandelbrot [1977, 1982], and relates to his concept of fractional dimensions. In computer graphics its principles are often employed as a means of fragmenting a surface or object in a pseudo-random manner in order to produce credible detail, without recourse to a large data bank. This can be seen to be very valuable with an object such as a mountain or cloud, where it is necessary to display a satisfactory level of detail at any magnification. To build a model of the Himalayas which was detailed over its whole extent, down to the last rock, would be an impossible task, but fractal techniques allow us to generate the required level of detail, in the chosen area, when required. (The key is self-similarity, since a rock could be seen as very much like a small mountain.) In the right circumstances this can be generated in real-time, and thus readily used in an animation or flight simulator. The technique has also been used to create clouds, planets and eroded surfaces.

Fractals have been used to turn the immaculate, idealised forms produced by modelling systems into real-world objects by the addition of dirt, rust, stains, corrosion and blemishes [Becket 1990]. The algorithmic generation of textures such as these can be made dependent on the surface geometry, so that scratches and rust, for instance, can be realistically positioned near exposed edges. The technique, as described, deals with the application of surface texture, and might be interestingly combined with the effects of wear and tear to provide a further area of investigation. Correct placement of marks such as stains does require some knowledge of the history of the stained surface, and Becket must have engaged in some unusual research to establish rules for the correct location of coffee drips, coffee rings from cup bases, and 'smearing transformations' to mimic cups being moved across the surface. The rule-based approach avoids the need to attempt complicated simulation and is relatively quick to apply.

The simplest example is the recursive subdivision of a triangle by randomly displacing a point on each of its sides and joining these three points with three straight lines. This creates four smaller triangles, which are then treated to the same process, and the iteration continues until a suitable level of decomposition is reached. If points in 3-space are similarly treated, fractal surfaces are generated, and the potential level of detail is infinite. A 4-sided pyramid could thus be transformed into a mountain, approximately retaining its original shape, with the displacement parameters determining its degree of self-similarity. Suitably rendered, scenes have been generated with high levels of realism using this basically simple technique.

The standard example of fractals in nature, is shown in the attempted measurement of a coastline, where the total length of coastline will increase as the measuring device is reduced. If, for example, a one metre measuring stick is 'walked' around the coastline it will map large rocks but will not be fine enough to cope with pebble-sized details. A one centimetre measuring stick would deal with pebbles (and therefore indicate a greater perimeter length) but could not negotiate individual grains of sand and so on, and so on.

10.4.1 ITERATED FUNCTION SYSTEMS

Fractals have been described as the language of geometry. They cannot be directly viewed like the elements of Euclidian geometry (i.e. the line and circle), but are expressed in algorithms. Jurgens [1990] describes how, "once one has a command of the fractal language, one can describe the shape of a cloud as precisely and simply as an architect might describe a house with blueprints that use the language of traditional geometry". In the same way that European languages are based on a finite alphabet, but do not carry meaning until they are built up into words and phrases, so Euclidian geometry can construct complex objects from its limited elements. Fractals, however, can be compared to a language such as Chinese which are made up of a potentially infinite range of symbols that have meaning themselves, the 'symbols' of fractal geometry being algorithms. Iterated function systems (IFSs) have already been used to employ this fractal language in the construction of natural objects, such as ferns, and research is likely to extend their use.

Although not specifically relevant to soft modelling, it is appropriate to mention another role of IFSs at the same time. Fractals represent a compact way of storing information which can be expanded to provide the description for a complex shape, pattern or object; IFSs can work backwards from a given image to provide a fractal which will imitate it. This method has produced compression ratios of 10,000 to 1 on the storage space required for some images, which is an important saving when an uncompressed image might require 130 Megabytes of memory. The method is proven on limited types of image as yet, and would seem useful with a non-algorithmic image (i.e. a painting) only in proportion to the degree of approximation that was acceptable. However, although the compression and decompression is expensive in computer time, the potential memory savings are considerable, and the method is being developed.

10.5 FINITE ELEMENT METHODS

It is commonly necessary in computer graphics, to generalise a line, shape or object into convenient size pieces within which further detail is ignored. A smoothly curved surface can never be more than approximated by a polygonised surface, even if it is defined at a sub-pixel scale. Even on an implicit surface, where every point is fully defined mathematically, it is inherent to the rendering process that the final image will be broken into units of a size dependent on the output device. Whilst high resolution output may offer a satisfactory appearance, surfaces do not have truly smooth continuity.

If an engineer wishes to test a model of a bridge (either a computer model or a constructed model) he can select points on the structure at which to apply and measure forces, and might expect to increase the accuracy of the test in proportion to the number of points used. He can only select a finite number of points, however, despite the fact that there are an infinite number contained in the model. The selection of sample points to produce a discretised model, which will give a true representation of the whole structure, is the essence of finite element analysis. It finds regular application in computer modelling, both intentionally and as an unintentional result of the modelling methods commonly employed.

In computer modelling a number of methods deform surfaces by applying deformation to a discretised model, perhaps a grid standing for a surface, and then reconstitute the surface by spline interpolation. Free-form deformation (FFD) [Sederberg 1986] applies local or global deformation by applying transformations to a containing cage of control points. In FFDs, a simple cage with few control points can be used to sculpt complex solids.

10.5.1 CLOTH

One of the animations that I always find fascinating is a short sequence showing a square of cloth being dropped. This mundane occurrence is elevated to the status of a minor ballet through the focus given it in a simulation by Jerry Weil [1986]. The cloth is lifted at discrete points and allowed to float gently down when dropped, later being given the potential to wrap itself over objects in its path, like a tablecloth being draped over a table. The potential of this synthesis is enormous as it points, amongst other things, towards complex cloth surfaces (e.g. clothes) being draped dynamically over complex, perhaps articulated, forms (e.g. people). Although the simulation is, in fact, only approximate, it is highly convincing, automatically creating folds that are far more realistic than the more common method of texture mapping a rigid surface.

The cloth is first represented as a grid of 3-D coordinates with constraint points defined, and an approximation is made to the surface within the convex hull of those points. The constraints on the cloth are then applied by 'relaxing' all points in successive stages and subsequently adding further points between the constraint points. These are placed along the paths of the curves ('catenary' curves) which threads would naturally adopt, and further stages determine the position of the initial grid points from which the polygonised surface can be constructed. A coarse grid can be used to keep calculations to a minimum and the remaining points then created by spline interpolation.

Different cloth stiffness can be built into the model to approximate different materials and various rendering techniques can be used, with cloth texture being added if desired. The method suggested by Weil, however, is that of raytracing cylindrical line segments representing the actual threads. The effect created is not without computational cost, but is very lifelike and amenable to development. Consider raytracing the shadow of a patterned net curtain, blowing in the wind, onto an interior scene!

10.6 TEXELS & FUR

Traditional methods of introducing fine detail into high resolution images cause severe aliasing problems, and an alternative approach is to treat the detail as texture rather than to try and model it geometrically. This is the solution to the long standing problem of rendering furry surfaces which is presented by Kajiya [1989]. He arrives at a very lifelike teddy bear by use of the 'texel', a three-dimensional texture map which can be rendered without the need for an underlying surface model, and in which the rendering time is independent of the complexity of the surface. More specifically, a texel is "a three-dimensional array of parameters approximating visual properties of a collection of microsurfaces" and could be used to describe a surface in the same way as a tree covered mountain. It can be seen as a close relation of the voxel, which, although only briefly mentioned here, is open to development.

10.7 STOCHASTICS

It is often appropriate to introduce random elements into the modelling process (Fig 10.7) in order to move away from the precision that geometry, or fixed rules, can lend. This is particularly relevant to the sort of models described in this chapter, in order that a simple set of rules can be used to produce a variety of waves, clouds or plants. Total, uncontrolled randomness would rarely be useful, but constrained stochastics (the employment of randomness within set limits) can be used to provide a predetermined level of variation on a basic theme and computers are good at producing an approximation to randomness. In a typical particle system, for instance, most of the parameters could be subject to random variation (i.e. the degree of randomness in the spatial initialisation would determine the spread of the initial particle cloud). It also becomes possible, and often entertaining, to regenerate sequences with fresh random variables, and produce very different results. A slight change can prove to have a dramatic effect, as chaos theory has shown.

If you don't mind what number is produced, you are looking for an arbitrary, rather than random, number. A random number is a precisely defined mathematical concept in which every number should have an equal likeliness of occurrence (which requires a limit to their range), and whilst a random number might be arbitrary, the opposite is not true. The nature of computers makes it impossible to generate truly random numbers and it is common instead, to access a data bank of pre-randomised numbers. Pseudo-random numbers can be generated simply with an accuracy that might be acceptable, but whilst you can't tell from a sequence of pseudo-random numbers that they are not random, if you know the formula in use then you can predict the next number. Since the computer will generate the same sequence each time, it is standard to 'seed' the number generator with a fresh number each time, although the same seed will provoke the same sequence. Also, the type of 'randomness' can vary: are you, for instance, sampling without replacement (i.e. as in 'Bingo'), or with replacement (in which case a selected number becomes available for reselection, and could be selected many times in a row).

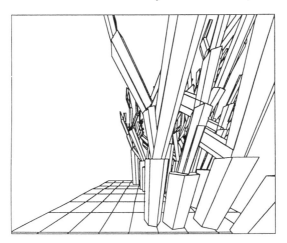

Fig 10.7
Stochastics was used to determine the number, size, position and orientation of trees and branches in this 'forest'

10.8 CONCLUSION

It can be seen, from the examples given here, that the non-geometric world can be represented in a computer model with increasing subtlety and sophistication. A flea-bitten dog might still be more difficult to model than a red cube, but as new hardware and improved algorithms make the former achievement more accessible, animation will have access to a much less restrained vocabulary. It is self-evident that many computer animation models produced to date have been influenced by the ease with which geometric primitives can be created and manipulated. Whilst, however, it is commercially necessary, and often artistically desirable, that limitations should exist, in talented hands the future of computer animation can prove much richer for the development of soft modelling.

CHAPTER 11

STATE-OF-THE-ART:
BEHAVIOURAL ANIMATION

There can be few dynamic scenes involving living creatures that can be explained purely by physics. The motivations and rationale governing the unfolding of a sequence of actions will often provide the motivation for an animation, and even when animating 'inanimate' objects it is often desirable that the objects should display intention and response. In another situation it might be necessary to attempt to simulate movement patterns occurring in 'real life' situations by attributing needs, desires and the means to satisfy them. An interesting example is "Electric Anthill", a simple interactive installation by Michael Travers [1989], in which aspects of an ant colony are enacted on a computer screen by ants homing in on a food source.

The behaviour of a ball in collision with a wall is determined by physical laws, though the speed of the ball, angle at which it hits the wall, surface of the wall and other variables effect its response. Different degrees of inflation will provoke different responses in otherwise similar balls in the same conditions. A cat in collision with a wall will be subject to the same physical laws as the ball, but is likely to show an additional, emotional response provoked by stimuli such as pain, fear and loss of dignity. The cat's behaviour is likely to be modified for a period of time after the collision, whilst the ball (unless damaged) will continue as it was before. The difference between the responses of the cat and the ball derives largely from the animal having a nervous system and brain which the ball lacks. The cat might also attempt to avoid the impending collision, an action which would require of it: a recognition of the existing conditions, an extrapolation from them to a recognition of future conditions, the ability to devise a method of avoidance, and the means to effect it. Such incidents fill the existence of all living things, and to have such behavioural traits (instinctive and acquired) automatically enacted by our actor moves the required level of animation another notch higher.

My dictionary offers several definitions of behaviour. Those which are helpful in the context of explaining behavioural animation are : "the aggregate of all the responses made by an organism in any situation", "a specific response of a certain organism to a specific stimulus or group of stimuli" and "the action, reaction or functioning of a machine, chemical substance, etc. under normal or specified circumstances" (*Collins English Dictionary* , 1986).

11.1 ARTIFICIAL INTELLIGENCE

There is a lot of interest in making computer models of animate objects in the real world act naturally. Much recent work has centred on attempts to impose physical laws automatically and with an increasing complexity. An area which has received a lot less attention, but which is now ripe for investigation, is that of artificial intelligence (AI), potentially, perhaps, able to build on the foundations offered by physically-based modelling towards the goal of total simulation.

The field of artificial intelligence is involved with building features associated with natural intelligence into machines. This implies a clear understanding of natural intelligence, of the mental and behavioural abilities that can be found in humans and other animals, and the history of the discipline shows that such an understanding is, at the least, incomplete. Mary Boden [1987] describes AI as being the use of computer programs and programming techniques to cast light on the principles of intelligence in general and human thought in particular. Minsky is often attributed (e.g. by Simons [1984]) with the quotation: "artificial intelligence is the science of making machines do things that would require intelligence if done by men".

A mechanist philosopher would point out that if all knowledge can be formalised then the human self can be matched, in principle, by a machine, and that analysing the problem is the only hard part. We are, however, understandably reluctant to confer the dignity of being thought intelligent on an evidently simple machine. Since the judgment of intelligence is more a reflection on what we understand than on what we, or machines, can do, it is not surprising that as soon as any process or performance has been mechanised it must be removed, with qualifications and apologies, from the list of intelligent (or creative) performances.

11.1.1 DISTRIBUTED AI

Whilst this next section is not yet important in the context of animation, I include it in the expectation that it will become so, as well as to indulge my own interest. Most AI research investigates how a single agent can exhibit intelligent behaviour such as problem solving using heuristic or knowledge based methods, planning, understanding and generating natural language, perception and learning. Several recent developments have together provoked interest in concurrency and distribution in AI; the development of powerful concurrent computers, the proliferation of multinode computer networks, and the recognition that much human problem solving and activity involves groups of people. Distributed artificial intelligence (DAI) is the subfield of AI concerned with concurrency in AI computations at many levels [Bond 1988]. A flock of birds is an example of a robust, self-organising distributed system.

DAI can be divided into three main areas. Research in Distributed Problem Solving (DPS) considers how the work of solving a particular problem can be divided among a number of modules, or 'nodes', that cooperate at the level of dividing and sharing knowledge about the problem and about the developing solution. A second area, called Parallel AI (PAI), is concerned with developing parallel computer architectures, languages and algorithms for AI. In a third area, called MultiAgent (MA) systems, research is concerned with coordinating intelligent behaviour among a collection of (possibly pre-existing) autonomous intelligent 'agents', how they can coordinate their knowledge, goals, skills and plans jointly to take action or to solve problems. The agents in a multiagent system may be working toward a single global goal, or toward separate individual goals that interact. Like modules in a DPS system, agents in a multi-agent system must share knowledge about problems and solutions. But they must also reason about the processes of coordination among the agents [Bond 1988].

An interesting tool relevant to DAI is the 'blackboard system', which is a set of processes, typically called knowledge sources (KSs), which share a common data-base or 'blackboard' of symbolic structures, often called (and indeed denoting) hypotheses. Each KS is an expert in some area, and may find a hypothesis it can work on, solve that hypothesis, create new hypotheses, and modify existing hypotheses. The set of processes thus c0-operate by sharing the common blackboard, rather like a group of human experts, each endowed with expertise and a piece of chalk, and using a common blackboard [Bond 1988]. I find the analogy very apt, not only as a description of a number of individuals co-operating, but also as a model of the way an individual might solve a problem over a period of time by solving sub-problems, leaving them to develop and interact on the mental 'blackboard', and adding fresh knowledge in the light of experience, until all the ingredients are present for a solution.

The basic questions that DAI must address are summarised, again by Bond[1988] as:

how to formulate, describe, decompose, and allocate problems and synthesise results among a group of intelligent agents;

how to enable agents to communicate and interact: what communication languages or protocols to use, what and when to communicate etc;

how to ensure that agents act coherently in making decisions or taking action, accommodating the global effects of local decisions and avoiding harmful interactions;

how to enable individual agents to represent and reason about the actions, plans, and knowledge of other agents in order to coordinate with them; how to reason about the state of the coordinated process (e.g. initiation and termination);

and how to recognise and reconcile disparate viewpoints and conflicting intentions among a collection of agents trying to coordinate their actions; how to synthesise views and results.

11.1.2 EXPERT SYSTEMS

Expert systems have been defined [d'Agapeyeff 1983] as "problem-solving programs that solve substantial problems generally conceded as being difficult and requiring expertise. They are called 'knowledge-based' because their performance depends critically on the use of facts and heuristics used by experts". The systems currently acquire a body of knowledge from humans who are expert in the subject area concerned, and whose skills in the area are formalised into a database. The domain of the subject area is necessarily limited, but within that area the expert system can offer intelligent advice and make intelligent decisions based on the information available in its database.

One of the main reservations about existing expert systems is their inability to stray outside their own limited domain. This immediately limits their application to search areas which have already been chosen by outside agents, although the possibility exists for a number of expert systems to interact (perhaps on a 'blackboard' or under the supervision of an expert system trained to supervise). If systems are allowed to develop by learning, and expert systems in related domains are allowed to cooperate, it is possible that expert systems themselves may prime future generations of expert systems.

The information in a system is stored as a collection of simple rules which can be searched in order to make inferences which will provide the basis for decisions, and can be 'weighted' according to probability of correctness e.g.

> Rule 1: If the dog is grey
>   then it may be a wolfhound (10% chance)
> Rule 2: If the dog is a wolfhound
>   then it is friendly (99% chance)
> Rule 3: If it is a wolfhound
>   and it lives at my house
>   then its name is Ogam

Having incorporated knowledge such as this, we can 'chain' forwards or backwards through the rules to draw inferences. If we start from the conclusion, we can 'backward chain' to find what evidence is available to enable that conclusion to be reached. If we start with the evidence, we can 'forward chain' to arrive at a conclusion. The emphasis on rule-based programming implies use of a language such as PROLOG, but interest is being shown in C++ as a potential language for creating expert systems [Hu 1989].

Within a specific domain an expert system could be designed to produce an animation from 'raw' data. For example, the daily television weather charts could be produced and animated directly from the relevant data, since the layout, symbols and house-style are all tightly defined, and the rules for applying them are relatively simple.

11.1.3 HUMAN INTELLIGENCE

In order to be able to approach the richness of human decision making, a system needs to be able to deal with different modes of thinking such as deductive (inference), inductive (classification) and abductive (guessing and testing); to be able to deal with uncertainty, weighted probabilities and 'fuzzy' logic [Zadeh 1965]; to deal with other representations of knowledge, such as 'frames' [Fikes 1985] which are data structures for representing stereotypical situations that can be organised into taxonomies of classes; and perhaps to be able to deal with ideas like 'naive physics' [Hayes 1969] where the system understands that, for example, water is wet. One further characteristic which we might want a system to possess, is the ability to learn. "An animal that learns is one which is capable of being transformed by its past environment into a different being and is therefore adjustable to its environment within its individual lifetime" [Weiner 1969]. If a system was empowered to learn, this learning could be programmed as ontogenetic (of the individual) or phylogenetic (of the race, or in the object-orientated case, of the class).

11.2 GROUPING

The title of Craig Reynold's stimulating paper 'Flocks, herds and schools: a distributed behavioural model' [1987] goes straight to the heart of the grouping issue. It immediately conjures up a vivid mental picture of natural groups with which we are all familiar, and points to the problem of understanding how a collection of individual intelligences can combine to create a group with a single behavioural momentum. He concerns himself primarily with flocking birds, describing a flock as a group of objects that exhibit the general class of polarised, non-colliding, aggregate motion (the term 'polarisation' is from zoology, meaning alignment of animal groups). He points out, however, how small modifications to his model renders it suitable for describing schools of fish, herds of animals, hybrid groups of imaginary creatures or even traffic patterns.

Natural grouping appears to arise from an instinctive belief that company is preferable to isolation. The 'safety in numbers' philosophy is of proven effect against predators. As an example, the number of animals in the vulnerable perimeter of a herd under attack by lions increases by only a linear factor when the total herd size increases by the square of the factor. (Grouping is, perhaps, less helpful to lemmings?) Whilst the motivation for grouping is an interesting and complex study, it might not be a necessary part of a simulation. If it is possible to deduce positional rules from the observation of natural grouping, then the application of these rules will result in a satisfactory mimicking of the grouping, whether of ants or commuters, bypassing the behavioural rationale. It is equally possible to contrive groupings in a system of actors by applying purely invented rules, so that starlings could 'flock' in a perfect cube with geometric precision, or particles could group in the form of a house (or of a starling).

Reynolds points out that "a flock exhibits many contrasts. It is made up of discrete birds yet overall motion seems fluid: it is simple in concept yet is so visually complex. It seems randomly arrayed and yet is magnificently synchronised. Perhaps most puzzling is the strong impression of unintentional, centralised control. Yet all evidence indicates that flock motion must be merely the aggregate result of the actions of individual animals, each acting solely on the basis of its own local perception of the world." A large number of individual intelligences subordinate their identity to the group gestalt, to a corporate intelligence. It might be considered as a particularly focused example of similar behaviour in human society, and perhaps as a prerequisite for, or even definition of, a society. It is highlighted in 'mob rule', 'team spirit' and warfare, but is also present in more mundane activities such as queuing or building communities.

Controlling the movement of a flock by scripting is clearly too complex in all but the simplest case, but a rule-based dynamic system should deal with it easily, in principle. Matching nature's 'constant time algorithm' is rather more difficult. With a constant time algorithm the speed of computation would not increase with the size of the flock, though in nature, of course, each additional flock member brings its own processor with it. A behavioural routine, however, which requires a comparison to be made with every other flock member, increases in work required as the square of the flock's population.

As a first attempt at simulating a natural group, it would be possible to control the path of an individual group member and require the other members to follow the leader, or, perhaps, surround the leader (Fig 11.2a).

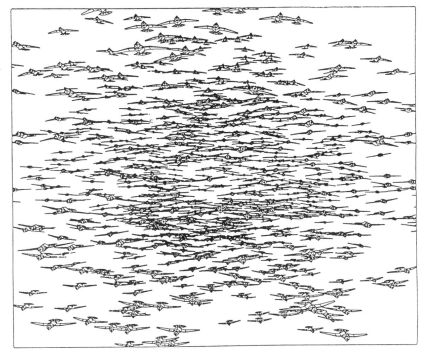

Fig 11.2a
The view from within Craig Reynold's flock (courtesy of Craig W. Reynolds, Symbolics, Inc.)

The weakness of such a model would be revealed when obstacles were encountered, since the leader's avoidance of an obstacle would not guarantee that those surrounding him also avoided collision. It

218

would certainly not permit a flock to split up and reform, in order to pass an obstacle as birds would. Another model might build attraction and repulsion (or negative attraction) fields around group members, which would bring them into a group but maintain a predetermined optimum gap between members. At the moment when all the fields had been brought to zero then the group would represent a 'relaxation' solution to the fields' constraints, but the same collision dilemma remains.

An expert system could provide rules which members must observe, but, in an open system, there is no guarantee that conflicts would not arise between the constraints proposed by the rules. Reynolds [1986] points out (in another context) that isolated constraints are easy to maintain, but multiple, interacting constraints can prove more difficult, if not impossible, to satisfy. This is because solving one constraint might violate another. A constraint system can be diagrammed as a network of dependencies. If the dependency diagram for a given situation forms an acyclic graph (no loops) it is possible to maintain all constraints simultaneously; but if there are cyclic dependencies it may be impossible to fully satisfy all the constraints at one time.

The rules Reynolds requires to be observed in his flock model, in decreasing order of precedence are:

1. collision avoidance: avoid collisions with nearby flockmates;
2. velocity matching: attempt to match velocity with nearby flockmates;
3. flock centring: attempt to stay close to nearby flockmates.

He points out that static collision avoidance and dynamic velocity matching are complementary, and that 'nearby' is a key word as it indicates that a flock member navigates by a local view of the world, rather than all flockmates being directly responsive to a single source of stimuli. He then goes on to explain how the flock rules are enforced by prioritised acceleration allocation. This is the means of handling the suggestions about which way to steer, which are generated by the three behavioural urges described by the rules. The easiest way to combine acceleration requests is to average them, and because they have 'strength' factors according to priority in a particular dynamic set of conditions this becomes a weighted average. This apparently produces reasonable results (Fig 11.2b) except in a crisis, when conflicts require a speedy solution.

Fig 11.2b
The flock maintains its identity whilst negotiating obstacles (courtesy of Craig W. Reynolds, Symbolics, Inc..)

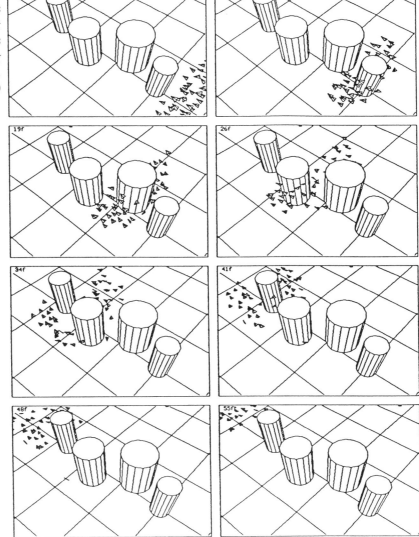

This is because acceleration requests lying in roughly opposite directions will largely cancel out and give rise to a very small turn which may not be sufficient to avoid a collision.

Prioritised acceleration allocation improves on this by considering requests in priority order and adding them into an accumulator, the magnitude of the request being added into another accumulator. The process continues until all the available acceleration is used, having ensured that the most pressing needs have been given as much acceleration as they need (or as is available). Reynolds found that an interesting result of his experiments was the discovery that a limited localised view of the world is actually a requirement for flocking.

An interesting, but apparently undocumented, project at Atari Systems Research is referred to by Wilhelms [1987a] and Reynolds [1986]. Unofficially nicknamed "fishbrains", it sought to create a dynamic aquarium simulation. Reynolds says of it that "an important aspect of the design of the characters was that they were required to react to each other in a variety of ways. One solution was to provide each character with a fair amount of internal state - the fishbrains might be hungry or full, alert or tired, calm or frightened". This brings into the arena the additional option of behavioural response determined by changing internal state, and it is interesting to speculate about a group response based on the internal state of its individual members.

11.3 GOAL SEEKING

In the context of movement control, the term 'goal seeking' is usually used to describe the progress through space of an object, from its starting position to its target position, encompassing its attempts to navigate an efficient, collision free route. It can also refer to its attempts to reach a more comprehensive target state which might include, for example, having accomplished tasks en route, or changed shape. The attempt to find a route is also known as 'trajectory planning' and this has been defined by Brady [1982] as the process of converting a task description into a trajectory. A trajectory is defined as a sequence of positions, velocities and accelerations. As the trajectory is executed, the tip of the end effector traces a curve in space and changes its orientation. This curve is called the path of the trajectory.

Intention in a system implies a future dimension. A system including goal seeking can not, therefore, be fully described by its past and present states alone. The two perspectives that can be taken on goal seeking are either that of the object itself or that of God: in the first instance each problem is navigated as it is reached, in the second instance an overview allows the whole journey to be mapped out in advance. This is an unrealistically complicated view to take in a dynamic simulation, and is usually employed only when negotiating a fixed environment with a single object. It might, however, be possible to have a basic overview which is updated in the light of experience.

An holistic approach to determining the optimal path is preferable, because although the shortest route between two points is the sum of the shortest sub-routes, the optimal path to a more complex goal is not necessarily made up of optimal sub-paths (the best team is not made up of the best individual players). It implies, however, a global perspective, with the problems already expressed, though it can be useful in many situations.

Obstacle detection is required in advance in order to implement a diversion, and can be carried out with an 'inflated' bounding box, either around the obstacle, or, more usually, around the actor. The degree of inflation determines how much warning is given of a forthcoming collision, i.e. a box much larger than the actor recognises imminent collisions earlier than one which is a snug fit. Whilst a spherical bounding box would be simple, and may be appropriate around an obstacle, a forward weighted system (corresponding to forward vision) seems more suitable for a moving actor. It could be a sphere transposed forward along the actor's direction vector, a cone (tapering towards the actor) or a shape more closely matching a particular range of vision.

Having recognised the presence of an obstacle, it is necessary to decide what the actor's 'view' of it should be. Should it be that of a blind man with a stick - knowing something is there, but not what it is; or that of the local god - knowing the full dimensions and position of the obstruction; or that of a camera - able to see the edges of the obstacle in each direction, but not able to see what is around the corner. The efficiency with which a path can be planned is determined by the amount of information available to the navigator. If the information is not complete then the path will be designed at random, or by algorithm (where a solution is guaranteed by following a defined set of rules or instructions [Simons 1984]), or by heuristic (using empirical strategies akin to 'rules of thumb' [Simons 1984]), with the option of allowing the actor to learn from his mistakes. Learning, problem solving, decision making and their application to path-finding, are all areas of interest within the fields of artificial intelligence, cybernetics and robotics.

If the obstacle is not stationary then some understanding of its own path must enter into the calculations, and if the moving obstacle is credited with a level of intelligence then it might even be necessary to consider its motives for taking a particular course. If two actors are trying to avoid one another, and are applying exactly the same rules to the problem, they can reach an impasse, escape from which may only be possible if their rules introduce a random factor at an appropriate moment.

It is likely that avoidance of the obstacle will not be the actor's only criterion. If other factors, such as grouping rules or the need (in a production environment) to be in a particular position at a particular frame, also need to be considered, then further control is necessary. It might then be appropriate to refer the problem to an arbitration function which can then try to resolve the differing desires. Similarly, if the actor has limited motor resources at his disposal, then it will be necessary for some agency to apportion them in the best way, having knowledge of what is 'best' in a given situation. This is the case with the flocks of Reynolds [1987].

11.4 VISION

Synthetic vision provides a means of supplying the actor with a valuable input for his use in dealing with a range of situations. If an actor can "see", the knowledge of the environment that he acquires is substantial and can be used for much more than for his obvious navigational advantage. If you think of the uses you make of your own sight, it is clear that the sense is of vital importance to our normal functioning (regardless of the fact that other senses, and devices, can partly substitute in its absence). The nature of the artificial vision with which our actor is imbued need not match that of a human to be useful, but could ultimately be wider ranging, extending, for instance, to a broader band of the electromagnetic spectrum than the human eye can see.

It is likely, however, that an early goal of an artificial vision system for a mobile actor will be obstacle recognition, and the handling of the subsequent avoidance, as already mentioned. It is also probable that the vision will initially be passive rather than controlled, i.e. the visual sensory mechanism will have a fixed relationship to the actor, rather than having the ability to 'look' in different directions and to focus. The actor will indiscriminately receive information within the limits set by the system parameters (which, in the case of a spherical bounding box model of vision, would be omnidirectional). Researchers in the field of robotics, as well as in our own, have looked at the vision of humans, birds, insects and fish, but have been less interested in duplicating the mechanism as in duplicating the effect.

Renault [1990] describes a system based on Displacement Local Automata (DLAs). These are similar to scripts written to describe specific instances, and which contain the information necessary to generate a suitable response. The script concept was introduced in the area of natural language processing, an example of a script being the attempt to book a hotel room, where all the actions and responses relating to that limited domain are specified (from entering the hotel, through conversing with the reception clerk, to finding the room). At a high level it is necessary to have specific knowledge corresponding to the current situation, unlike the basically algorithmic handling of perception and navigation at a low level. In the case of Renault's actor the task is to move automatically in a corridor avoiding objects and other synthetic actors, and to that end his DLAs include 'displacement-in-a-corridor', 'obstacle-avoidance', 'crossing-with-another-synthetic-actor' and 'passage-of-a-door'. The DLA concept permits the description grain (the level of detail) to be increased and decreased by tuning a more general DLA, and allows simple situations to be dealt with by combining DLAs.

The DLAs must either activate themselves (perhaps having identified the need from a situation 'chalked' on a 'blackboard') or be activated by another agent - a controller. In the first case, the DLA would be responsible for taking relevant action (and possibly coordinating that action with those of other DLAs which are operating), in the second instance (as used by Renault) the controller is the thinking part of the system. The DLA method has proved capable of dealing with collision avoidance in a dynamic environment and Renault concludes of the project that "this is certainly a new interesting vivarium for artificial intelligence".

11.5 STIMULUS-RESPONSE ANIMATION

The behaviour of an actor can be described in terms of his response to stimuli within his environment and that response may be qualified by his internal state (if he is credited with one). It is described in psychological literature how simple movements of geometric objects can be interpreted by observers as the intentioned behaviour of intelligent/emotional creatures [Lethbridge 1989], and the movement of objects as simple as particles becomes mysteriously organic when the rules governing the movement are hidden [Mealing 1989]. It is intriguing to see how simple rules mimicking animal behaviour (such as moving towards the light, avoiding obstacles), and mimicking internal states (such as hunger and anger) can interact to produce complex movement patterns which give the appearance of animate intelligence.

It might be that a system capable of causing actors to respond according to stimuli could be used to simulate animal behaviour, though the understanding of the mechanism of such behaviour is incomplete, and could be expected to provide no more than an external approximation. This level of simulation, however, could be used in the construction of animations where actors, or groups of actors, were given behavioural traits and left to interact with themselves and with their environment. These behavioural traits could exist in conjunction with dynamic behaviour and constraints, and provide a behavioural 'background' for task-directed control.

The actors could be given the 'virtual' senses with which to recognise a range of stimuli, corresponding to (or extending beyond) those recognised by a higher animal. As well as 'seeing' the position, size, colour and direction of obstacles and fellow actors, sounds could be 'heard', winds 'felt', emotions 'sensed', and invisible scalar fields (such as of barometric pressure or population density) recognised. The potential responses could be simply directional, using internal motors, or more comprehensive such as changing form or colour. Movement in any direction might be qualified by low-level routines defining gait patterns or other motion characteristics, so the stimulus-response (s-r) level of animation could be used to drive complex actors with their own embedded motion rules. The ability of the actor to sense his environment might be modelled in different ways, with different degrees of correspondence to the real world. For instance the actor in a 'sensory' world can be constantly aware of his surroundings, but in an object-orientated world must rely on messages being passed between himself and his environment. Lethbridge [1989] points out that the external metaphor need not map to the algorithm used internally.

Wilhelms [1989] describes a method of interactively implementing behavioural control, by providing an interface which allows the operator to map between sensors and effectors present in the objects (the effectors usually have the effect of the internal motors described already, but could alter other qualities). Since both sensors and effectors can be present in different parts of the object, different sensors will simultaneously register different distances from an obstacle, and the appropriate effectors will receive different strength inputs which will contribute to avoidance of the obstacle. Sensors and effectors are connected through nodes (which are functions that can modify the signals passing through them) thus forming a network. A diagram of the network can be interactively modified by the user to set the behaviour which will control the animation. The sensors respond according to their location and orientation on the object, according to their distance from the stimulus, and according to the range of simultaneous stimuli present.

Having nodes between the sensors and effectors permits more complex mappings than if they were directly connected, as the parameters of the node function can be altered to fine-tune the response. The nodes can have multiple input and output connections to accommodate a rich variety of connections to the (potentially) multiple sensor outputs and effector inputs. A range of node types is implemented, such as an 'avoid' node which passes output values that increase exponentially as objects approach. Another node type is 'random', which can break up cycles that can occur and also take the smoothness out of a motion. (It is interesting to compare with Lethbridge [1989] who avoids stochastics on the grounds that the complexity of his stimulus environment makes repetitive behaviour rare. His concern, in that instance, is with the appearance of the behaviour, Wilhelms' [1989] is with the appearance of the movement.)

11.6 ARBITRATION

The potential conflicts of interest in behavioural systems between, for instance, pursuing a target, avoiding a collision and refuelling (or feeding), require a mechanism to arbitrate on simultaneous requests to response devices. The subtlety required of this arbitration increases with the number and range of the inputs to it, and must play a large part in the apparent conviction of the system's behaviour.

Consider how the complex human system copes with meeting an oncoming human in a doorway. The need for collision avoidance is clear to both pedestrians, but the means of achieving it requires (usually unspoken) co-operation. Often one party will step aside due to a decision based on the dress, sex, age or manner of the other (and conditioned by background, training and experience), but both parties may either step aside or step forward (their behavioural systems are balanced?), in which case a fresh assessment of the situation is made. We have probably all been in a situation where a short stalemate arises from both parties repetitively taking the same action. In an even more anonymous situation such as confronting someone on a pavement, who moves left, who moves right and who carries straight on? How far apart are the first evasive measures initiated? How seldom do you actually make contact with someone on a crowded pavement?

11.7 CONCLUSION

We are moving towards a high level of animation control, which might be closer to the direction given to human actors. An actor can be given a goal, which might be merely positional - "reach XYZ", or perhaps rather more philosophical - "survive". He can 'know' the rules governing his existence - to avoid collisions, to eat actors half his size. His responses can be modified by age and anger. He can be 'conditioned' to operate as a communal or a lone organism. If his performance is not satisfactory, the 'director' can amend his motivation and replay the scene.

CHAPTER 12

STATE-OF-THE-ART:
SYNTHETIC HUMANS

One of the longest standing goals in computer animation is the lifelike simulation of human beings. Each year the films shown at conferences such as SIGGRAPH illustrate research developments taking us nearer that goal, and in the last few years a number of the improvements have, for the first time, been very convincing. Human gait is an example where one cannot now, within a limited range, distinguish current computer simulation from animation rotascoped from film of a live figure. The search for means of simulating humans also feeds a more general aspiration to create believable fantasy figures, which are often built from exaggerations of human form.

The human being is a complex, potentially self-propelled object. It comes in a variety of sizes and in two main types (or 'sexes'). It comprises a large, roughly symmetrical collection of articulated components in proportions which vary with age and sex. The joints are constrained in their range of movements, the skeletal levers are powered by groups of muscles inside the convex hull and the whole structure is covered by a flexible membrane (or 'skin'). The thickness, taughtness and texture of the membrane, the constraint limits of joints, and the relationship of components in a neutral state (or 'posture') all vary with age, sex and environmental conditioning. All these factors effect the efficiency and style variation of the object's mobility pattern (or 'gait). Additionally the colour of the object is conditioned by racial, genetic and environmental factors.

The object has motivation and emotions, is goal-directed, enters into complex spatial and psychological relationships with other like objects and with the rest of its environment, and is self-reproducing. It gathers information from its environment through senses including tactile, auditory and visual, it learns, it makes decisions based on current and past states, and it can operate in conjunction with others of its species to arrive at corporate decisions. It obeys complex grouping rules and communicates through language and expression. We may need to recognise that it is often clothed. It is not going to be easily modelled using cubes.

Even this rudimentary description of some of the more obvious features of a human being, makes it immediately clear that the task of synthesising such an object is going to be formidable. Synthesis is "the process of combining objects or ideas into a complex whole" (*Collins English Dictionary*) and it is apparent that the construction of the complex whole needs to be decomposed into a number of manageable sub-tasks. We will look here at the current state of resolution of some of these sub-problems, discover that a number of disciplines are involved in their solution, and will later extrapolate into the near future.

The minimum properties that the synthetic human should possess will vary according to the situation in which it is to be used. In order to make an ergonomic evaluation of an environment the figure does not need expression or colour, for example, and may not require any sophisticated modelling of skin. To be viable as a surgical model, the figure might need a full set of internal organs, perhaps including circulating blood, but may not need any mobility or speech facility. To recreate a scene from a soap opera, the external appearance of the figure might have a high priority, with intelligence far less important.

Boisvert [1989] suggests that synthetic actors should match the appearance and behaviour of real persons, have their own personality, be directed by task level commands, be conscious of their environment, be able to walk, speak, have emotions and grasp objects, and that their faces should naturally deform during motions. This is not a complete list of attributes, but includes many that would be desirable in an actor available for an animation. He also adds, provocatively, that existing people, dead or alive, can be recreated as synthetic actors, and his point is illustrated with an animation of a synthetic Marilyn Monroe.

12.1 LOCOMOTION

Making a character walk must be one of the oldest problems in animation, and one of the primary means of establishing characterisation. The exaggerated gaits of Felix the Cat, Popeye, Roadrunner and other cartoon characters immediately give us strong clues about the actor's identity, and the gait definition is often arrived at by extrapolating from the animator's first hand experience of the root character. In the early days of the Walt Disney studios, even the most senior animators were required to attend life drawing classes in which the models were animals, and Bambi was derived from direct observation of young deer brought into the film studio and drawn from life. For any animator there can be no substitute for looking and drawing, and even photography should be an addition rather than a replacement. Even the characterisation of an anglepoise lamp in "Luxo Jnr." must owe a lot to the artist's observation of people and things moving in the real world.

It is easier, however, to make a potato walk 'convincingly' than to make a human figure walk in a believable manner. This is because we have so much first and second hand experience of walking that we instinctively recognise any aberrations in the complex gait cycle. For this reason it is often the human characters in a cartoon that are the least effective. Rotascoping (tracing off film) is one way of improving the appearance of the motion, but this requires film to have been shot from all the angles which will later be required to be drawn. Kinematic rules can be derived, which are visually credible, but which increase in complexity as the changes involved in walking uphill, downhill, or on a camber are added. Consider deriving rules to explain the changing stride pattern of an accelerating horse!

These walking rules for a simple figure are proposed by Peter Balch [1989a]: Each leg is either down on the ground or up off it. If one leg is down, the other must be up. If the up foot is more than a certain distance in front of the point below the centre of the body then we start to place it down on the ground. Similarly if the down foot is more than the same distance behind the point below the centre of the body then we start to lift it up. On level ground, this 'certain distance' is one half of the step length. If the ground slopes the distance is lessened by the difference in heights under the two feet. If the foot is up and is in front of the centre of the body, it moves forward at twice the speed of body movement.   If it is up and is behind the centre of the body, it moves forward at such a rate that it will be directly under the body just as the other foot passes under the centre. (This helps keep both legs in antiphase.) The body moves forward at a constant rate and the down leg is kept straight.   The height of the up foot increases linearly as the foot rises, stays constant, then decreases linearly as the foot is put down.

Whilst a skilled animator can achieve a passable appearance of human locomotion, he must either produce a large number of key frames or specify in terms of joint rotations over time.   The latter method requires coordination of movements within each limb, within the body as a whole, and a recognition of the figure's interaction with its environment. The complexity of specifying walking kinematically is very great and to be a realistic option requires inverse kinematic algorithms to work backwards from the end position to produce suitable joint angles. This is far from intuitive, and often specified in terms of forces and torques, whilst the animator will usually want to describe the desired locomotion at a high level, in terms of obvious visual characteristics. (This is, of course, making presumptions about the uses that are likely to be made of such a system.   Instead of the implied animator merely requiring the appearance of a figure walking, the application could be medical or ergonomic, in which case   the specification of forces and torques might be appropriate.) Although movements like walking and running are conceptually well understood, a complete dynamic solution is complicated by problems like balance and coordination. On the other hand, kinematic animation tend can prove inflexible and tends to produce a weightless, unrealistic movement, and a system combining dynamic and kinematic would be helpful.

KLAW (Keyframe-Less Animation of Walking) is a system developed by Bruderlin [1989] which uses dynamic analysis to deal with movement control but allows high level specification.   The operator determines the velocity, step length and step frequency and can set 28 "locomotion attributes" which individualise the gait (such as lateral distance between the feet and list of the pelvis). The business of moving the figure using the parameters defined by the operator is dealt with by dynamics and the system proves to produce extremely convincing movement. It deals satisfactorily with starting, stopping and with changing stride lengths and tempos, though modifications to the dynamic model would be required for running. It is also suggested that it would adapt to modelling locomotion systems with more than two legs, and is being extended to deal with other motion tasks, such as grasping, standing up and turning.

An interesting diversion from the problem of legged locomotion is attempting to mimic the motion of legless creatures such as worms and snakes. Gavin Miller [1988] simulates the movement with a simple mass spring model. Directional friction allows the leading mass to move forward as the spring expands, and allows the trailing mass to move forward when the spring contracts, a number of spring mass sections linked together becoming a worm. By keeping the total volume of the worm constant, the contracting sections bulge and the stretching sections narrow. A snake's skeleton leads to a different movement pattern from a worm, and is simulated on the mass spring model by sending compression waves down each side of the model 180 degrees out of phase. The model is responsive to changes in grip, and to external forces such as gravity, and is very realistic in simulating the three most common of the four basic ways in which a snake moves. The realism is clear in the animations "Eric the dynamic worm", "Her Majesty's secret serpent" and "The Audition" by Miller.

12.2 TASKS

It would be useless to choreograph the figure without reference to its environment. In a constraint based system the orientation of each body part can be specified relative to its neighbours or to the actor coordinate system or the world. The gesture of a hand may be defined relative to the arm, but for a foot to be flat on the floor, it must reference the world coordinate system regardless of the orientation of the pelvis [Boisvert 1989]. Even the most commonplace of tasks involving our synthetic actor, is likely to require his interaction with the rest of his world, and this is likely to require the solution of many apparently simple problems. What could be simpler than closing the door, sitting down in an armchair and picking up a cup of tea? If you try and explain how you manage to accomplish these tasks, they start to sound anything but simple, yet are dealt with in real life at an almost reflex level. It is also true that authentic movement is about far more than just mechanics, experience playing a big part in causing toddlers to walk differently from adults, for example, and a synthetic human might even benefit from learning how to use his limbs by trial and error.

It would often be desirable for the animator to specify movement with commands such as "sit down" and "close the door", but there is no single sequence of movements which will satisfy either of these instructions in more than one case. In each instance, the spatial position and current pose of the actor will effect his response, as will the position, height and orientation of the chair or door. A solution requires both cognitive and motor problem solving [Zeltzer 1988]. An application which would immediately benefit from the solution of this problem is that of ergonomic environment evaluation, such as occurs in the design of an aircraft cockpit.

Badler [1990] describes the problems of ergonomic simulation and evaluation by what is now called a 'human factors engineer'. In his system he works with a seventeen section torso, with each section having its own joint limits, and as well as being able to watch the figure attempt a task within its domain, it is possible to see the figure's view. Objects seen by foveal and peripheral vision can be distinguished. A task for the figure, such as taking a load from a surface in front of it and lifting it above its head, can be modified by changing the figure's strength or the load's weight. It is fascinating to see that these changes lead to the adoption of changing motion strategies, rather than with just repetition of the same movement path through the action. You don't try and lift a hundredweight the same way as a pound, it is necessary to bring a heavy load closer to the body than a light one, before raising it up. In this model it is possible to measure and display the comfort/discomfort levels of the figure, and the torques at each moment in any joint, in all degrees of freedom. "The strength model dictates acceptable kinematic postures. The resulting algorithm offers torque control without the tedious user expression of driving forces under a dynamic model" [Lee 1990]. (Instinctive anticipation of a the weight of a load is also a factor in real life, and a mistake at this pre-lift stage can prove disastrous, since experience will have lead to muscles being primed to counteract the expected load.)

A discipline which is centred on human movement is ballet, and a number of people have attempted to use the computer as a choreographic aid. Whilst no systems have (yet) come close to matching the subtlety and expression of real dancers, they can be effectively used to plan and animate dance sequences. The relative crudeness of the animation, however, probably requires an experienced eye to be able to extrapolate from it to a human performance. COMPOSE is an interactive system for the composition of dance from menus of postures and sequences [Schiphorst 1990] which addresses itself to the provision of a suitable environment for the creative process in this context. A specific attempt is made, therefore, to allow the artist to engage and interact with the idea, rather than with the tools of the interface. Whilst one would hope this was always the case, it is particularly important in an environment such as this that the animator is not constrained by having to deal with the mechanics of articulation. The rationale behind animation in this context is quite different from that implied in the previous part of the chapter. The task could, perhaps, be described as 'inverse scripting', in that the process is not concerned with acting out of a pre-existing script but with composing a script by interaction with the screen dancers and (probably) a piece of music.

The COMPOSE main screen shows a menu of simple figures, from a library of 500 stances, an adjustable view of the stage area, and a range of menus and controls. For each scene the dancers' stances are positioned using the mouse, and their facings adjusted, with the option of creating fresh postures by interactively positioning the limbs and torso of a figure on a second 'body' screen. Composition can be created spatially on the stage or temporally in a timeline; splines are fitted to a mouse-drawn movement path, and can be edited; the timing is initially linear but can be subsequently adjusted. It is intended to develop a knowledge base for the system together with the ability to reason about the knowledge contained in it, so that the system will develop level of intelligence.

12.3 APPEARANCE

Once models have started to deal satisfactorily with the mechanics of human movement, it becomes a higher priority to investigate the subtleties of surface change brought about by that movement. Another little gem from the researchers in Ohio is "Bragger Bones" [Chadwick 1989]. This hip little cartoon character swaggers down the street (in his SIGGRAPH t-shirt and shades!) with biceps bulging as his arms flex and with cheeks puffing out and relaxing. As well as increasing realism in an animation, the ability of the surface of the figure to deform in accordance with internal and external forces is in the great cartoon tradition of elephants inflating into balloons and cats being squashed paper thin under ten ton weights. The prototype system ("Critter"), which produced Bragger Bones, builds the figure in physical (and conceptual) layers. These layers maintain a relationship defined by parametric constraints and describe how the figure moves in general in response to specifically defined movements. By putting a lot of emphasis on defining the layers and their relationship, the animation can be scripted at a high level and the lower levels can look after themselves.

The four layers defined for Critter are: the behaviour layer, at which motion is specified; the foundation layer, where the skeleton is found; the shape transition layer, where the muscle and fatty tissue are found; and the surface layer, where Critter has skin, fur or clothing. The muscle layer surrounding the skeleton is distorted by Free Form Deformation (FFD). This method surrounds the object with a three-dimensional, cubic lattice which deforms like a jelly (jello) cube, distorting objects embedded in it accordingly.

Surprisingly, perhaps, since the geometry of the area seems easier to understand than much of the face, the eyes are the least convincing part of many facial models. It may be that eye contact is such an important part of human interaction that we are particularly familiar with that region of the face. Also that we are skilled at making intuitive interpretations of mood from subtle eye-area clues, and are, therefore, more tuned to representational deficiencies. This might provide a clue to the practical problems of satisfactorily modelling a human. Not that we fully match all its visual properties (although that is an ultimate aim) but that we devote most care and attention to the features which are most telling in real-life observation. How many people could you recognise by their eyes alone? how many fewer by their ears? how many with paper bags over their heads?

I remember seeing on exhibition stands a few years ago, stationary figures convincingly giving a sales monologue for the product they represented. On closer inspection they proved to be immobile white models on whose faces were projected movie film of a real actor speaking the lines. They remained convincing after the artifice was revealed, and demonstrated how strong the right visual clues can be.

12.4 FACIAL ANIMATION

A major vehicle for communicating the internal state of a person is the face (Fig 12.4). Emotions are expressed by variations of the surface topology, the lips and mouth externalise speech and the general topology distinguishes one person from another. To be able to convey anger, happiness or fear is a challenging task, and to recreate the appearance of speech another. Both are being attempted with some degree of resolution, and the vision of a synthetic human actor, driven only by a Shakespearean text, is not wholly remote.

The first obvious problem in creating a facial animation, is getting the data from which to construct the face model. Measurements of a real face can be taken with a laser scan or other 3-D digitising technology, but a method accessible enough for anyone to use is photographic. The subject's face can be divided into suitable polygons drawn onto the skin, and photographed in front view and side view. The X,Y values of the points making up the polygons can be extracted from the front view and the Z values added by matching the points in the side view. It might be acceptable to build just one side of a face and mirror it along a vertical axis to create the entire face, since in a model such as Keith Waters' [1987] it will be possible to operate the muscles on each side of the face independently.

But how should the division of the face into polygons be established? In a static model it is only necessary to deal with changes of surface plane at a degree of subtlety appropriate to the rendering method, but if the model is to be animated then the articulation or deformation of the polygons must be considered. The underlying structure which gives rise to the surface characteristics can be taken into account. Bone, subcutaneous fatty tissues and epidermis could all be modelled in the cause of a dynamic model [Waters 1989] but the effects of analysing muscle structure and deriving muscle vectors alone is impressive. Waters [1987] arrives at "a model for the muscles of the face that can be extended to any non-rigid object and is not dependent on specific topology or network".

He points out that previous parameterisation techniques have dealt principally with the surface characteristics rather than with the underlying dynamics, and that the main alternative to parameterisation is key framing. This is very data intensive (as each positional extreme,

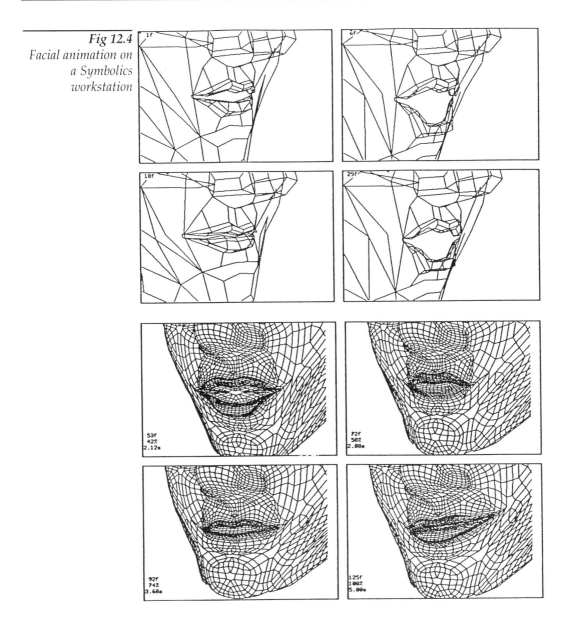

Fig 12.4
Facial animation on a Symbolics workstation

or difference between extremes, has to be completely specified) and is lacking in the specific manipulation required for subtlety. Amongst other things, his model has been applied to the caricatured head of Margaret Thatcher from "Spitting Image" (the satirical/political TV puppet show). The Waters [1989] model for facial tissue, which offers increased realism, replaces the representation of skin as an infinitesimally thin membrane with a three-dimensional lattice. In this, the nodes of the lattice are connected by springs (whose conduct is governed by Hooke's law), and by varying the spring constants in each of three layers in the lattice, the elasticity of the skin can be approximated and muscle action applied.

The use of a polygonal mesh for mimicking facial soft tissue is used by Pieper [1989] in the context of a plastic surgery simulator. This is an application which most people would not think of when picking up a book on computer animation, but serves to reinforce how diverse are the uses of the discipline. To be able to contribute to the health and wellbeing of people requiring cosmetic surgery, or to assist in the training of their surgeons, makes all the flying logos seem an acceptable loss-leader.

A display which has caught the attention at recent exhibitions of computer graphics hardware, demonstrates real-time animation of a shaded facial model, in this case on Silicon-Graphics hardware. A range of lip, mouth, eyebrow and nostril movements are realistically and smoothly variable, and in the hands of an experienced puppeteer generate surprising life and character using a simple interface. The team that produced this system (The Performance Animation System [deGraf 1989]) also used it to convert the oldest living cartoon character, Felix the Cat, to a three-dimensional model, with two puppeteers controlling eight different functions using controls such as joysticks [Sørenson 1989]. Surprisingly, it was in some ways harder to animate Felix than a realistic person, despite the fact that he was basically a sphere plus nose, ears and tufts of fur, with eyes and mouth flush to the head. In order to preserve the characterisation of the 2-D original, it was necessary for there to be a collection of different mouths for different purposes, and for the mouth to slide around the head so that it always faced the camera. Using the same system, however, ninety seconds of lip-sync was completed for another project in less than a week.

The localised muscle action controlling the lips and jaw

requires special consideration in order that realistic synchronisation to speech can be attained. Phonemes (individual speech units) can be associated with lip positions, and work with the deaf long ago led to the compilation of lip-reading charts. Books on hand drawn cartooning usually include illustrations of mouth positions corresponding to speech. It is not sufficient, however, merely to match phonemes to textbook lip positions, as the preceding and following phonemes must also be considered.

12.5 CHARACTERISATION

In the context of caricature, it is necessary to focus on, and exaggerate, features which characterise an individual; to identify the ways in which the subject deviates most from a physical mean, rather than the ways in which he conforms to it. Similarly, a characterisation might develop the extremes of expression or behaviour of the character. Although this chapter has implied only the accurate simulation of humans the animator has it in his power to ammend and distort the simulation. The traditional animator's techniques such as "squash" and "stretch" can be applied to models built using the methods described here, or joint limitations can be set to allow a knee the freedom to bend forward if the animator so chooses.

It is important to recognise that the construction of a synthetic human, in whole or part, has merely provided a passive actor ready for direction. Whilst the direction in an ergonomic simulation would be imposed by the forces inherent in the scene, direction in a narrative context requires creative skills very different from the skills used in creating the model. It is disappointing to see how often demonstrations of innovative scientific development in our field are let down by poor visual presentation, simply because the research basis of the work does not allow for artistic skills in the production team. There is no reason why the programmer should expect to be a good designer, or the animator should be a skilled computer scientist, but it is necessary to recognise when additional skills are required and to acquire or import them. The Pixar team (Chapter 2.10) is a classic example of a group containing all the required skills and this shines through in their work.

240

CHAPTER 13

THE FUTURE TODAY

The pace of development in computing means that predictions about the future are likely to be overtaken by fact in months rather than years. Machine speeds seem to double every time you open a new computer magazine, storage quadruples and prices halve. Today's state-of-the-art is standard in tomorrow's home-micro. When I started writing this book I pencilled in a chunk of this 'Future' chapter to describe 'virtual reality', which was just emerging, but since then most of the material I proposed has been covered in daily newspapers and popular TV science programs. I therefore talk about the future in the confident expectation that it will have become history by publication day.

13.1 VIRTUAL REALITY

At the 1989 SIGGRAPH conference I saw a man moving objects that weren't there. He wasn't a mime artist, and he was neither drunk nor 'high' (or at least if he was it wasn't relevant), though what he was doing has immense potential and yet has been likened to a dream experience. (It has also been likened to a drug experience though with the caveat, expressed at SIGGRAPH '90, that it will take a long time before it approximates the price/performance ratio of LSD!) The clue to what he was doing lay in the strange electronic mask and glove that he wore. He was trying out the latest human/computer interface, the DataGlove. Instead of viewing the representation of a three-dimensional computer generated scene on a two-dimensional screen, he was entering into the scene itself, and interacting with the objects therein, he had entered a 'virtual' reality. Picking up one object that wasn't there and stacking it on another that wasn't there either, but with total conviction. Spectators were able to follow the results of his efforts through a traditional 2-D animated screen display.

The obvious uses for this infant technology are remarkable, the less obvious uses are staggering, and despite the fact that it has only just reached the marketplace in 1989 it is expected to revolutionise many disciplines. Surgeons will be able to practice convincing operations on 'virtual' patients, astronauts can already practice space manoeuvres on the ground, anyone can be a 'virtual' racing driver in his own living room, and the animator can define an actor's path through 3-space with a sweep of his hand. Whilst the ultimate video game scenario is one promise offered, there are many more uses for the DataGlove and its allied technology, both mundane and outrageous. You can tell that something quite different is afoot when technical authors start quoting Marshall McLuhan, go on to describe the founder of VPL (the DataGlove company) as a guru and sage, and feel obliged to mention his dreadlocks. Jaron Lanier is the man in question, with Tom Zimmerman and Young Harvill being credited with the invention and development of the DataGlove. Virtual reality has grown from concepts such as 'artificial reality' (a term coined some years back by Myron Krueger) and is currently typified by its enabling encumbrances like the glove, mask and suit.

The DataGlove is an input device which is worn like a glove and translates hand and finger movements into electric signals. Combined with an absolute position and orientation sensor, the glove translates movements made by the operator's hand into information which can be used to duplicate the movements in the computer's 3-space. It is thus possible to control movement in the computer scene by hand movement, and one obvious application is to create a computer model of a hand which can mimic the operator's hand. It is then easy to create an object in the computer's scene and to grasp it with the model hand which inhabits that same scene, under the control of the DataGlove. The glove is also an output device, as tactile-feedback devices can give the operator the same touch clues as he would expect from manipulating a real object. Whilst the glove can be used with a 2-D VDU screen to display what is happening in the scene, this falls short of providing the total control which participation in the 3-D scene would give. The glove is therefore used in conjunction with a stereoscopic headset which provides a separate screen for each eye and allows the user to look around the scene as he would in real life, presenting fresh views as it senses the head being moved, and utilising all the spatial depth clues that the user would normally expect.

The gloves can, as you would expect, be used in pairs, and a DataSuit has also been constructed to allow the whole body of the operator to interface with the machine. The only obvious limitation on the feedback from these devices at the moment is the lack of force-feedback. It is possible to feel the surface of an object, but not to feel its weight when 'picked up'. A more effective force-feedback device is the 'joystick' built by Richard Feldmann of the National Institutes of Health, which is a T-shaped bar held in space by nine taut wires. The T-bar can be manipulated by the operator and forces and torque feedback can be returned to the operator through tension on the wires. This sort of feedback might be essential if the interface was being used to keep its operator out of a hazardous environment, for example if containers of radioactive material had to be moved by robot under the operator's control. Forces and torques can be applied to a hand control, but currently only as part of a substantial machine rather than in the compact and mobile form required (Iwata [1990] describes a surface-mounted device which applies reaction forces to the fingers and palm of the operator). The possibility of using 'memory metals' to push against the skin in the DataGlove has been considered as a response to the force-feedback limitation [Foley 1987]. No doubt someone has also considered bypassing the body as a feedback interface, and going direct to the brain.

NASA has a team working on virtual reality worlds, which must have at least two obvious attractions for them. One is the possibility of rehearsing elements of space missions on the ground, and the other is of using parallel environments where an astronaut can work in a safe virtual world that mirrors a real world in open space. The possibility of control being exercised from a virtual world on the Earth must also have been considered, although interactive feedback would be delayed by current signal transmission methods. This project, together with the Aspen Movie Map project which initiated the research into virtual reality, first used video before moving to computer graphics, (the town of Aspen could be toured at will from a computer via a videodisc). There are other examples of virtual worlds being used already, for instance the ability of architects to 'walk' about buildings that have not yet been constructed, but it is the encompassing interactivity of the new technology that sets it apart.

Sam Kiley described, in *The Sunday Times* (17 June 1990) an experience in which he had 'flown' using the DataGlove technology and added "The equipment I was playing on cost $250,000, but Lanier plans to bring the price down to an affordable level. By hooking up with a toymaker, Age Inc. of New York, 18 months from now, Lanier's outfit in Silicon Valley could be releasing technology on to the market which could be more influential than television and more fun than the telephone - at about half the price of a video recorder. Computer buffs predict that by the end of the century, most households will have access to computer universes they will create themselves." As well as being able to build your own dream world to retreat to, there will be off-the-shelf worlds as accessible as videotapes, in which you will be able to play golf with Arnold Palmer and dance with Marilyn Monroe, or vice versa if you prefer.

I am tempted to say that you could BE Palmer or Monroe, in the same way that articles describing virtual reality talk about BEING a lobster, for instance. However, whilst your body could drive a model of the figure of your choice, you would be acting that person rather than feeling what it was like to be them. Of course you might expect to share the same reactions from people you meet in your virtual world as would the person you are mimicking, and this would constitute part of the feeling of being that person. Lanier has broader visions of what you might become. In an interview in *Whole Earth Review* (Fall 1989) he says "The computer that's running the Virtual Reality, will use your body's movements to control whatever body you choose to have in Virtual Reality, which might be human or might be something quite different. You might very well be a mountain range or a galaxy or a pebble on a floor. Or a piano ... I've considered being a piano. I'm interested in being musical instruments quite a lot. Also you can have musical instruments that play reality in all kinds of ways aside from making sound in Virtual Reality. That's another way of describing arbitrary physics. With a saxophone you'll be able to play cities and dancing lights, and you'll be able to play the herding of buffaloes made of crystal, and you'll be able to play your own body and change yourself as you play the saxophone. You could become a comet in the sky one moment and then gradually unfold into a spider that's bigger than the planet that looks down at all your friends from high above." It is also promised that there will be virtual mirrors available in these virtual worlds, which will presumably enable you to amend the body you are inhabiting while you watch.

In a panel session at SIGGRAPH 1990, entitled 'Hip, Hype and Hope - the three faces of virtual reality' a number of interesting suggestions were made. Warren Robinette was sure that the head mounted device will display to all the senses, the most important perhaps being sight, hearing, smell and force-feedback. He suggested that the future experience would be like the telephone, TV, hi-fi, cinema and video games all rolled into one; that it would enable synthetic experience to be superimposed onto the real world; that it came close to X-ray vision (think of the virtual surgery example); and that anyone's vision could be made available to everyone. His example of the latter, was the view from someone on a hill being passed to someone hidden behind the hill to enable that person to see 'through' the hill, with obvious military overtones. William Bricken suggested, amongst other things, that the cumbersome pixel-view headset would be replaced by a device inscribing the image directly on the retina with a low-level laser, and that we should be able to address the fabric of space as well as objects in that space. He also pointed out that the technology has become commercially available before the scientific community understands what it is. The session was at one stage described as the most significant event in the history of humanity, and virtual reality as the first scientific tool of metaphysics, but it was also pointed out that we are getting very excited about something we know next to nothing about (probably only 20 people having spent more than 15 hours in VR).

The consequences of believable virtual worlds are mixed and, as yet, little understood. Considered superficially as a home entertainment medium they might be more addictive than television, but even if they provided further incentive to stay at home every night they would require the use of imaginative participation and could be a powerful learning medium. As well as trips to your private holiday island (weather at your discretion, of course) you could tour the virtual Tate Gallery whenever you chose, and your incentive to keep fit might be increased by joining in with Jane Fonda in her exercise session. If the virtual world eventually provides a totally convincing sensation, will it still be necessary to have the real experience? If all experience can be brought to you, what reason will there be to go anywhere? Such questions have already been asked in science fiction and soon we might be testing out the answers. As far as the present is concerned, we still have the problem of rendering the images representing the virtual world in convincing detail at sufficient speed. At the moment the choice is between interaction in a simple scene and viewing a post-processed complex scene (a current VR system just on the market, at the same cost as a low price workstation, can display 30K polygons per second at 20 fps with a resolution of 640 x 400). We can, however, confidently assume that hardware improvements will alleviate the problem.

13.2 INTERFACES

Other interface developments that are already being tested present information to the user in the form of 'head-up' displays, typically in a pilot's helmet. Representations of the scenery the pilot is flying over can be presented with greater clarity than might be possible in reality because of weather conditions or night flying. Related data can also be presented in the same display as the scene, and the display will follow the pilot's head. Eye tracking will allow the pilot to select from menu choices presented with the scene, and voice recognition provides another possible input device. The DataGlove can be part of a new interface, with pointing or sign language being readily interpreted as input.

A head-up display helmet for an aircraft technician might incorporate a mixture of the real world of a stripped down engine, a diagrammatic version using VR technology and overlays of relevant written instruction. The system would recognise the context of the technician's operations and use an expert system to make available appropriate information, either visibly or audibly, on request. The ability to access the information otherwise held in dozens of manuals, at the moment of need, and in a form which might be superimposed on the user's live view of the situation, has equal potential for a mechanic, surgeon or football coach.

Flight simulators could easily change from being massive and very expensive mockups of real cockpits mounted on hydraulic rams, to individual units comprising DataGloves, a headset and a chair driven by small rams. A dozen pilots could all fly the same virtual plane at the same time in the same room, and to change aircraft it becomes necessary only to change the data file which sets the virtual cockpit display and aircraft characteristics. It would not even be necessary to have a real joystick, as a virtual one would be indistinguishable. The same system would perhaps be applicable to any seated simulation, and with the addition of a DataSuit and force-feedback could be used for any simulation at all. The same unit would be used for instructional training and entertainment.

13.3 DIGITAL DOUGH

If a 3-D lattice was created to define an object, then the object could be deformed by moving points in that lattice. If the points were interconnected with springs then the deformations would transmit through the solid and the consistency of the object could be defined by the tension of the springs. (We have already looked at skin models using this principle and Sederberg [1986] describes a method for free-form deformation of solid geometric models by displacing control points in a surrounding frame.) If we now let this object exist in a virtual world accessible to the DataGlove, then it can be hand-modelled like clay - a sort of digital dough. By putting on the gloves we can squeeze, stretch and shape the object like a sculptor, and, by changing the tension of the springs at any time, can change the object's consistency. This becomes a much more intuitive modelling method than those with a more visible mathematical basis.

13.4 ERIC

If we take an articulated human figure model, as previously described, and let its parts be defined as digital dough, then we have a lay figure which can be hand modelled to suit any requirements. We can make it short and fat, tall and skinny, with a big head or large feet, can create caricatures or likenesses, and could easily 'tweak' the quantities of dough available in any particular area. Once sculpted to taste, the figure can be animated using all the existing techniques, including dynamics, but the glove technology also offers the option of combining them with interactive positioning. The figure could be taken through its movements like a puppet, set in key-frame positions which could be interpolated between, even being deformed during the movement. The degree of refinement of the figure would be determined by the closeness of the lattice points, but since we are looking to the future we can assume the hardware to cope with anything.

We can now create a scene with animated actors as simply as a child can play with clay, but with the additional option of using 'traditional' modelling techniques when appropriate. We can define characteristics such as gait pattern with 'conventional' methods or by real-time demonstration using the figures themselves (the figures have become plural, because it is, of course, trivial to clone a crowd). Facial expression can be similarly controlled, and artificial intelligence can be attributed as desired.

It might be useful to have a dynamic articulated figure always available for use from within any program. It could wait in the desktop to be called on to demonstrate, or to test for ergonomic soundness, equipment designed on the computers, and as this is the first task for which it is being considered the ERgonomic figure In our Computer will be called ERIC. If ERIC was called with no application running, he would exist in an empty three-dimensional desktop world, and if called from within an application, would have to map his world to that of the application. He would be controlled and rendered by his host application, but we will conveniently ignore the interfacing problems involved in doing so. ERIC's digital dough properties would be switchable, so that DataGlove techniques could be used to customise your own ERIC (perhaps creating an ERICA), but need not be available during his use. His proportions could also be entered numerically to ensure the accuracy needed for scientific testing.

He would, of course, be a contestant in computer games, and could be programmed to learn if required, or to diplomatically lose to the operator. He could, with his cloned siblings, take part in team pursuits, and be used to test out strategies in sports or wargames. Networked games would allow you to test your ERIC against anyone else's, and events similar to computer chess contests would become common. ERIC and his friends would become the animator's flexible actors, capable of being exploded, squashed and metamorphosed indefinitely without any problems from unions. They might even be persuaded to act out the complete works of Shakespeare that you have on disc. As a human/computer interface ERIC might be the perfect go between, being able to communicate more eloquently than any icon.

13.5 HARDWARE

Hardware will be faster, smaller, more powerful and, at the same time, cheaper. The magnitudes of each change are unpredictable, but looking at the pattern of the past 40 years suggests an exponential growth curve in many areas. Pocket-sized workstations might not get given away free with petrol (what petrol?) but they will become commonplace. The resultant increase in portability will not just add to convenience, but will change attitudes to computers, an ever-available handheld box losing the preciousness of a desk-bound machine available during office hours. Increased networking, particularly using telephone and satellite links, moves towards the idea that all computers could ultimately be linked to produce a single global machine with massive computing power and access to all recorded knowledge.

Speech input will reduce much of the need for keyboards (currently effecting the minimum size of machines) but will not be appropriate in all situations, and a virtual keyboard might prove a useful spacesaver. For individual viewing, screens can be built into glasses or contact lenses, or perhaps replaced by holographic displays, and resolution will be sufficiently high to be indistinguishable from non-electronic media. HDTV will soon prepare the general public to expect greater image quality and eventually a watercolour and computer generated image could look the same.

Storage capacity will be massive and solid-state in the relatively near future, and data will be stored in very compressed form. Data compression will be one of the first hurdles to be crossed in the development of the next generation of systems and it is possible that brain-function analogies may lead to new data access techniques, providing the additional handling speed that will be required.

Distributed intelligence and parallel processing are likely paradigms if we extrapolate from current technologies, but a number of people have speculated on biological computers. Durham [1987] suggests that there is nothing implausible about the idea that biological processes and materials should be used to construct computing devices on a scale 100 or 1000 times smaller than today's VLSI chips. He quotes James McLear: "If you took all the information in all the computers existing in the world today and used biomolecular technology, it would fit into one sugar cube". Macro-engineering is being seriously considered as a means of constructing things at an atomic level.

13.5.1 NANOTECHNOLOGY

The beginnings of nanotechnology are attributed to suggestions made in 1959 by Richard Feynman, the term now used to describe the ultraminiaturisation which he envisaged coming from the Greek word for dwarf, and the prefix 'nano' denoting 10^{-9} (a nanometre therefore being one thousand-millionth of a metre). Nanotechnology deals with manufacturing technologies and machine systems with dimensions and tolerances in the range 0.1 to 100 nanometres, this is a range from the size of an atom to the wavelength of light. Picotechnology (pico = 10^{-12}) is a sub-nanometric technology dealing with the manipulation and modulation at the level of individual atomic bonds and orbitals, and work has already been carried out at resolutions of 1 to 10 picometres [Schneiker 1988].

The applications of nanotechnology extend far beyond our immediate concerns as computer animators, but the potentially extreme diminution of hardware can interest us. It is suggestive of increased power, accessibility and perhaps even democratisation of access. This new technology is also interwoven with ideas about self-replicating systems, and one wonders about parallel systems and networks being able to extend themselves by replicating their own processors and nodes.

13.6 MULTIMEDIA

Multimedia, and its predicted growth, have been mentioned several times in the book, but the media to be included in future systems might include holography, virtual reality and references to other senses than sight and hearing. The first ventures will probably be called 4-D multimedia, and will give Hypercard-like, interactive access to sensory microworlds. The distinction between video, animation and participation will become irresistibly blurred. Interactivity will become the norm, and the currently somewhat self-conscious interaction that is developing through the use of CDs and hypermedia will become smoothly intuitive.

Alvey Ray Smith suggested in *Byte* magazine (September 1990) that "much modelling will be made redundant by the selection, from electronic catalogues, of ready-made models. The user becomes a 'spatial editor' inserting the model(s) into the 3-D scene, sizing and customising to taste". This principle is likely to apply to much in the multi-media area, and with world-wide data banks linked electronically there will be a massive amount of visual, audio and written material to use (and to abuse).

13.7 CONCLUSION

Eighty per cent of the information we receive comes through our eyes, sight is our key sensory medium.

Computer hardware is now able to support highly detailed and sophisticated visual imagery and will become universally available.

Animation provides an extra dimension to still images, for without diminishing their information content it allows them to be discursive (in the same way as spoken language).

Film, television, and now multi-media, have led us to subsume the moving picture into our vocabulary of communication.

Computers allow us to bring all this together to provide one of the most powerful tools yet devised for education, communication and dissemination - that of computer animation.

The medium will be well used, and it will be badly used. It will enable great discoveries to be made, and it will allow great deceits to be perpetrated. It is just starting.

APPENDIX A

BOOK RECOMMENDATIONS

The following books are singled out from the bibliography as being particularly recommended.

'Computer graphics for designers and artists' [Kerlow 1986] is a clear, simple and well illustrated introduction to computer graphics, intended for those with a visual background, that goes into enough depth to be very useful.

'Television Graphics - from pencil to pixel' [Merritt 1987] is a heavily illustrated book, full of good examples and explanations of TV computer graphics including animation.

'Animation - a guide to animated film techniques' [Noake 1988] gives a very well illustrated guide to traditional and modern animation methods, and ends with a chapter on computer animation.

'Animation - from script to screen' [Culhane 1988] offers a methodical guide to the complete process of creating an animation. Mainly dealing with traditional methods, but with a chapter on computer animation, it includes a number of practical appendices on issues such as running a business.

'Computer graphics' [Hearn 1986] is a particularly balanced and readable account of the subject area. It has good diagrams, illustrations and coding examples.

'Computer graphics - principles and practice (2nd Edition)' [Foley 1990] is an update of one of the "bibles"of CG. Extensive, authoritative, up-to-date and with many colour plates

'Computer graphics - systems and concepts' [Salmon 1987] is one of many books dealing with computer graphics theory ,but is more comprehensive than many in dealing with input, hardcopy and HCI. Also deals with the GKS graphics standard.

'Fundamentals of three-dimensional computer graphics' [Watt 1989] is one of the few books devoted specifically to 3D. It is comprehensive, well written and up-to-date.

'A programmer's geometry' [Bowyer 1983] brings together all the geometry required for computer graphics, with straightforward explanations and simple diagrams.

'Computer graphics - an introduction to the mathematics and geometry' [Mortensen 1989] is a particularly comprehensive account o the maths relating to computer graphics, and includes straightforward introductions to vectors, matrices, etc., for those not familiar with them.

'Soft computing' [Reffin Smith 1984] provides a useful antidote to mainstream computer writing. It is intelligently questioning and deals with visual aspects of the medium.

'Que's computer user's dictionary' [Pfaffenberger 1990] is a very good guide to computing terms. Its range is more practical than most, including major applications and machines. It offers explanations rather than definitions, and adds many helpful tips and cautions.

APPENDIX B

DYNAMICS FORMULAE

This appendix gives the most basic formulae necessary to create a dynamic point mass. Wilhelms [1987c] 'Dynamics for everyone' gives a concise account of the area from which you can develop things further.

Newton's laws of motion

Formulated in 1687, they can be stated as follows.

1. An object continues in a state of rest or constant velocity unless acted on by an external force.

2. The resultant force acting on an object is proportional to the rate of change of momentum of the object, the change of momentum being in the same direction as the force.

3. If one object exerts a force on another then there is an equal and opposite force (reaction) on the first object exerted by the second.

(The first law was discovered by Galileo, and is both a description of inertia and a definition of zero force.

The second law provides a definition of force based on the inertial property of mass.

The third law is equivalent to the law of conservation of linear momentum). [6]

Chapter 9.1 introduces the Newton/Euler method as a simple

means of numerical integration, but with the limitation that inaccuracies arise if the time-step used is not relatively small. The simplicity of the method, however, often outweighs the requirement to keep increments small.

The dynamics of a particle can be stated as:

$$F = m\,a$$

F = force in Newtons (kilograms-metres/seconds^2)
m = mass in kilograms
a = acceleration in metres/seconds

This is a vector equation representing the scalar equations for each of the cartesian axes:

$$f_x = max$$
$$f_y = may$$
$$f_z = maz$$

If, therefore, the particle mass and applied force are known, then:

$$a = F/m$$

is the vector to find the acceleration.

If the present velocity (v) at time i is known, then to find the velocity a bit (∂t) further on in time, we have the vector equation:

$$v_{i+1} = v_i + a_i \partial t$$

Given the new velocity, the vector equation to find the new position (p_{i+1}) is:

$$p_{i+1} = p_i + v_i \partial t + 1/2\,a_i \partial t^2$$

To move a particle, therefore, we need only to initialise its position and mass and apply the external force acting on it, probably as a 3-D vector. This external force may be the sum of a number of forces acting on the particle, such as the force of gravity which is about 9.81 metres/second^2 on Earth, acting towards the Earth's centre, times the particle's mass.

ie $f_{grv} = (0,-9.81,0)m$

If you want to detect collisions a simple check to implement uses a spherical bounding box and computes the distance of each object from each of the others in turn. If the distance is less than the sum of the radii of the two bounding spheres, then the spheres intersect, i.e.

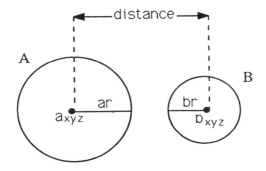

$$\text{distance} = \text{sqrt}(\ \text{sqr}(a_x - b_x) + \text{sqr}(a_y - b_y) + \text{sqr}(a_z - b_z))$$
$$\text{collision} = \text{distance} < (ar + br)$$

or to avoid the expensive square-root calculation, this can be ammended to:

$$\text{collision} = (\text{sqr}(a_x - b_x) + \text{sqr}(a_y - b_y) + \text{sqr}(a_z - b_z)) < \text{sqr}(ar + br)$$

The response to a collision can be calculated analytically by considering the linear velocity, angular velocity, mass, centre of mass and inertial tensor of the colliding masses, which is computationally expensive but usually applied only once for each collision (linear and angular momentum must be preserved and a new direction vector sought).

conservation of momentum: $\quad m1v1_i + m2v2_i = m1v1_{i+1} + m2v2_{i+1}$
Newton's exponential function : $\quad v2_{i+1} - v1_{i+1} = -c(v2 - v1)_i$
c is coefficient of restitution $(\ 0 = \text{inelastic},\ 1 = \text{elastic}\ )$
   Nb 'elastic' means not deforming

these equations can be solved for xyz, for example:

$$vx_{(i+1)} = (2(m_x v_x)_i + (m_x 1 v_x 1)_i - (m_x 2 v_x 1)_i) / (m_x 1 + m_x 2)$$

This would lend itself very readily to a simulation of gas molecules in an enclosed space, when, if the coefficient of restitution is one, the molecules would ricochet off the walls and one another indefinitely:

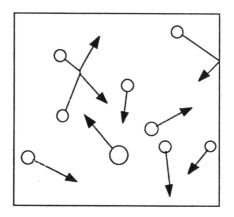

An object could also be bounced off a plane using the surface normal (N) of the plane :

$$V_{new} = -2(N.V)N - V$$

THE MAKING OF PENCIL TEST

Galyn Susman
Apple Computer, Inc.

This paper is reproduced by kind permission of Apple Computer, Inc. and is included as an interesting record of the complete process of making a computer animation. In particular, it includes an indication of the problems that must be dealt with during production, often to tight deadlines. Since the paper was circulated at the Bristol Animation Festival in 1989 (in conjunction with an impressive demonstration), and it describes a project from 1987/8, it can be understood that significant improvements have been made in much of the hardware and software now available.

ABSTRACT

The Advanced Technology Group at Apple Computer, Inc. recently produced an animation entitled Pencil Test, created entirely with Macintosh II and Macintosh Plus equipment. This paper discusses the challenges and obstacles faced, and the set of solutions chosen in producing an animation on a platform that had not previously been utilized by the animation industry. Animation is both an entertaining and effective communication tool. The conclusions set forth in this paper present some of the issues that need to be addressed to facilitate easier creation of animation on personal computers.

1. INTRODUCTION

In the fall of 1987 Apple's Advanced Technology Group decided that it was time to create a production quality animation for SIGGRAPH. The goal was to produce a piece of 3D character animation with high quality rendering. The challenge was to create this piece entirely on Apple computers, specifically on the Macintosh II. In just six months we formed a group that designed, produced, and scored our first animation, Pencil Test , which debuted at SIGGRAPH in July 1988.

The 3D animation problem can conveniently be divided into six steps: design, modeling, animation, rendering, sound and the final transfer to some medium.

Design is the creation of a story and script, storyboards (pictorial representations of changes in action), and animatics (video recordings of the storyboard that show the timing of the transitions).

Modeling is the creation of three-dimensional models for every object and character shown in the storyboards.

These models, along with the animatics, are used to create the animation , where all of the objects are placed, scaled, and rotated to their actual positions within a scene. A scene consists of all actions that take place from one camera position (or sequence of camera positions as in a pan, zoom, or fly-by). As soon as the camera alters its position, orientation, or path of motion, there is a change of scene. All camera and object movement within a scene is achieved by defining key-frames (set positions, scales and orientations of an object throughout a scene). A keyframe animation system interpolates between key-frames to produce all of the intermediate frames.

Rendering takes these frames along with the models and generates two-dimensional images from the three-dimensional mathematical descriptions. In computer animation this generally involves modeling a natural environment where there are lights and a camera, and objects have color, material properties and even textures. A software rendering package will then take this information and, depending on the algorithm, generate images as simple as cartoon frames or as rich as photographs.

These images are then transferred to some medium, usually film or videotape. In some cases this tape needs additional editing. For example, for special effects like fades or for overlayed credits, this tape must be taken to an editing studio where these effects can be achieved.

The sound track is usually designed while the graphics are being produced. Generally, a professional recording studio is used to record and lay the sound track to tape.

2 OVERVIEW

The high-end systems that are typically used for animation projects have large, integrated software packages to create animations. There is no such software for the Macintosh. Instead we used existing programs to solve parts of the problem and integrated them with custom software (Fig 1). We chose to do all of the design by hand. For modeling we chose Super 3D from Silicon Beach Software. We convinced the author of Twixt, a public domain animation package from Ohio State University, to port his code to the Macintosh for us (MacTwixt). The majority of rendering software was written in-house. We used a scanner and SuperPaint from Silicon Beach Software to create some of the textures. The credits were generated during the rendering process and we chose Microsoft Word to format them. A big breakthrough occurred when we realized that we could create the entire sound track on the Macintosh, something that high-end systems generally do not address. In producing the sound, we used one package for editing sound effects (Sound Designer by Digidesign), another for composing the score (Professional Performer by Mark of the Unicorn), and a third for cuing the sound to video tape (Cue Sheet by Digidesign). Finally, there was no software or hardware in place to help us transfer our piece to video tape; we had to provide these ourselves. All of the components shown in Figure 1 that are not discussed in this paragraph were written by us specifically for this project.

3 DESIGN

Though the primary motivation for this work was technical, we were not without artistic goals. We wanted our piece to tell a story; to be funny and endearing. The design we developed had to accomplish this while allowing for the limitations of the software and the hardware. We were working with beta, alpha, and pre-alpha software, and many of the tools were relatively primitive by Apple standards. To achieve

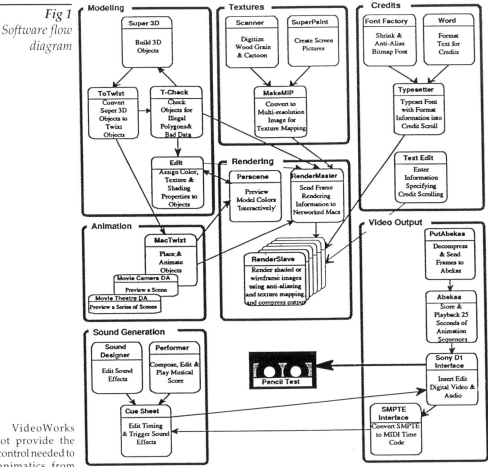

Fig 1
Software flow diagram

Note 1. VideoWorks does not provide the timing control needed to stage animatics from handdrawn storyboards, and it is much too complicated to use for such a basic process. Upon reflection, HyperCard probably would have sufficed if we had scanned the storyboards and then written a script that allowed timed playback and manipulation.

simplicity, we decided that our story would have only one primary character. The rest of the objects would, for the most part, remain stationary and have few or no movable joints.

With these criteria in mind we wrote a script that we thought would be reasonable to work with and still satisfied our artistic goals. Unfortunately, there was no existing software for the Macintosh to aid in the process of storyboarding and creating animatics [note 1], so we

262

contracted an artist to do this work for us. When we received our first set of storyboards and started to work with the character, we realized that as unadorned as our initial design had been, it wasn't going to be simple enough. The main character had been visualized as an articulate, curvy pencil that bent and twisted in all directions (Fig 2a). All we had to work with was a polygonal modeler and an animation package that did not allow us to animate control points on a flexible object. If we wanted to model the pencil with splines we were going to have to write an animation package that let us animate splines. We reconsidered the motions for the pencil and came up with the segmented polygonal design as it exists today (Fig 2b).

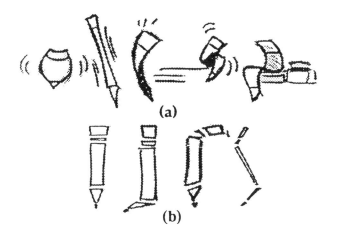

(a)

(b)

Fig 2
Character design (a) original curvy design, (b) final segmented design

In all we devoted about two months to design, including writing the script, creating storyboards, shooting the animatic, and designing the character and objects. At this point we were ready to begin modeling.

4   MODELING

Modeling was the one phase of this project where we solicited involvement from as many people as possible (with the hopes of encouraging further participation). Any interested party could model one of the many objects that appeared on the desk (Fig 3). Because the majority of these people had no previous modeling experience, we needed a modeler with a simple user interface and straight-forward tools like revolution and extrusion. In addition, the modeler had to have a published data format or at least export the model data in ASCII so that we could import our models into the animation and rendering software. Based on these criteria we chose Super3D by Silicon Beach Software.

Fig 3
Sample modeled
objects

Though the version of Super3D that we worked with was a beta version, the software was relatively reliable and easy to work with. It maintained the click and drag interface of the Macintosh in the 3D environment by having a third scroll bar that controlled motion in the Z dimension. The scroll bars controlled rotation, while clicking on pan and zoom icons controlled the translation and scale. There were, however, a few setbacks working with this package. One of the greatest difficulties was the lack of visual feedback. Because the only solid visual feedback was a flat shading mechanism, approximated for an eight bit frame buffer, it was very difficult to tell if an object was closed or inside out. Smooth shading and data consistency checking should be included in this kind of modeling package to guarantee a model's data integrity. Data anomalies did appear and greatly hindered us later in the project.

Super3D exported its data in a very intelligible ASCII format that we could easily parse and convert. Our first (but certainly not our last) data conversion program, ToTwixt, was written to take this output and convert it into a format that the animation software could use. The objects could then be placed within the 3D environment.

5   ANIMATION

From the start it was never really clear what the quality of the rendering was going to be for the final piece. However, we did know that limitations in rendering time would not allow for photo-realistic rendering. This increased the importance of concentrating on the quality of the animation. If the story wasn't successfully told by the expressiveness of the main character and the information carried in the sound it would not be understood. We needed an animation package that would allow us to squash and stretch our objects and define transformational relationships between objects. It also had to create good curved interpolations for the paths of motion.

It was fortunate that MacTwixt satisfied these criteria, for it was the only 3D animation package available to us (by coercion) on the Macintosh. Working with MacTwixt was a new experience for us point-and-click Macintosh users. It had a command line interface and lacked the ability to move objects relative to their current position (i.e. move object x one unit to the right). In addition, the software was not able to do real-time playback of animation. Drawing one 1/4 screen wireframe image on the screen took anywhere from 2 to 15 seconds. This made it impossible to view our motion.

As a result, we wrote a desk accessory (MovieCamera) that we could run with MacTwixt [note 2] to capture all of the drawing commands and play them back in something approximating real-time (timed to the refresh rate of the monitor). In this way we could see clips of the basic wireframe animation and study our motion. However, that was not quite good enough. We then wanted to see a series of scenes strung together. MovieCamera was modified to save the captured bitmaps in a file and another desk accessory was written (MovieTheater). That could take a collection of these files and string them together for playback. By playing back the scenes in sequence we were able to get an idea of the overall timing.

Note 2.   MacTwixt does not run under MultiFinder, which is why MovieCamera had to be a desk accessory if it was to be used simultaneously with MacTwixt.

After scenes had been animated, MacTwixt would write out scene files, which were a collection of transformation matrices for every object at every frame. Depending on the scene, this process could take anywhere from one to twenty-four hours, an unexpected delay [note 3]. We minimised this process by editing these scene files by hand for simple changes, and by writing out very small subsections of scenes and cutting them into the larger files for more complex changes. These scene

Note 3.   This was due to a bug in the ported version of Twixt and not an inherent limitation in the MacTwixt application.

265

files were the frame descriptions used by the renderer.

6 RENDERING

Our plan was always to get the best quality rendering possible in the allotted development time (approximately three months). At the very least we had to have smooth shading, and we aimed for Phong shading which would produce specular highlights. We also needed texture mapping because much of the information relating to the story was told by texture maps appearing on the Macintosh screen (Fig 4). Anti-aliasing was also necessary or the quality would not suffice for the SIGGRAPH Film and Video Show. Though it was not clear how time-consuming the rendering process was going to be, we knew that we would need a distributed system to allow for time to render several versions of the film. With this in mind we initiated the renderer project and the distributed systems project.

Fig 4
A texture mapped screen showing the Macintosh in the startup sequence

6.1 PREPARATION

Before we could render any of our objects we needed to modify them to include various rendering attributes. We wrote a program called Edit that allowed us to assign colors, smooth edges, material properties and surface textures to the objects.

Some early rendering tests revealed topological inconsistencies

266

in our model data. The anomalies fell into three categories: zero area polygons and multiple neighbor polygons causing cracks in the shaded models; open solids (where one or more polygons of the model were missing) resulting in holes in the shaded model; and reversed polygon normals, appearing as holes or causing the entire object to appear inside-out. To fix some of these problems we wrote TCheck, a program that would read in the objects, remove zero area polygons, and flag all the other bad data. All models that failed to pass TCheck were rebuilt in Super3D. This cycle was extraordinarily time consuming. Each object was broken into its subparts and all the subparts were run through TCheck. Any part found with bad data was rebuilt and checked until all of the parts were renderable. Then the object could be reassembled, and read into Edit to be recoloured and resmoothed.

An early addition to our rendering environment was a program to preview rendered objects. Parscene began as a model that parsed scene description files from MacTwixt and object description files from Edit. It then converted them into a form usable by the renderer. At this point it was expanded to be an interactive front end that allowed us to read in a scene and display the frames on a 24-bit monitor, using an experimental 24-bit version of Color QuickDraw for the Macintosh II and a prototype 24-bit video card. Once this was accomplished we added an interface that allowed us to interactively move the camera, add and manipulate lights, and experiment with different rendering methods. We could also remove one degree of freedom and use the mouse to move the camera and lights.

6.2 RENDERER

All of the rendering code was written in-house. The renderer we implemented provided flat shading, smooth shading, and Phong shading. Multiple (four) colored light sources were implemented; up to three sources of white light were used in Pencil Test. A 24-bit Z-buffer was used to eliminate hidden surfaces (16-bit was not able to resolve front-most polygons in the ranges with which we were working).

Texture mapping allowed planar mapping of textures onto polygons [note 4] MipMapping was the fundamental technology used here and a utility program called MakeMip was written to create multiple resolution MipMaps from texture files (RLE or PICT format).

Note 4. We did not implement mapping onto arbitrary curves because we did not have any objects constructed with patches.

267

These input files could be either scanned data (the woodgrain for the desk) or painted images created with SuperPaint (screen shots for the Macintosh).

Anti-aliasing was achieved by rendering each frame at higher than target resolution (4, 9, or 16 times) and then decimating the image with a digital filter (Lanczos Windowed Sinc Function) to the target resolution [note 5]. As a result, even machines with eight megabytes of memory could not compute a whole frame with a large number of objects and textures at nine times the resolution. We therefore modified our renderer to render small bands of the image. This became very useful when setting up network rendering because it allowed us to render on more memory limited machines. We also implemented anti-aliased wireframe output for the production of flicker-free wire-frame test [note 6].

Note 5. This is clearly not the fastest method of doing anti-aliasing. However, it was the most quickly implemented, given the limited amount of time that we had remaining to develop the piece. Certainly, one of the first changes to our system will be to implement a faster method of anti-aliasing.

Note 6. There are several additions we would have made to the renderer if we had had more time. The obvious is an enhanced anti-aliasing algorithm. Another would have been a cheap implementation of shadows. Without shadows our objects sometimes appeared as though they were floating in a space slightly above the desk.

6.3 OPTIMIZATIONS

Because rendering is so time-consuming we needed to take any shortcuts available to speed up rendering time. The first of these shortcuts was to convert the computations of the renderer from floating point to fixed point. However, peculiar results like tearing textures indicated that we were exceeding the numeric range of our fixed point numbers. As a result, the radix location for any given variable depended on the number range for that variable, meaning that we had to keep track of the radix location for every variable. However, we found that we achieved an order of magnitude performance improvement using fixed point over the hardware floating point on the Macintosh.

An additional performance improvement was added to the Phong shading algorithm: Gouraud shading was automatically used instead of Phong shading if a quick test indicated negligible specular reflection in a given polygon.

6.4 EXTRAS

The credits were done by formatting a high resolution bitmap and then decimating it to the target size (as was done with our anti-aliased frames). The text was laid into a long scroll file whose scan-lines

268

were indexed by frame number. Once the section of credits was determined it was composited onto the background frame. This compositing (blending, not overwriting) meant that we could lay the credits onto any colored background.

A few special effects were achieved. To avoid having to do post-production, we implemented our own fade to black. The only trick here was realizing that the Y value in YUV is not a pure luminance value. Decreasing this Y value does not bring all color to black. As a result, all of the components had to be scaled.

We also implemented a cheap form of motion blur for one scene involving a fast camera pan that produced rough motion. The difficulty here was that we were not set up to render fields (our animation files were keyed to the frame rate and our renderer shaded full frame images). Our solution was to first reduce the vertical resolution to that appropriate for fields, and then estimate the motion difference between frames and approximate the blur of the horizontal pan with a horizontal smear.

6.5 DISTRIBUTED SYSTEM

Fortunately, we anticipated that we were going to require a distributed rendering system to be able to compute frames in a realistic amount of time. This was later confirmed when timings showed that it took approximately thirty minutes to render a frame (96 days to render the entire film on one Macintosh II). However, when the project began there was no renderer to work with, so the distributed computational environment had to be implemented as an independent module from the renderer. The environment set up was a master/slave system where the master handled the data and file management, and the slave controlled the actual rendering. The master was a modified version of Parscene (see section 6.1) that parsed the scene file and broke it into individual frames. The slave was a generic module that attached to any program to handle I/O, data transfer and program initiation. Because this slave was generic we were able to continually modify the renderer and simply attach new versions to the slave. This process was so robust that we could even substitute renderers while the slave programs were running [note 7]. The slave program communicated with the master, telling the master its available resources, such as memory. The master

Note 7. It would be simple to take a slave and attach it to any distributed process.

then selected an appropriate job (e.g. a frame renderable within the slave's memory constraints) and passed back the name of the current rendering program, the frame file to render as well as the location of this file and the output file. The slave would then fetch objects and textures from a file server and initiate the attached renderer. The output frame was passed back to the server where it was stored until recording.

In the end we were able to have 25 to 30 Macintosh IIs running at any given time. There were approximately 5000 frames to be rendered, each frame taking anywhere from 20 to 40 minutes to compute (depending on the amount of texture mapping and the number of reflective surfaces). One complete turn of the animation could be completed in just over three days.

7 SOUND

The sound track to Pencil Test needed to be much more than pretty background music. It was very important that the sound effects be dramatic because they were conveying parts of the story that were not represented graphically (e.g. you are aware of a human presence even though you never see a human figure). The accompanying music needed to be finely tuned to these sound effects to help emphasize but not overpower them. At the same time the music needed to help set the mood and pace of the piece. This careful timing required sequencers and an electronic cue sheet.

Sound effects were gathered from existing prerecorded sources and from hand-recorded sounds. We discovered immediately that a normal sound taken out of context (like a footstep) is unrecognizable without visual cues and the natural acoustic environment that normally surrounds it. We therefore needed to record greatly exaggerated sounds. For example, the footsteps of a person leaving the room were recorded by having a large person walk loudly across a cafeteria table. The sounds were then edited using Sound Designer by Digidesign and external effects boxes (reverb, etc.) all controlled with a Macintosh Plus.

The music was performed and edited using Professional Performer, a Macintosh sequencer. This program enabled easy experimentation with ideas of sequences and orchestration. Once the music was created, it was carefully cued to the timing of the animation. Individual bars of the music were fit to actions within the film. This stretching and scaling of time on a bar by bar basis required a powerful sequencer.

Though the sound effects were synchronized to particular frames of action within the film, much additional tweaking was needed to compensate for the psycho-acoustical properties of the effect, i.e. the moment you expect to hear the sound based on what you see. This often required bumping sounds backwards and forwards by as much as five frames from the actual event, and demanded at least half frame accuracy. All of this was done with Cue Sheet and the Opcode Time Code machine (which performed with 100% reliability). This kind of editing requires VITC equivalent timecode, which is a vertical interval timecode that is frame accurate (a longitudinal time code can not maintain accuracy when single-stepping through tape). In general, a thorough understanding of SMPTE, differences between drop frame and non-drop frame striping and other additional timing complexities were needed to lay the sound to tape. This volume of expertise should be hidden from the user in future systems.

We have received many favorable comments on how well the music and the sound effects worked with each other. It was important to make sure that the music did not cover sound effects that gave pertinent information to the story line. Yet too much sound and not enough score tended to slow down the motion of the piece. The synergy was due to the sound effects people and the music people working together constantly, not because of a particular software package. However, the software was well enough integrated to allow the various people to work together and share information.

8   OUTPUT

8.1. IMAGES TO TAPE

When it came time to put the animation to tape we faced some very large problems. First, the Macintosh has no direct video output so we could not transfer the frames in the analogue domain. Second, to save the entire film in RGB format without some kind of compression would have required seven gigabytes of storage (about 10,000 floppies). Finally, to transfer these digital frames to a digital frame store over

Ethernet would take minutes a frame, translating into days for the entire film.

To circumvent the lack of video output we decided to use the Abekas A60 to transfer our files to tape. The Abekas is a digital sequence store that can be written to one frame at a time, and can play back 25 seconds of digital video in real-time. The Abekas' frame store saves frames in YUV format. A procedure was written to convert our RGB frames to YUV. These frames were then compressed using the standard Macintosh PackBits routine, packing each component separately (a scan line of Y, a scan line of U and then a scan line of V). We were able to compress the entire video down to approximately 1.7 gigabytes from the original 7 gigabyte figure. This fit easily on our 2.4 gigabyte file server (four 600 megabyte Racet drives).

Though this compression solved the storage problem, these frames still needed to be transferred to the Abekas. To accomplish this we wrote our own Ethernet protocol to communicate with the Abekas. This worked reasonably well when communication was happening between two nodes on the same subnet, but it failed miserably when trying to cross bridges. This limited the number of machines we could actually use for rendering [note 8]. Shipping compressed frames to the Abekas over Ethernet still turned out to be a very time-consuming process. For every frame it took about 10 seconds to decompress the frame and another 10 seconds to transfer it to the Abekas. We finally reduced this time by abandoning Ethernet altogether and transferring the images via SCSI. This reduced our transfer time to about one second.

Once the images were on the Abekas they could be recorded, in real-time, onto video tape. For recording we used a Sony D1 digital tape drive. By using a digital medium we were able to prevent one generation loss in the recording process.

Note 8. This number was further limited because of bugs in the file server. For some unknown reason, the file server could handle no more than 30 clients.

8.2 GOTCHAS

While these steps solved all of the known problems, we still encountered a few unknowns that were almost devastating to the project. The most pronounced of these was the 'disappearing file syndrome'. With only a few days left until the submission deadline we found that some of our files began to disappear. They still occupied space on the disk, but the directories no longer had any record of them. Fortunately we were using the D1 for recording, and this became our backup device. As soon as we rendered something, we shipped it to the Abekas and then transfered it to the D1. If there were problems with individual frames in a scene, we could copy the scene from the D1 to the Abekas where we could replace those frames and then transfer the entire scene back to tape. However, by the time we grasped what was happening we had lost about one third of the film and many of the frames needed to be rerendered.

8.3 SOUND TO TAPE

Once all of the graphics were laid to tape we were ready to lay down the sound track. Our original intention was to use a Macintosh-controlled 24-track studio for recording. However, after laying the first pass of the sound track to tape in such a studio, we realized that with two Macintoshs and three samplers we could record the entire sound track live with a mix down instead of taking the time to lay all of the sound effects onto different tracks of tape. In addition, synchronizing to the 24-track tape deck was no simple feat, whereas controlling the samplers with the Opcode machine was much more reliable. However, to record live, all of the sound effects had to be staged and divided between the three samplers to avoid generating overlapping sounds. This was done by hand with a giant multi-colored scheduling chart. Though this was manageable for a three minute piece it would be a nightmare for anything longer. Using the information from this scheduling chart, the cue sheet was filled with the location and destination of the music and sound effects, and the sound was loaded into the sequencers. The score was then ready to be laid to tape. This was an entirely Macintosh-driven process. In fact, there were no people in the sound lab when the music was laid to tape because everyone went into the graphics lab to watch the video, a dramatic climax to end our production!

9 CONCLUSIONS

One of the most prominent problems throughout the creation

of the piece was the lack of data interchangeability between software packages. Different stages of the project produced 19 distinct file formats (Fig 5), with the development of all conversion software up to us. This is completely unmanageable for an animator and even for most engineers. However, in the personal computer environment it is unreasonable to expect a single developer to provide an all-in-one package doing modeling, animation, rendering, I/O, etc. The environment is such that developers produce high-quality solutions for particular portions of the animation process, giving the user the flexibility to pick the packages that best meet her needs. Therefore, someone, preferably Apple, should define a common data format for modeling and animation and encourage the development of animation frameworks that provide presentation and data integration [note 9].

Fig 5
File flow diagram

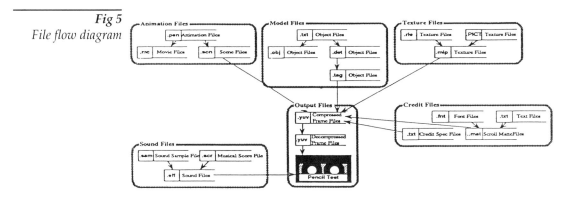

Note 9. This problem also holds true outside of Apple. Developers for high-end workstations like the Silicon Graphics Iris machine tend to supply one-package solutions, and there are several such packages. However, there are no common data formats that would allow an animator to select a modeler, an animation module, and a renderer, each from a different vendor.

Sound technology seems to be much further ahead than the graphics technology, and Apple has taken a lead here in promoting interchangeability. There are already timing and music data standards that are well accepted, and passing music and sound effects from one program to another is virtually standardized. Synchronising to video is possible because there is already a mechanism for synchronizing to prerecorded material, a process that requires precision beyond that of video frame rates. However, there is still room for progress. A clearly defined interface to sound does not yet exist. The concepts of cut and paste, duplicate, etc. are very well understood methods of manipulating graphics, but the same ease of use and standard interaction protocol for sound is not in place. Apple should provide basic techniques for interaction with time ordered operations like sound and animated graphics.

Regardless of the speed of your computer, it is always possible to find a rendering algorithm that is complex enough to prevent rendering from happening in real-time; if you are using a personal computer this is almost a given. A standard method for using a distributed system to perform rendering (or any other computationally intensive activity) is an attractive solution, allowing differing qualities of animation to be produced in a reasonable amount of time. This applies not only to distribution across a network, but also to coprocessors within the host machine. We made a start at solving this problem by designing a generic slave that could be attached to any distributed task. Further efforts are needed to make distributed computing a standard on low-end machines [note 10].

Finally, to this date, the phrase 'tools for computer animation' has been synonymous with 'packages for the creation of high-end 3D animation'. In focusing on solutions to complicated 3D animation problems, we have been overlooking some of the more basic problems. Software does not exist to manage the hoards of information that is generated for an animation. For example, there is no software to generate animatics from storyboard drawings or to manage scheduling data for music and sound effects. In addition, people have not been using computers to produce exciting 2-1/2D animation environments, something that is feasible for personal computers to achieve in real-time. Currently, the 2-1/2D world consists of basic motion control animation (moving bitmaps). Consider all the exciting work that could be done with animating splines and filled regions! Furthermore, interesting work can be done by combining the 3D and 2D environments which will reduce rendering time to something more manageable.

We need to be creative in finding new solutions for real-time interactive animation. In some ways, this may be the most challenging problem.

Note 10. In the same vein, if frames are not going to be produced in real-time it is essential that personal computers provide some sort of frame-by-frame control along with the video output to allow standard recording equipment to be used. This is the area where enormous amounts of money are spent. To get work to video tape, one needs to buy a frame-by-frame controller or high-end video editing equipment. Both are expensive and neither is a reasonable solution for low-end computing.

10 ACKNOWLEDGMENTS

The following people made the project and paper possible: Jim Batson, Ernie Beernink, Mark Cutter, Sam Dicker, Toby Farrand, Jay Fenton, Jullian Gomez, Shaun Ho, Sampo Kaasila, Lisa Kleissner, Al Kossow, Mark Krueger, John Lasseter, Bruce Leak, Mark Lentczner,

Tony Masterson, Steve Milne, Eric Mueller, Terri Munson, Daian Onaka, Wil Oxford, Jack Palevich, Steve Perlman, John Peterson, Mike Potel, Steve Roskowski, Andrew Stanton, Scott Stein, Carl Stone, Nancy Tague, Larry Tesler, Victor Tso, Ken Turkowski, Dave Wilson, John Worthington, Larry Yaeger.

11 REFERENCES

Foley, James D., and Andries van Dam, *Fundamentals of interactive Computer Graphics*, Addison-Wesley Publishing Company, Inc., Reading, Mass. (1984). Chapters 9, 15 and 16.

Magnenat-Thalmann, Nadia, and Daniel Thalmann, *Computer Animation*, Springer-Verlag, Tokyo (1985).

Williams, Lance, "Pyramidal Parametrics", SIGGRAPH '83 Proceedings, *Computer Graphics*, vol. 17, no. 3, July 1983.

Wyszecki, Gunter, *Color Science: Concepts and Methods, Quantative Data and Formulae*, John Wiley & Sons, Inc., New York (1982).

GLOSSARY OF COMMON USAGE

1-Dimensional When referring to spatial dimensions: having length but no breadth, such as a straight line.

2-Dimensional (2-D) When referring to spatial dimensions: having two dimensions (length and breadth, or length and height), such as a plane.

2 1/2-Dimensional (21/2-D) Usually referring to an animation created in several flat layers to give some of the depth effects of true 3-D.

3-Dimensional (3-D) When referring to spatial dimensions: having three dimensions (length, breadth and height), such as an object.

3-Space Three-dimensional space.

4-Dimensional Usually referring to three spatial dimensions plus the added dimension of time.

Actor A term now used to refer to anything in an animation which moves (though originally having a far more specific definition).

ADC Analogue to Digital Converter.

AI Artificial Intelligence is involved with building features associated with natural intelligence into machines.

Algorithm A set of instructions given to the computer in order for it to do a specific task. In other contexts a recipe or a knittingpattern could be   described as an algorithm.

Aliasing (see spatial aliasing, temporal aliasing).

ALU Arithmetic and Logical Unit. The computer component which carries out the arithmetical calculations.

Analogue (analog) Dealing with events as continuous rather than as sequences of separate moments (see digital).

Animatic A presentation of storyboard frames, at appropriate time intervals, in order to get some 'feel' of an intended animation.

Animation The presentation of images over time to give a sense of movement.

Aliasing (see spatial aliasing, temporal aliasing).

Anti-aliasing The removal of aliasing artifacts, most commonly involving the smoothing of jagged edges on output displays.

Artifact Used to describe some part of the image which has been inadvertently created, or is unsatisfactory as a result of deficiencies in the system, and constitutes an error.

ASCII (Pronounced "askey") An internationally agreed set of characters as produced by a standard keyboard.

Axis The line about which an object rotates.

B-rep Boundary Representation method for creating objects by defining a polygonised surface mesh.

Back-face culling A simple, but crude, hidden line removal method.

Bandwidth Strictly a measure of the range of frequencies in a given situation, the term is more generally used to describe the breadth of information a system or device can handle.

Behavioural animation An animation in which the actors respond to stimuli in a scene as a result of their inbuilt rules. Simple, animal-like behaviour, for example, can be effectively simulated.

Bezier He invented a mathematical description of a curve, based on the definition of a few points, for use in the car industry. It is widely used in computer graphics, often in a context where the curve is to be 'tuned' interactively, to create 2-D lines, 2-D and 3-D paths and 3-D surfaces.

Bicubic patch A means of describing a curved surface using cubic functions. Typically a surface may be divided into a number of patches with suitable continuity at boundaries.

Bit From 'binary digit'. The basic unit of computer information (which can be represented by either 0 or 1).

Bit map   The representation of the screen image in memory, stored as pixel intensities.

Blitter   A hardware device, usually a 'chip', designed to speed the movement of bit maps around the screen.

Boolean operations   Operations based on the logical relationships of AND, OR and NOT (union, difference and intersection). In CSG modelling, for instance, the logical operators can be used to join or cut existing objects into new objects.

Bounding box   A simple spaceframe which can act as a temporary substitute for a more complex object in order to simplify calculations when a quick approximation (of a movement, for example) is needed.

Buffer   An area of memory (which may be internal or external) temporarilyreserved to hold information which is currently required. A frame buffer, for example, holds the displayed image as a matrix of intensity values.

Bump mapping   By perturbing surface normals across a flat surface suitable rendering algorithms will produce what appears a bumpy surface.

Byte   A set of (usually eight) contiguous bits.

Cartesian coordinates   Two dimensional points which can be located by reference to calibrated horizontal (X) and vertical (Y) axes. In three dimensions an additional axis (Z) establishes depth.

Canonical position   The expected, default position of an object on creation and before it is moved. Normally centred on the origin and with key facets orthogonal to axes.

Cel animation   A traditional animation technique in which each frame is drawn on a transparent cel. The term has been carried forward into the computer animation.

CGI   Computer Generated Imagery.

Chip   A miniature electronic circuit, typically the size of a postage stamp.

Chromakey   A technique in which a prescribed colour in a scene allows itself to be replaced by another layer of visual information. Typically, a particular blue in a video shot has another scene electronically superimposed.

Clock rate   The rate at which operations are carried out by the CPU.

Colour cycling A limited illusion of movement can sometimes be created by changing selected colours in the palette in a defined sequence.

Compositing Assembling a number of separate visual elements together in a single scene. Synchronised live action, computer generated material and a painted background might be brought together in each frame of a sequence.

Constraints Limitations applied, particularly to the movement of an object.

Continuity The degree of smoothness with which line and surface sections join.

Convex hull The 'skin' created by enclosing all the extreme points of an object.

Coordinates (See Cartesian coordinates, polar coordinates and spherical coordinates.)

Cosine shading (See Lambert shading.)

CPU Central Processing Unit. The heart of the computer.

CRT Cathode Ray Tube. Provides the screen of most monitors.

CSG Constructive Solid Geometry. A modelling method in which primitives, such as cubes and spheres, are combined using Boolean operations.

Cushioning The acceleration or deceleration which may be added at either end of a movement (and which adds realistic softening to otherwise abrupt changes of speed).

DAC Digital to Analogue Converter.

DAT Digital Audio Tape.

Data compression The algorithmic reduction in size of data files. Since images with large palettes and high resolutions contain a large amount of data, the issue of reducing the data size to manageable proportions, and of being able to store and retrieve it fast enough for real time animation, is of great current interest.

de Casteljou Inventor of an alternative method of describing curves to that of the more well known Bezier.

Default state The state in which something will exist until it is consciously changed.

Degrees of freedom of movement The number of singular ways in which an object can move. For example, a particle has three degrees of freedom of movement (along X,Y or Z), a rigid body has six (along X,Y and Z plus rotation around X,Y and Z).

Desktop A visual metaphor used in a WIMP environment whereby the VDU screen is organised as if it was a real desktop.

Digital The representation of something in the form of separate digits. Compare the digital watch with one having continuous sweep hands (see analogue).

Digitiser (3-D) A device for acquiring and inputting spatial data about the surface of an object. Currently relatively slow and expensive, the method of use can be to manually triangulate the surface of the object and then use a stylus to collect the coordinates of the vertices thus created.

Digitising tablet An input device with a flat, sensitive surface which can be drawn on with a stylus in the manner of a pencil and paper. A puck may be used to acquire 2-D coordinates from drawings aligned on the tablet.

Disc drive A secondary storage device in which data are saved on a removable rotating disc (which can be conveniently stored or used to transfer data between computers). The most common storage medium is magnetic but optical drives are developing.

Distributed AI Artificial intelligence attributed to a group rather than to an individual e.g. to a flock of birds or to the farm of transputers in a parallel computer.

Dithering   One means of simulating a larger palette of colours than is actually available.

DMA   Direct Memory Access.

DRAM   Dynamic Random Access Memory.

DTP   Desktop Publishing.

DTV   Desktop Video.

DVI   Digital Video Interactive technology.

Dynamics   The branch of mechanics dealing with the way masses move under the influence of forces and torques. Increasingly used to drive animations by the application of physical laws (see kinematics).

Easing   Another term for cushioning.

Expert system Provides a means of solving 'significant' problems by applying rules to a data bank of relevant information culled from human experts in the field concerned.

281

Explicit control   Low level control where the animator has to specify every detail of every frame (see implicit control).

Extrusion   A swept surface method of modelling, where a 2-D template is dragged through 3-space along a path, in the simplest case at right angles to the plane of the template.

Facet   A planar surface which constitute one face of a polygonised model.

Fairing   Another term for cushioning.

Feedback   Information returned as a result of an action which can then cause future actions to be modified.

FFD   Free Form Deformation. A method of deforming an object by applying transformations to a cage of control points. Objects can be created by using FFDs on primitives, and the same principles can be used to animate a change of shape.

Firmware   The embodiment in hardware of a function normally associated with software. For example some frequently used rendering algorithms might be built into a chip in order to gain substantial speed increases.

FLOPS   FLoating Point Operations per Second.

fps   Frames Per Second. E.g. The PAL standard observed in the UK requires a VTR to run at 25 fps.

Fractal   A term used to describe the self-similarity of some phenomena when viewed at different levels of detail. The principle is typically used in computer graphics to generate mountains, clouds and such like, from a very small data base.

Frame   A single image from an animation sequence or film.

Frame buffer   A piece of specialised memory (which may be internal or external) reserved to hold one or more images for quick access and/or processing.

Fuzzy   As well as describing visual phenomena which are not clearly defined, the word is applied to a branch of logic which can be used for decision making in unclearly defined situations, and is likely to find use in animation/simulation in this context.

Genlock   To synchronise two video signals. Also used to describe the hardware which does the job.

GKS   Graphics Kernal System. A 2-D graphics standards that has been established by the International Standards Organisation (ISO).

GUI   Graphical User Interface.

Gouraud shading   A shading model which improves on Lambert shading by smoothing intensity across surfaces.

Granularity   A rough description of the level of detail at which an operation is conducted (e.g. rough-grained = low level of detail, fine-grained = high level of detail).

Hard disc   A sealed unit for secondary storage which is constructed internally like tiers of disc drives.   It combines larger storage space (typically 20 - 160 Megabytes) and relatively quick access.

Hardcopy   Output in permanent form such as on paper or film.

Hardware   Refers to the physical components of a computer system i.e. the boxes that sit on your desk.

HCI   Human Computer Interface.   The boundary between the machine and the user at which they communicate with one another.

Hidden line/surface   It can be visually confusing to display all edges of a model as in wireframe, and a number of algorithms exist to remove lines or surfaces which we would expect to be obscured when viewed from a specified direction.

High level   In this context, a high level operation is one in which the operator does not need to involve himself with the details of how the operation is carried out.   (See low level.)

HDTV   High Definition TeleVision (several proposals exist for a standard, all in excess of 1000 scan lines).

IC   Integrated Circuit.   An electronic circuit (or circuits), of microscopic size, built into a single chip.

Icon   A graphical symbol designed to be identified with a particular function of the system.

IFS   Iterated Function System.   Used to derive a simple set of fractal rules from complex data, such as an image, and thus allow potentially extreme data compression.

Illegal colours   Colours which can be generated on screen but are outside broadcastable range.

Image mapping   A means of applying a picture to a surface or of wrapping a picture around an object.

Implicit control   High level control where the animator specifies the starting conditions and constraints and leaves the system to deal with the movement (see explicit control).

283

Inbetween ('Tween') To produce the required number of frames in between the key frames. Refers to both the process and the frames created.

Incremental Developed in steps (or increments).

Input Information entered into the computer.

Interactive Allowing the user to respond to the running of an application with fresh input while it is in progress.

Interlaced A raster scan in which alternate scan lines are refreshed on each pass. This means that less information needs to be handled at any one moment than in a non-interlaced scan, but that the complete image is refreshed less often.

Interpolation The calculation of values at predetermined intervals between two end values.

Inverse dynamics Working backwards from known end forces to find the correct joint positions.

Inverse kinematics Working backwards from the desired end position to find acceptable joint positions.

I/O Input/output.

Iteration Repetition, usually of a piece of a computer program (in which case it is called a loop). Something that computers are particularly good at doing.

Jaggies An informal term for the jagged lines in a pixelated image which it is usually desirable to minimise.

JPEG algorithm Joint Photographics Experts Group algorithm for data compression of still images.

Keyframe A frame, from a sequence, at which a significant event (such as a change of direction) takes place. Keyframes are traditionally drawn by the leading animator, and the inbetween frames created by juniors (or by the computer).

Kinematics The study of movement without regard to cause (see dynamics). To animate kinematically involves the specification of everything in the scene at any moment in time by the animator himself, though techniques such as key-framing can assist.

Lambert shading A basic shading model in which each facet is evenly shaded according to the angle at which the light hits it.

Lathe The term is sometimes used instead of 'spin'.

Line test A test of the pace and feel of a piece of animation by creating it in wireframe without time-consuming shading or rendering.

Lofting Connecting cross-sections through an object by triangulating a surface between their edges.

Lookup table A way of storing pixel information which is memory efficient for limited palettes.

Low level A level of operation where the operator is required to become involved with the detail of the machine or process. (See high level.)

Lurp An abbreviation of 'linear interpolation' (to interpolate in a straight line).

Mach banding A phenomenon in which a smoothly shaded surface appears to have dark streaks on it.

Mapping (See bump mapping, image mapping, reflection mapping, texture mapping.)

Metamorphosis A change of physical form, often easily animated by interpolation between the start and end forms.

Micon An animated icon.

MIPS Million Instructions Per Second.

Model animation Animation by the manipulation of real 3-D models.

Modelling The construction of objects in a scene prior to rendering or choreographing movement.

Motion blur The apparent blurring of a moving object typified in still photographs. It is sometimes seen as appropriate to duplicate the phenomenon in separate frames of an animation.

Motion control rig A specialised camera, moving along overhead tracks, which can be controlled on a precise path relative to a constructed scene. Computer control of such a rig enables accurate synchronisation with computer generated material.

Mouse A common input device which fits in the palm of the hand and is rolled over a flat horizontal surface to control the movement of a screen cursor.

MPEG algorithm Motion Picture Experts Group algorithm for data compression of motion picture images.

Multimedia A term used to describe the mixed use of still and moving visual media, together with sound, normally under the control of a computer and potentially created by computer.

Multi-tasking The ability of some computers to work on several tasks at the same time. In fact, although things appear to be happening at the same time, the machine is normally swapping from one task to another to optimise use of available CPU time. Not to be confused with parallel computing.

Non-interlaced A raster scan in which each scan line is refreshed on each pass (see interlaced).

NURB Non-Uniform Rational B-spline. A type of B-spline which is particularly flexible in interactive use.

Normal See surface normal.

NTSC Broadcast standard used in USA and Japan.

Object orientated Describes a type of programming language, which is growing in popularity, in which program elements are considered as separate objects which can communicate with one another. The term is also used to refer to an image which is defined as a number of separate parts and their relationships to one another (as opposed to one defined by its pixels).

Object space The 3-D space of the object's world.

OCR Optical Character Recognition.

Octree A data structure which records the spatial position of elements in an object (or of objects in a scene). Hierarchical methods avoid the need to individually deal with every unit of the space.

OOPS Object Orientated Programming System.

Origin The point at the centre of a coordinate system where X,Y and Z all equal zero.

OS Operating System.

Output Material printed or displayed by the computer.

Paging Swapping chunks of memory back and forth from secondary storage to RAM in order to run programs bigger than the available RAM can hold at one time.

Painters' algorithm A simple method of removing hidden surfaces by overpainting.

Paint system An electronic simulation of the materials used for drawing and painting, with which the operator can create images on the computer screen.

PAL Broadcast standard used in much of Europe.

Palette The range of colours available. Dependent on hardware and software constraints, the range can stretch from 2 to more than 6,000,000.

Path The course along which something moves.

Parallel architecture A design of computer in which a number of tasks can be carried out simultaneously i.e. 'in parallel'. Sometimes refered to as 'non-von' since it is a departure from the traditional von Neumann computer architecture.

Parallel processing The simultaneous processing carried out in a parallel computer, (see parallel architecture).

Parameter A value which, when varied, changes another.

Particle A single point in 3-space. Theoretically infinitely small, but often treated as a small mass limited to three degrees of freedom of movement.

Particle system A system containing a number of particles (typically between ten thousand and a million) which might be used to model 'soft' objects or to animate flow through a medium for example.

PC Personal Computer.

PDL Page Description Language e.g. PostScript.

PHIGS Programmers' Hierarchical Interactive Graphics System. A 3-D graphics standard established by the American National Standards Institute (ANSI).

Physically based modelling The representation of a model in terms of its physical attributes, such as mass and forces. Such a model can be controlled by the application of the laws of physics, and is thus ideal for simulation.

Phong shading A smooth shading method which incorporates specular highlights.

Picon An icon made of a small picture.

Pixel From 'picture element', the smallest element out of which a screen display is made.

Plotter An output device in which a pen, or selection of pens,is raised and lowered whilst being carried across the surface of a piece of paper. Traditionally associated with engineering and architectural drawing.

Polar coordinates A point in two dimensions can de defined by its distance from the origin, and the angle between the positive X axis and a line from the origin to the point.

Polygon A planar figure bounded by straight sides.

Post production Work, such as editing, carried out after the initial work has been produced.

Precision errors Errors arising from the inability of the computer to accurately store numbers beyond a certain length. If the result of a calculation is a long decimal number the machine might need to truncate it for storage, thus introducing a small error which could become exaggerated in further calculations.

Primitive A simple object (such as a cube or sphere) which is provided in a modelling system. A limited number of primitives provide basic units for the production of more complex models.

Puck A device similar to a mouse, but with a cross-hair sight for accurate alignment, used for the input of points (for instance from a drawing). See 'digitising tablet'.

Radiosity The radiosity interchange method is a ponderous but effective shading method which is particularly good at dealing with diffuse light.

RAM Random Access Memory.

Raster image Often used to describe a pixel based image (in which the image is recorded as a collection of pixel intensities) as opposed to one which is vector based (and can therefore be displayed at the best resolution of the output device).

Raster scan The scanning of a monitor screen by the electron beam.

Ray tracing A simple, though currently time consuming, rendering method which automatically produces 'realistic' shadows and reflections.

Real time A one to one relationship between display time and real-life time.

Recursion A self-referential process such as when a computer program calls itself. (A traditional computing joke is that the entry in a dictionary under 'recursion' should say "see recursion".)

Reflection mapping A means of applying a picture of an object's surroundings (or imaginary surroundings) to its surface in order to simulate reflection.

Refresh rate The rate at which an image is redrawn on a screen.

Render To make the internal mathematical model of a scene visible. Usually referring to the algorithmic realisation of the effects of lighting, surface colour, texture, and reflection.

Resolution Although a number of factors effect resolution, it is generally taken to describe the apparent level of detail an output device is capable of resolving.

RGB   A colour system where all colours are defined as a mixture of red, green and blue (as in a TV).

RISC   Reduced Instruction-Set Computing.

ROM   Read-Only Memory.

Rostrum stand (animation rostrum)   A movable, vertically mounted camera pointing down at artwork held on a movable base.

Rotascoping   The process of tracing moving images, one at a time, off a screen.

Sampling theory   The branch of mathematics which explains aliasing.

Scanner   A 2-D image input device which scans an image in the same way as a photocopier.

Scientific visualisation   The translation into visual form of scientific data, in order to make it more comprehensible. This is becoming a particularly important skill as our ability to generate vast quantities of data increases.

Screen space   The two dimensional space of the screen image. See 'object space'.

SECAM   Broadcast standard used in France, Russia and elsewhere.

SIGGRAPH   ACM (Association of Computing Machinery) Special Interest Group in Graphics.

Simulation   In this context, an animation in which the aim is to accurately model an event by applying physical laws.

SIMD   Single Instruction Multiple Data. An architecture for parallel processing.

Soft modelling   The modelling of non-geometric, often natural, forms.

Software   Refers to the programs, expressed in machine readable language, that control the hardware.

Solid texture Instead of texture being applied to the surface of an object the texture pattern runs right through the volume of the object.

Spatial aliasing   A problem of discontinuity arising from trying to match correct locations to the nearest available point on an output device. See jaggies.

Spatial occupancy enumeration A volume modelling method where the object is defined by the presence or absence of voxels.

Spherical coordinates   An extension of the polar coordinate system which deals with 3D by incorporating an extra angular measurement.

Spline   A flexible strip of wood used to create smooth curves (originally in shipbuilding), the same result is now achieved mathematically.

Sprite   A piece of screen image which has its own identity and can thus be readily moved around. It provides the basis for much computer games animation.

Spinning   Process of creating a swept surface by rotation of a 2-D template around an axis.

Staircasing   (see jaggies)

Stochastic   Random within prescribed limits. Stochastics are often employed to produce variations on a basic theme.

Stop-frame   Animation generated one frame at a time, with pauses for each new frame to be composed or generated.

Storyboard   A sequence of pictures illustrating key moments in the script.

Stylus   A pen-like device used in conjunction with a digitising 'tablet, mainly used for the freehand creation and input of images.

Sub-pixel   Theoretical division of a pixel into smaller units for the purpose of calculations.

Super sampling   Conducting calculations at a finer resolution than the output device will be able to implement. Used as a means of dealing with aliasing by sampling at a sub-pixel level.

Surface normal   A vector orthogonal to a surface. Central to many computer graphics calculations.

Swept surface   A 3-D surface created by passing a 2-D template through 3-space.

Temporal aliasing   A problem of discontinuity arising from trying to match accurate moments in time to the nearest available time-point on an output device (such as a VTR running at 25 fps). An example of the problem this causes is the stagecoach wheel appearing to rotate backwards.

Teleological modelling   An extension of physically based modelling to include goal-orientation. The attributes of an object include a knowledge of how it should act.

Texture mapping   Used to describe both the wrapping of a 2-D representation of texture onto a surface in object space, (although this might be better referred to as image mapping) and the transfer of an external bump map to a surface.

Texture space The space inhabited by the 3-D textural information used in solid texturing (where the texture runs through the object like grain through wood).

Texel TEXture ELement. A single unit of texture (which might be compared with a pixel or a voxel).

Transformation The alteration of shapes or objects by applying geometrical rules to their coordinates, e.g. translation (movement in a straight line), scaling and rotation.

Transputer A chip for parallel processing, containing its own memory and processing unit.

Triangulation Division of a surface into triangular facets. The division is often required because a triangular facet is necessarily planar, and non-planar facets would create problems during other calculations (such as at the rendering stage).

VDU Visual Display Unit. Normally refers to the monitor screen.

Vector Usually referring to the storage of image data in terms of relative measurements (which can therefore be displayed at the best resolution of the output device) as opposed to storage of an image in terms of pixel intensities. In mathematics a vector is a value having magnitude and direction, and in modelling a point can be represented by a vector and transformed using matrices.

Vertex A point in 2-D or 3-D space which is connected to others in order to build shapes or facets.

Viewing transformation The mathematical conversion of 3-D information so that it can be presented in 2D, as if viewed from a given point (with perspective).

Virtual Appearing to be something it is not. Hence virtual memory describes the use of secondary storage as if it was main memory and virtual reality describes a simulated situation which aims to be indistinguishable from one of real life.

ViSC Visualisation in Scientific Computing.

Visualisation Making complex information (often being large quantities of scientific data) understandable through presentation in a visual form.

Volume visualisation The rendering of 3-D volumes by voxel methods (see spatial occupancy enumeration).

Von Neumann architecture The traditional computer architecture in which operations are carried out sequentially (as opposed

291

to concurrently).

Voxel From 'volume element'. A cubic unit of 3-D volume defined at a size appropriate to the required resolution, sometimes described as the 3-D equivalent of a pixel.

VR Virtual Reality (See virtual.)

VTR Video Tape Recorder

WIMP Windows, Icons, Menus and Pointers used in an interface.

Wireframe A representation of an object using only the edges of its constituent polygons.

WORM Write Once Read Many. Refers to a storage device from which information can be read but to which it cannot be written.

WYSIWYG What You See Is What You Get. Describes a system where the screen representation exactly represents the hard-copy output. The two are otherwise often not the same since the device resolution determines how accurately images can be shown, and this represents a common problem in many graphics situations (such as DTP).

X-axis The horizontal axis in a Cartesian coordinate system.

Y-axis The vertical axis in a Cartesian coordinate system.

Z-axis The axis representing the dimension of depth in a 3-D Cartesian coordinate system. In its most usual presentation the Z-axis can be thought of as going back at rightangles to the vertical plane on which the X- and Y-axes exist. (This is a left-handed system. In a right-handed system the Z-axis would come forward from the XY plane.)

Z-buffer An area of memory holding the depth (Z) values of each surface as represented at each pixel location.

Zel Occasionally used to refer to a unit of depth.

BIBLIOGRAPHY

d'Agapeyeff A 1983
Expert systems, fifth generation and UK suppliers
NCC Publications

Badler Norman 1990
Ergonomic simulation and evaluation
SIGGRAPH course notes: Human figure animation: approaches and applications

Badler N., Barsky B. & Zeltzer D. (Eds) 1991
Making them move - mechanics, control and animation of articulated figures
Morgan Kaufmann Pub. Inc.

Balch Peter 1989a
Human movement
Program Now (magazine) May

Balch Peter 1989b
Kinematics
Program Now (magazine) June/July

Baran Nick 1990
Putting the squeeze on graphics
Byte (magazine) December

Barnsley Michael & Sloan Alan 1988
A better way to compress images
Byte (magazine) January

Barr Alan 1989a
Introduction to physically-based modeling
SIGGRAPH course notes - Topics in physically-based modeling

Barr Alan 1989b
Teleological modeling
SIGGRAPH course notes - Topics in physically-based modeling

Barzel Ronen & Barr Alan 1988
A modeling system based on dynamic constraints
Computer Graphics Vol. 22 N0 4 Aug.

Becket Welton & Badler Norman 1990
Imperfection for realistic image synthesis
The Journal of Visualisation & Computer Animation Vol. 1 No 1 Aug.

Boden Margaret   1987
Artificial intelligence and natural man (2nd Edn)
Basic Books Inc.

Boisvert D., Magnenat-Thalmann N. & Thalmann D.   1989
An integrated control view of synthetic actors
New advances in computer graphics (Eds: Earnshaw & Wyvill)
Springer Verlag

Bond Alan & Gasser Les (Eds)   1988
Readings in distributed artificial intelligence
Morgan Kauffman Inc.

Bowyer Adrian & Woodwark John   1983
A programmer's geometry
Butterworths

Brady Michael *et al.* (Eds.)   1982
Robot motion: planning and control
MIT Press

Bruderlin Armin & Calvert Thomas   1989
Goal-directed, dynamic animation of human walking
Computer Graphics Vol. 23 No 3 July

Cavigioli Christopher   1990
Image Compression: Spelling out the options
Advanced Imaging October

Cavigioli Christopher   1991
JPEG Compression: Spelling out the options
Advanced Imaging March

Chadwick John, Haumann David & Parent Richard   1989
Layered construction for deformable animated characters
Computer Graphics Vol. 23 No 3 July

Chin Norman & Feiner Steven   1989
Near real-time shadow generation using BSP trees
Computer Graphics Vol. 23 No 3 July

Cook Robert, Porter Thomas & Carpenter Loren   1984
Distributed ray tracing
Computer Graphics Vol. 18 No 3 July

Culhane Shamus   1988
Animation - from script to screen
Columbus Books Ltd.

deGraf Brad 1989
 Notes on human facial animation
 SIGGRAPH course notes: State of the art in facial animation
Durham Tony 1987
 Computing Horizons
 Addison-Wesley
Fikes R & Kehler T 1985
 The role of frame-based representation in reasoning
 Communications of the ACM Sept. Vol. 28 No 9
Foley James 1987
 Interfaces for advanced computing
 Scientific American Oct.
Foley J., van Dam A., Feiner S. & Hughes J. 1990
 Computer Graphics - principles and practice (2nd Edition)
 Addison-Wesley
Fournier Alain & Reeves William 1986
 A simple model of ocean waves
 Computer Graphics Vol. 20 No 4 Aug.
Gardner Geoffrey 1985
 Visual simulation of clouds
 Computer Graphics Vol. 19 No 3 July
Getto Phillip 1987
 The Clockworks: an object oriented computer animation system
 SIGGRAPH course notes
Glazzard Nick 1987
 Particle systems: methods, implementation techniques and experiences
 Computer Graphics 87
 Online publications
Goodman Arthur 1983
 The colour coded guide to micro computers
 Macdonald & Co
Greene Ned 1989
 Voxel space automata: modeling with stochastic growth processes in voxel space
 Computer Graphics Vol. 23 No 3 July
Haeberli Paul & Akeley Kurt 1990
 The accumulation buffer: Hardware support for high-quality rendering
 Computer Graphics Vol. 24 No 4 Aug.

Halas John (Ed) 1974
Computer Animation
Focal Press

Hayes P 1984
Naive physics manifesto
Expert systems in the micro-electronic age (Ed. D Mitchie)
Edinburgh University Press

Hearn Donald & Baker M. Pauline 1986
Computer Graphics
Prentice-Hall

Hodgson Paul 1990
The 20th century box
Apple Business (magazine) Sept.

Hu David 1989
C/C++ for expert systems
MIS Press

Inakage M. 1988
Particals: an artistic approach to fuzzy objects
New trends in computer graphics
Springer Verlag

Isaacs P M & Cohen M F 1987
Controlling dynamic simulation with kinematic constraints,
  behaviour functions and inverse dynamics
Computer Graphics Vol. 21 N0 4 July

Iwata Hiroo 1990
Artificial reality with force-feedback: development of desktop virtual
space with compact master manipulator
Computer Graphics Vol. 24 No 4 Aug.

Jern Michael 1990
The visualisation of scientific data
Eurographics UK Conference: Tutorial

Jurgens Harmut, Peitgen Heinz-Otto & Saupe Dietmar 1990
The language of fractals
Scientific American (magazine) Aug.

Kajiya James & Kay Timothy 1989
Rendering fur with three dimensional textures
Computer Graphics Vol. 23 No 3 July

Kass Michael 1989
Comments during lecture
SIGGRAPH Physically-based modelling course

Kerlow Isaac & Rosebush Judson   1986
Computer graphics for designers and artists
van Nostrand Reinhold

Kernighan Brian W. & Ritchie Dennis M.   1988
The C programming language
Prentice Hall

Lansdown John   1987
Computer Graphics
(Teach Yourself Books) Hodder & Stoughton

Lasseter John   1987
Principles of traditional animation applied to 3D computer
animation
Computer Graphics Vol. 21 No 4 July

Lee P., Wei S., Zhao J. & Badler N   1990
Strength guided motion
Computer Graphics Vol. 24 No 4 Aug.

Lethbridge Timothy & Ware Colin   1989
A simple heuristically-based method for expressive stimulus-
response animation
Computers & Graphics Vol. 13 N0 3

Levitan Eli   1977
Electronic Imaging Techniques
Van Nostrand Reinhold Co

Lozano-Perez Tomas & Wesley Michael   1988
Algorithm for planning collision free paths among polyhedral
obstacles
Communications of the ACM Vol. 22 No 10 Oct.

Magnenat-Thalmann Nadia & Thalmann Daniel   1983
MIRA-3D: A three-dimensional graphical extension of PASCAL
Software - Practice and Experience Vol. 13
John Wiley and Sons Ltd.

Magnenat-Thalmann Nadia & Thalmann Daniel   1985
Computer animation
Springer Verlag

Mandelbrot Benoit   1977
Fractals: form, chance and dimension
W.H.Freeman & Co.

Mandelbrot Benoit   1982
The fractal geometry of nature
W.H.Freeman & Co.

McCormick B. H. *et al.* **(Ed)   1987**
  Visualisation in scientific computing
  Computer Graphics Vol. 21 No 6 Nov.
Mealing Stuart   1989
  Acting naturally
  CASCAAD Middlesex Polytechnic (MA dissertation)
Mealing Stuart & Yazdani Masoud   1990
  A computer-based iconic language
  Intelligent Tutoring Media Vol.1 No 3
Merritt Douglas   1987
  Television Graphics - from pencil to pixel
  Trefoil
Miller Gavin   1988
  The motion dynamics of snakes and worms
  Computer Graphics Vol. 22 No 4 Aug.
Miller Gavin & Pearce Andrew   1989
  Globular dynamics: a connected particle system for animating viscous liquids
  SIGGRAPH course notes: topics in physically-based modelling
Moore Mathew & Wilhelms Jane   1988
  Collision detection and response for computer animation
  Computer Graphics Vol. 22 No 4 Aug.
Mortenson M E   1989
  Computer graphics - an introduction to the mathematics and geometry
  Heinemann Newnes
Nakamae E, Kaneda K, Okamoto T & Nishita T   1990
  A lighting model aiming at drive simulators
  Computer Graphics Vol. 24 No 4 Aug.
Newman William M. & Sproull Robert F.   1984
  Principles of interactive computer graphics
  McGraw-Hill
Noake Roger   1988
  Animation - a guide to animated film techniques
  Macdonald Orbis
Oppenheimer Peter   1986
  Real time design and animation of fractal plants and trees
  Computer Graphics Vol. 20 No 4 Aug.

Papathomas T., Schiavone J. & Julesz B. 1988
Applications of computer graphics to the visualisation of meteorological data
Computer Graphics Vol. 22 No 4 Aug.

Pfaffenberger Bryan 1990
Que's computer user's dictionary
Que Corporation

Piegl Leslie & Tiller Wayne 1987
Curve and surface constructions using rational B-splines
Computer-aided Design Vol. 19 No 9 Nov.

Pieper Steve 1989
Physically-based animation of facial tissue
SIGGRAPH course notes: State of the art in facial animation

Platt John 1989
Constraint methods for physical systems
SIGGRAPH course notes:Topics in physically based modeling

Prusinkiewicz P., Lindenmayer A. & Hnana J. 1988
Developmental models of herbaceous plants for computer imagery purposes
Computer Graphics Vol. 22 No 4 Aug.

Reeves William 1983
Particle Systems - a technique for modelling classes of fuzzy objects
Computer Graphics Vol. 17 No 3 July

Reeves William & Blau Ricki 1985
Approximate and probabilistic algorithms for shading and r endering structured particle systems
Computer Graphics Vol. 19 No 3 July

Reffin Smith Brian 1984
Soft computing - art and design
Addison Wesley

Reffin Smith Brian 1989
Beyond computer art
Leonardo (magazine) supplemental issue: Computer art in context

de Reffye P., Edelin C., Francon J., Jaeger M. & Puech C. 1988
Plant models faithful to botanical structure and development
Computer Graphics Vol. 22 No 4 Aug.

Reilly Paul 1990
  Towards a virtual archaeology
  Communications in Archaeology: a global view of the impact of
  information technology Vol. 1: Data Visualisation
  (Papers for the Second World Archaeological Congress)
Renault Olivier, Magnenat Thalmann Nadia & Thalmann Daniel 1990
  A vision-based approach to behavioural animation
  The Journal of Visualization & Computer Animation Vol. 1 No 1 Aug.
Reynolds Craig 1986
  SIGGRAPH course notes: *Advanced computer animation*
Reynolds Craig 1987
  Flocks, herds and schools: a distributed behavioural model
  Computer Graphics Vol. 21 No 4 July
Ritchie Simon 1989
  C++ graphics
  Computer graphics 89
  Blenheim Online Publications
Rogers David F.   1989
  Procedural elements for computer graphics
  McGraw-Hill
Rooney Joe & Steadman Philip (Eds) 1987
  Principles of computer aided design
  Pitman Publishing / The Open University
Salmon Rod & Mel Slater 1987
  Computer graphics - systems and concepts
  Addison-Wesley
Schafer Mark 1989
  Displacement animation
  Computer Graphics 89
  Blenheim Online Publications
Schiphorst T., Calvert T., Lee C., Welman C. & Gaudet S 1990
  Tools for interaction with the creative process of composition
  SIGGRAPH course notes: Human figure animation: approaches
  and applications
Schneiker Conrad   1988
  NanoTechnology with Feynman machines
  Artificial life - Langton Christopher (Ed)
  Addison-Wesley

Sederberg Thomas & Scott Parry   1986
Free-form deformation of solid geometric models
Computer Graphics Vol. 20 No 4 Aug.

Shoemake Ken   1985
Animating rotation with quaternion curves
Computer Graphics Vol. 19 No 3

Simms Karl   1989a
Particle animation and rendering using data parallel computation
SIGGRAPH course notes: Topics in physically based modelling

Simms Karl   1989b
Notes on combining dynamic and kinematic techniques for animating particle systems
SIGGRAPH course notes: Topics in physically based modelling

Simons G L   1984
Introducing artificial intelligence
NCC Publications

Sørensen Peter   1989
Felix the cat. Real time computer animation
Animation Magazine   Winter

Swain Bob   1987
Mickey mouse comes to town
Computer Images (magazine) May/June

Thalmann Daniel & Magnanet-Thalmann Nadia   1986
Artificial intelligence in 3D computer animation
Computer Graphics Forum 5

Tizzard Keith   1988
C for professional programmers
Ellis Horwood

Tokoro M & Ishikawa Y   1984
An object-oriented approach to knowledge systems
Proceedings of Fifth generation computer systems
Elsevier

Travers Michael   1989
Electric Anthill
Computer Art in Context
Leonardo (Supplemental Issue)

Uchiki Tetsuya, Ohashi Toshiaki & Tokoro Mario   1983
Collision detection in motion simulation
Computers and Graphics Vol. 7 No 3-4

Vince John 1984
Dictionary of computer graphics
Frances Pinter
Vince John 1986
The PICASO system
CAMPUS (Middlesex Polytechnic)
Waters Keith 1987
A muscle model for animating three-dimensional facial expression
Computer Graphics Vol. 21 No 4 July
Waters Keith 1989
A dynamic model of facial tissue
SIGGRAPH course notes: State of the art in facial animation
Watt Alan 1989
Fundamentals of three-dimensional computer graphics
Addison-Wesley
Watt Mark 1990
Light-water interaction using backward beam tracing
Computer Graphics Vol. 24 No 4 Aug.
Watts Susan 1989
Parallel tracks to standard processing
New Scientist 12 Aug.
Weil Jerry 1986
The synthesis of cloth objects
Computer Graphics Vol. 20 No 4 Aug.
Weiner Norbert 1969
Cybernetics: or control and communication in the animal and the machine
M.I.T. Press
Weiner Richard & Pinson Lewis 1988
An introduction to object-oriented programming and C++
Addison Wesley
Weinstock Neal 1986
Computer Animation
Addison Wesley
Wilhelms Jane 1987a
Towards automatic motion control
IEEE CG & Applications Vol. 7 No 4 April
Wilhelms Jane 1987b
Using dynamic analysis for animation of articulated bodies
IEEE CG & Applications Vol. 7 No 6 June

Wilhelms Jane 1987c
 Dynamics for everyone
 IEEE CG & Applications Vol. 7 No 6 June
Wilhelms Jane & Skinner Robert 1989
 An interactive approach to behaviour control
 SIGGRAPH course notes: Human figure animation. Approaches and
 applications
 Witkin Andrew, Fleischer Kurt & Barr Alan 1987
 Energy constraints on parameterised models
 Computer Graphics Vol. 21 No 4 July
Witkin Andrew & Kass Michael 1988
 Spacetime constraints
 Computer Graphics Vol. 22 No 4 Aug.
Zadeh L A 1965
 Fuzzy sets
 Information & Control No 8 pp 338/353
Zadeh L A 1983
 Commonsense knowledge representation based on fuzzy logic
 Computer Oct. pp 61/65
Zeltzer David 1988
 Motor problem solving for three dimensional computer animation
 SIGGRAPH course notes: Synthetic actors

INDEX